German
Grammar
Handbook

Christopher Wightwick

Berlitz Publishing
New York   Munich   Singapore

German Grammar Handbook

CONTACTING THE EDITORS

Every effort has been made to provide accurate information in this publication, but changes are inevitable. The publisher cannot be responsible for any resulting loss, inconvenience, or injury. We would appreciate it if readers would call our attention to any errors or outdated information by contacting Berlitz Publishing, 193 Morris Avenue, Springfield, NJ 07081, USA. Fax: 1-908-206-1103. email: comments@berlitzbooks.com

Cover Photo © Punchstock/Stockbyte

Second Printing
Printed in China by CTPS, July 2010

The Author and Series Editor:
Christopher Wightwick was formerly principal inspector of Modern Languages for England and UK representative on the Council of Europe Modern Languages Project.

CONTENTS

How to use this Handbook   ix

A   *Putting ideas into words*

1   *Classes of words: parts of speech*

1a	What kind of word is it?	2
1b	Content words and structure words	2

2   *Getting it down on paper: spelling and punctuation*

2a	Spelling and sounds	4
2b	The German alphabet	4
2c	The main spelling rules	4
2d	Punctuation	7

3   *Linking ideas together*

3a	Compound words or phrases?	10
3b	Compound words	10
3c	Side by side: words in apposition	13
3d	Quantities, measurements and prices	14

B   *Putting a sentence together: syntax*

4   *Recognizing sentences*

4a	What is a sentence?	18
4b	The subject of a sentence	18
4c	The predicate of a sentence	19
4d	Sentences and clauses	19
4e	The order of words and phrases: syntax	20

5   *Linking clauses together*

5a	Clauses with conjunctions	28
5b	Relative clauses	32
5c	Indirect speech	32
5d	Indirect questions	33
5e	Indirect requests and commands	34

6   *Asking for information: direct questions*

6a	What is a direct question?	35
6b	True or false: Yes/No questions	35
6c	Checking up: tag questions	35
6d	Asking for details: question-word questions	35

C   *Actions and states: verbs and their uses*

7   *What verbs do*

7a	Full verbs	40
7b	Auxiliary verbs	40

8   *What verbs govern: their role in the sentence*

8a	What does a verb govern?	41
8b	Self-sufficient verbs	41
8c	Verbs linking equals: the complement	41
8d	Verbs with one object	42
8e	Verbs with two objects: direct and indirect objects	45
8f	Objects which refer to the subject: reflexive verbs	47
8g	Verbs + preposition + noun phrase: prepositional objects	48
8h	Verbs + infinitives of other verbs	52
8i	Wanting someone else to do it: verbs + subordinate clauses	57
8j	Impersonal verbs	57
8k	Feelings and sensations: idioms with **haben** and **sein**	57

9   *Attitudes to action: modal verbs*

9a	The function of modal verbs	59
9b	Modal verbs in action	59
9c	The parts and meanings of modal verbs	61

10   *Verb forms not related to time: non-finite forms*

10a	The infinitive	68
10b	The present and past participles	70

11   *The passage of time and the use of tenses*

11a	What do tenses tell us?	75
11b	One word or two? Simple and compound tenses	75
11c	Doing or done to? The active and the passive	75
11d	The active tenses	75

12   *Statements of fact: past, present and future*

12a	The present tense	77
12b	The past tenses	78
12c	The future tense	81

13 Requests and commands: the imperative

13a	What does the imperative express?	83
13b	What you are to do: second person imperatives	83
13c	Instructions and firm commands	84
13d	Wishes and suggestions	84

14 Areas of uncertainty: *der Konjunktiv*

14a	**Konjunktiv** or subjunctive?	86
14b	The tenses of the **Konjunktiv**	86
14c	What did they say? Indirect speech	87
14d	What if? Conditional statements (**Konjunktiv II**)	89

15 Things done to you: the passive

15a	What does the passive express?	92
15b	The tenses of the passive	92
15c	By whom? How? With what?	93
	The agent, the means and the instrument	
15d	The passive with intransitive verbs	93
15e	What is going on? Passive verbs with no subject	94
15f	Alternatives to the passive	94
15g	Action or description? The descriptive passive	96

16 Types of German verbs

16a	Predictability: regular or irregular?	98
16b	Weak and strong verbs	99
16c	Weak verbs	99
16d	Strong verbs	101
16e	Compound verbs	105

17 The formation of tenses: how are verbs conjugated?

17a	The basic form (base) of simple tenses	111
17b	Tense endings	112
17c	Compound tenses	113
17d	Formation of the imperative	117

18 Verb tables

18a	**haben** to have	119
18b	**sein** to be	121
18c	**werden** to become/will	122
18d	**gewarnt werden** to be warned	124
18e	List of strong verbs	125

D   *People, things and ideas: nouns and noun phrases*

19   *Labeling the world: nouns*

19a	What does a noun do?	132
19b	Adding details: the noun phrase	132
19c	Individual names and general labels:	132
	proper and common nouns	
19d	Names of people	133
19e	Geographical names	134
19f	Nationalities and languages	136
19g	Nouns formed from other parts of speech	137
19h	Nouns governing phrases and clauses	141

20   *Classes of German nouns: the three genders*

20a	What is meant by gender?	143
20b	What does it mean? Gender groupings by meaning	143
20c	Gender benders: nouns with double gender	145

21   *One or more? Singular and plural*

21a	Predicting the plural	147
21b	Plural groupings	147
21c	Double plurals	151
21d	Plurals with no singular	152
21e	Singulars for plurals	152

22   *The role of the noun phrase in the sentence: the four cases*

22a	What are cases?	154
22b	Case endings on nouns	154
22c	Uses of the nominative case	155
22d	Uses of the accusative case	156
22e	Uses of the genitive case	157
22f	Uses of the dative case	158
22g	Masculine nouns with irregular case endings	159

23   *Specifying nouns: determiners*

23a	What are determiners?	162
23b	Case endings on determiners	162
23c	Which ...? What sort of ...?	162
	Interrogative determiners	
23d	Already known: the definite article 'the'	164
23e	Unknown individuals: the indefinite article 'a(n)'	166
23f	Pointing and showing:	167
	demonstrative determiners 'that, this' etc.	

23g	How much? How many?	170
	The indefinite quantifiers 'some, all' etc.	
23h	Belonging together: possessive determiners	175
	'my, our' etc.	

24 Describing nouns: adjectives

24a	What do adjectives do?	177
24b	Accompanying the noun:	177
	adjectives within a noun phrase	
24c	At a distance: adjectives as separate elements	180
24d	Adjectives used as nouns	180
24e	More and most: comparative and superlative	182
24f	Adjectives formed from other parts of speech	187
24g	Adjectives governing phrases and clauses	189

25 Representing nouns: pronouns

25a	What pronouns do	192
25b	Personal pronouns	192
25c	Reflexive pronouns	195
25d	The indefinite pronoun 'one'	197
25e	The impersonal pronoun 'it'	197
25f	Which one? Interrogative pronouns	199
25g	Pointing and showing: demonstrative pronouns	200
25h	How much? How many? Indefinite quantities	202
25i	Belonging together: possessive pronouns	206
25j	Relative pronouns	206
25k	Natural and grammatical gender:	210
	problems of agreement	

26 Giving vent to your feelings: exclamations and interjections

| 26a | Exclamations | 211 |
| 26b | Interjections | 212 |

E Linking and modifying meanings: prepositions and adverbial expressions

27 Linking noun phrases into the sentence: prepositions

27a	What does a preposition do?	216
27b	Prepositions and the cases they take	216
27c	Prepositions followed by clauses	226

28 *Types of adverbial expression*

28a	What is an adverbial expression?	228
28b	Adverbs	228
28c	Adverbial phrases	229
28d	Adverbial clauses	230

29 *What adverbial expressions do*

29a	The role of adverbs in German	231
29b	What do adverbials affect?	231
29c	What effect do adverbials have?	232

F   **Using numbers**

30 *Numerals*

30a	Counting: cardinal numbers	238
30b	Arranging in order: ordinal numbers	241
30c	Dividing into parts: fractions and decimals	242

31 *Times and dates*

| 31a | Clock times | 244 |
| 31b | Days, months and years | 245 |

G   **Index**

How to use this Handbook

This *Grammar Handbook* can be used in two main ways.

• If you want to get a *general picture* of some aspect of German grammar, start with the list of Contents on page iii. You can then read through the relevant sections of the text. The many *cross-references* [shown by ➤ plus a paragraph number] will lead you to other, related topics.

• If you want to find out about a *specific grammatical point*, look it up in the extensive General Index at the end of the book. This gives the paragraph numbers for all the important items of grammar and for many German structure-words. To help you to find what you are looking for, items are often listed more than once, under different headings.

The *Handbook* gives a great deal of information about grammatical forms and structures, but above all, it is designed to show how they fit in with what you want to say or write. This shows in a number of ways.

• *Grammatical terms* are treated as convenient labels and used whenever necessary, but the Handbook does not assume that you already know what they mean. All terms are explained in everyday language in the most relevant paragraph, which is marked ⒟ (for Definition) in the General Index.

• The chapters are grouped into six parts (A to F), each of which deals with an area of language. This helps to show how various aspects of grammar are linked.

• Many *chapter and paragraph headings* use short descriptive phrases as well as grammatical terms.

• A key feature is the way in which grammatical points are *illustrated by examples* which make clear how they are used. Wherever it makes sense to do so, these sentences are linked together by a common context, and they often form short narratives or dialogues which help to fix them in the memory.

• The examples are drawn from a wide range of situations and occupations, so they provide you with a stock of useful expressions which you can adapt to suit what you want to say. If any construction is mainly used in more formal contexts, this is made clear in the text.

Finally, because all examples are translated into English, they provide a convenient way of testing your knowledge. Simply cover the translation and try to produce the German original. If you get a structure wrong, check it in the text and try again later.

A
PUTTING IDEAS INTO WORDS

1   *Classes of words: parts of speech*

2   *Getting it down on paper: spelling and punctuation*

3   *Linking ideas together*

Classes of words: parts of speech

1a   What kind of word is it?

It is often impossible to say what class a word belongs to (what *part of speech* it is) until it is used in a sentence. On the other hand, understanding a sentence may well depend on knowing what part of speech a word is, so it is useful to be able to recognize them. In this *Handbook* we define each part of speech mainly by what it does – what it refers to, and its function and position in the sentence. If you can also recognize a part of speech by its form, for example, by its endings, then this is described as well.

1b   Content words and structure words

Four classes of words, the *content words*, contain most of the meaning of the sentence. The others, the *structure words*, do of course add to the meaning, but they do it mainly by the way they relate to the content words. There is some overlap between these two groups, but the distinction is useful all the same. The following table shows the two groups with their English and German names, the paragraph number where they are first defined, and some examples. The German terms are given for information – they are not used in the text.

Note   German has two sets of grammatical terms, one derived from Latin, the other native German. The first set is much more like English, but the second set often gives a better idea of the function of a word than the Latin terms.

(i)   Content words

Verbs
Verben, Zeitwörter [►7a]
Meine Großmutter *spricht* und
***liest* Deutsch und Englisch.**
My grandmother *speaks* and *reads*
German and English.

Adjectives
Adjektive, Eigenschaftswörter
[►ch.24]
Sie findet sie *interessant* und
nützlich.
Sie finds them *interesting* and *useful.*

2

Nouns
Substantive, Hauptwörter [➤19a]
***Sprachen* sind ihr *Hobby*.**
Languages are her *hobby*.

Adverbs
Adverbien, Umstandswörter
[➤ch.28]
Sie spricht *schnell* und *gut*.
She speaks *fast* and *well*.

(ii) Structure words

Pronouns
Pronomina, Fürwörter [➤ch.25]
Sie* schenkt *mir* oft *etwas
Interessantes.
She often gives *me* something
interesting.

Determiners
Begleiter des Substantivs
[➤ch.23]
Mein* Lieblingsgeschenk ist *ein
Buch über *alle* Völker *der* Welt.
My favorite present is *a* book about
all the peoples of *the* world.

Prepositions
Präpositionen, Verhältniswörter
[➤27a]
***In* diesem Buch kann man viel**
***über* Sprachen lesen.**
In this book you can read a lot *about*
languages.

Conjunctions
Konjunktionen, Bindewörter[➤5a]
***Weil* sie Sprachen liebt, hofft sie,**
***dass* ich sie studieren werde.**
Because she loves languages, she
hopes *that* I will study them.

Exclamations
Interjektionen, Ausrufewörter
[➤ch.26]
***Na und!* Ich mag lieber Mathe.**
Auwei!
So what! I prefer math/maths. *Oh
dear!*

Getting it down on paper: spelling and punctuation

2a Spelling and sounds

This chapter describes the main features of German spelling and punctuation. It does not deal directly with German pronunciation, as attempts to describe sounds on paper are more likely to be a hindrance than a help.

2b The German alphabet

The order in which letters are listed in German dictionaries is the same as in English. The list below gives their pronunciation, using standard German spelling. Note that the **e** at the end of a letter name is pronounced as though doubled, as in the German word **See**. It is useful to know the German alphabet when spelling names and addresses, for example on the telephone.

A	a	J	jot	S	ess
(Ä	ä)	K	ka	ß	ess zett
B	be	L	ell	T	te
C	ze	M	emm	U	u
D	de	N	enn	(Ü	ü)
E	e	O	o	V	vau
F	eff	(Ö	ö)	W	we
G	ge	P	pe	X	ix
H	ha	Q	ku	Y	ypsilon
I	i	R	er	Z	zett

Note   The three vowels with Umlaut (**Ää, Öö, Üü**) [➤2c(i)] are separate letters, with their own typewriter keys, but they are not listed separately in the alphabet.

2c The main spelling rules

In most ways German spelling is quite predictable. Even where there are irregularities, they usually only affect a few words.
• Spelling rules do not apply to people's names.
• Important exceptions or inconsistencies are dealt with wherever they occur throughout the *Handbook*.

SPELLING AND PUNCTUATION 2c

(i)   Letters needing care

ä/e   Pronounced similarly, especially when short. Long **ä** is a more open sound than long **e**. Many words with **ä** are related to stems with **a**.

c   Used mainly in the combinations **ch, ck, sch** and **tsch**. By itself **c** is used only in foreign words, when it is pronounced like **k** before **a, o, u** and consonants, and like **z** or **s** before **e** and **i**.

f/v   Usually pronounced the same. **V** is used: in the many words with the prefix **ver-**; at the start of about a dozen other native German words (e.g. **Vater, Veilchen, Vetter, Vieh, viel, vier, Vogel, Vogt, Volk, voll, von, vor**); in foreign borrowings.

s/sch   The sound 'sh' is spelled **s** in words which start with **sp** (like **sprechen** or **Sport**), or **st** (like **stehen** or **Straße**). Otherwise it is spelled **sch**, as in **schwimmen**.

y   Only used in foreign borrowings. It is found as a vowel in words of Greek origin like **System** or **Physik**, when it is pronounced like **ü** or (by some people) **i**. In a few modern borrowings like **Yacht** or **Yoga** it is an initial consonant, pronounced like **j**.

b/d/g   Pronounced **p/t/k** respectively at the end of a word (though **-ig** is often pronounced **-ich**). This means that the pronunciation of many words changes when an **-e-** ending is added.

(ii)   Long and short vowels

German vowels are pronounced long:

(A) Usually before a single consonant: **fragen, träge, leben, wider, bot, Öl, duzen, für**. The main exceptions are some one-syllable structure words [►1b], like **das, in, mit, ob**. Before **ch,** vowels are sometimes long, as in **Sprache** or **Buch**, but more often short: **lachen, Fächer, sprechen, sicher, kochen, Löcher, Küche**.

(B) When followed by **h** (which is then never pronounced): **fahren, fährt, gehen, ihr, ohne, stöhnen, Kuh, Bühne**.

(C) In the few words with double **a, e** or **o** and the many words with **ie**: **Paar, Meer, Boot, wieder**. Note that **aa** and **oo** + Umlaut reduce to **ä** and **ö**: **ein Saal - zwei Säle, das Boot - das Bötchen**.

(iii)   Single and double letters

The following rules should be noted:

(A) ck is written instead of **kk** and (except in some foreign words) **tz** instead of **zz**: **Brücke, Katze** but **Jazz, Pizza**.

(B) Apart from endings and compounds, no German word contains the combinations consonant + double-consonant or double-consonant + consonant. Learners often write, for example, **der Artzt** for **der Arzt**, forgetting that **tz** counts as a double consonant.

(C) Two words can even make a compound which results in triple-consonant and vowel. If such a compound is split at the end of a line of running text, the new line begins with just one consonant, i.e. the last one of the three. (A vertical bar is used here to show the split.)

das Bett + das Tuch	➜	**das Betttuch (Bett|tuch)**
schnell + der Läufer	➜	**der Schnellläufer (Schnelll|läufer)**
brennen + die Nessel	➜	**die Brennnessel (Brenn|nessel)**
Stress + die Situation	➜	**die Stresssituation (Stress|situation)**

(iv) *ss or ß?*

SS is always used when writing in capitals. Otherwise, the following rules apply:
•**ß** is written instead of **ss** after a long vowel or a dipthong (vowel combination). (Fuß, Füße, Fußweg, groß, großes, Großhändler, fließen)
• After a short vowel **ss** is written, also at the end of a word. (küssen, küsst, Kuss, kussecht, gewiss, gewisser, Gewissheit)
• All words ending in -**nis** as well as some foreign words are written with only one **s**, even though their plural forms are written with **ss**. (Zeugnis - Zeugnisse, Geheimnis - Geheimnisse, Bus - Busse)

Note   **ß** is not used when **ss** is formed at the join between the two halves of a compound.

das Glas + der Splitter	➜	**der Glassplitter**
die Rettung + joining -s-		
+ die Station	➜	**die Rettungsstation**

(v) *Capital letters*

Capitals are used for the first letter of:

• a word at the start of a sentence, as in English;
• all nouns, not just the names of persons and places [➤19c];
• any other part of speech used as a noun. Especially with adjectives, the rules about capitalization are complex [➤24d(iii)].

beim Essen	while eating [➤10a(iii)]
eine Sechs	a six [➤30a(ii)]
das Für und Wider	the pros and cons
alles Gute!	all the best!
etwas Verdächtiges	something suspicious
das Ich und das Es	the ego and the id

2d Punctuation

The main punctuation marks in German are:

.	der Punkt
,	das Komma
;	der Strichpunkt
:	der Doppelpunkt
?	das Fragezeichen
!	das Ausrufezeichen
( )	die Klammer (-n)
„ "	die Anführungsstriche (unten/oben)
-	der Bindestrich

(i) Periods/Full stops

The period is used, as in English, at the end of sentences, and also:

• after ordinal numbers [➤30b]: **der 16. September**;
• after abbreviations like **Dr. Ing**. for **Doktor Ingenieur, bzw**. for **beziehungsweise** 'or', **vorm./nachm.** for **vormittags/nachmittags** 'a.m./p.m.', but not after initial letters like **EU** for **Europäische Union** 'European Union' **USA**, **UN**.

(ii) Commas

The use of the comma differs significantly from English.

(A) Its main function is to mark off each separate clause in a sentence from the next [➤4d]. Commas are therefore written:

• between main clauses with different subjects. Main clauses which share a subject are separated by either a comma or **und/oder**, but not both [➤5a(i)].

Wir standen alle auf, und ich holte meine Sachen und lud sie ins Auto.	We all got up, and I fetched my things and loaded them into the car.

Note: This comma can also be left out

7

• between the main clause and any type of subordinate clause. Subordinate clauses linked by **und** or **oder** do not have a comma between them.

Da Heiner noch nicht da war, fürchtete ich, dass er den Ausflug vergessen hatte oder dass sein Wagen eine Panne hatte.	As Heiner had not arrived yet, I was afraid that he had forgotten the outing or that his car had broken down.

• between the main clause and a **zu** + infinitive clause. Exceptions to this rule are given in paragraphs 8h(ii) and 10a(iv).

Ich versuchte mehrmals umsonst, ihn telefonisch zu erreichen.	I tried several times without success to reach him by phone.

Note: This comma can also be left out.
• between the main clause and longer participle clauses[➤10b(v)].

Das Schlimmste fürchtend, fuhr ich zu seinem Haus hinüber.	Fearing the worst, I drove over to his house.

(B) Commas are also normally written:
• between two or more adjectives before a noun if they are felt to be equally important, that is, if they could be linked by **und**.

Da saß Heiner vor seinem Haus in einem knallroten, teuren Wagen. Es war der neueste italienische Sportwagen.	There sat Heiner in front of his house in a bright red, expensive car. It was the newest Italian car.

• to separate exclamations (but see (iii) (C) below), explanatory remarks and the like.

„Aber Heiner, um Gottes willen, hast du denn unseren Ausflug vergessen, Mensch?", rief ich.	"But Heiner, for heaven's sake, have you forgotten our outing, man?" I exclaimed.

• in decimals, where English uses a decimal point [➤30c(iii)].

„Magst du meine neue 3,5-Liter-Kutsche?", fragte er gelassen.	"Do you like my new 3.5-liter wagon?" he asked unperturbed.

(iii)   Other punctuation marks

(**A**) The semi-colon is rarely used in German. A comma or period is usually preferred.

Ich schwieg einen Augenblick, ich war nämlich sprachlos.	I was silent for a moment; I was in fact speechless.

(**B**) A colon, not a comma, is used to introduce direct speech.

Schließlich sagte ich: „Mann! Du bist mir aber einer!"	Finally I said, "Man! You really are something else!"

(**C**) Opening quotation marks are placed on the line, not above it as in English (see the examples given above). Hence the expression **Anführungsstriche unten/oben** for 'Open/close quotes'.

(**D**) Question marks are used as in English, at the end of direct questions [➤ch.6].

„Hast du unseren Ausflug wirklich vergessen?"	"Did you really forget our outing?"

(**E**) An exclamation point/mark is used:
• after exclamations and commands. If the command is more like a request, many Germans would now put a period [➤13b(ii)].

„Sei mir nicht böse, Karl!", sagte er. „Lies das!" Und reichte mir einen Brief.	"Don't be angry at me, Karl," he said. "Read that!" And handed me a letter.

• after the opening words of a letter, though a comma is now frequently used instead.

„Sehr geehrter Herr Klotz!", las ich. „Sie haben den ersten Preis im Lotto gewonnen!"	"Dear Mr. Klotz," I read. "You have won first prize in the lottery!"

(**F**) Use of hyphens: ➤3b(iii).

Linking ideas together

3a   *Compound words or phrases?*

All languages have ways of combining word meanings so as to express more complex ideas, either by joining two words together to form one compound word or by linking separate words to form phrases. German does of course employ phrases in this way, but the particular strength of the language is its capacity to make compound words.

3b   *Compound words*

This section illustrates some of the ways in which compound nouns and adjectives are formed. Compound verbs, made either with prefixes or with particles, are dealt with in Chapter 16 (see references below). Compound adverbs are discussed briefly in paragraph 28b(ii).

Note   1) In any German compound, the last component plays the leading role. That is to say, it is the final part of the word that decides the gender (if a noun), takes endings and makes stem changes (if any).

2) The examples in paragraphs (ii) and (iii) below show some of the qualities of German compounds.

• The English equivalents sometimes use two words, sometimes one, perhaps with a hyphen. German compounds are written as one word, normally without a hyphen [but ➤(iii) below]. This can produce some very long words, but this is only really noticeable in writing.
• English often uses words of Latin or Greek origin (for example, 'anemometer, pugnacious, anemic') where German uses easily comprehensible combinations of everyday words.
• Especially with adjectives and adverbs, English often has to use a phrase to render the meaning of a German compound word.

➤   *for-* + get → forget: verbs formed with fixed prefixes ➤16e(i).
get *up*: verbs linked to particles ➤16e(ii).
mis- + govern + *-ment* → misgovernment: nouns formed with prefixes and suffixes ➤19g(iii) and (iv).
un- + read + *-able* → unreadable: adjectives formed with prefixes and suffixes ➤24f(i) and (ii).

(i) *Nouns*

Compound nouns [➤19a] can be formed with any other part of speech, but noun + noun is the most common combination. After nouns ending in **-e** (and a few others) there may be a linking **-n-**; after some other nouns (e.g. feminine nouns ending in **-heit, -keit, -schaft** or **-ung**) a linking **-s-** is used.

Noun + noun

die Presse + die Karte	➔ **die Pressekarte**	press card
die Kasse + -n- +		
das Buch	➔ **das Kassenbuch**	cashbook
die Rettung + -s- +		
das Floß	➔ **das Rettungsfloß**	liferaft
der Wind + der Messer	➔ **der Windmesser**	anemometer (wind-speed meter)

Verb stem + noun

schreib- + der Tisch	➔ **der Schreibtisch**	(writing) desk

Adjective + noun

schnell + der Zug	➔ **der Schnellzug**	express train

Adverb + noun

sofort + die Hilfe	➔ **die Soforthilfe**	emergency aid

Preposition + noun

für + die Sorge	➔ **die Fürsorge**	care, welfare

Exclamation + noun

Pfui! + der Ruf	➔ **der Pfuiruf**	boo

(ii) *Adjectives*

Many compound adjectives come from the corresponding noun. In other cases the compound gives an adjective a particular slant which may be translated by a single English word but which is often best rendered by a phrase.

Noun + adjective

das Wasser + dicht	➔ **wasserdicht**	watertight

PUTTING IDEAS INTO WORDS

der Streit + lustig	→ streitlustig	argumentative, aggressive
das Blut + arm	→ blutarm	anemic
die Kreide + weiß	→ kreideweiß	white as chalk

Verb stem + adjective

| lern- + begierig | → lernbegierig | eager to learn |
| stink- + langweilig | → stinklangweilig | deadly boring (colloquial) |

Adverb + adjective

| hoch + interessant | → hochinteressant | most interesting |
| früh + reif | → frühreif | precocious |

Preposition + adjective

| ohne + gleich + -en | → ohnegleichen | unparalleled, like nothing else |

(iii)   *Hyphens*

Hyphens have various functions in German. The precise rules are often complex and not at all important for learners. In general, hyphens are used:

(A) between syllables when a word has to be split across two lines in a piece of running text. (In the examples given below a vertical bar | is used to show the split, as these words would not normally have a hyphen.)

• Compounds are split at the join so that the new line starts with the second (or later) part.

Geschäfts	leute	business people
Miet	vertrag	lease
Mikro|wellen|herd	microwave oven

• With simple words, including those with suffixes, the basic principle is that the new line begins with just one consonant or with the second of two separate vowels. The diphthongs **ai, au, äu, ei** and **eu** are not split, nor are **ch, sch,** or **ck**.

Öff|nung	opening	**Bäu|me**	trees
Bäcke|rei	bakery	**bers|ten**	burst
Ver|schie|de|nes	various things	**spre|chen**	speak
bö|ig	gusty	**wa|schen**	wash
freu|dig	joyful	**grü|ßen**	greet
le|cker	tasty	**küs|sen**	kiss
Fens|ter	window		

(**B**) to break up a compound which contains, for example, the name of a person or organization, an abbreviation, a figure or a prepositional phrase.

die Mercedes-Werke	Mercedes factory
die Fritz-Thyssen-Stiftung	Fritz Thyssen Foundation
die SPD-Fraktion	SPD (Social Democrat) party
der 10-Kilometer-Lauf	10-kilometer race
das Vor-sich-hin-Starren	staring into space

(**C**) to avoid repeating a part which two or more compounds have in common.

An- und Verkauf von Silber- und Goldwaren!	Silver and gold objects bought and sold!
Das ganze Hin- und Herlaufen hatte mich total erschöpft.	All that running back and forth had completely exhausted me.

3c   *Side by side: words in apposition*

Sometimes we use one noun phrase immediately after another to give further information about it. This explanatory phrase is said to be in apposition. In German, the second phrase is separated from the first by a comma. It is normally in the same case as the first phrase.

Hans Wollmer, *der Präsident der Studentenvereinigung*, ist ein Freund von Dr. Bäumler, *dem Seminarleiter*.	Hans Vollmer, *the president of the student union,* is a friend of Dr. Bäumler, *the leader of the seminar.*

Note   1) This also applies to phrases introduced by **wie** 'as' or **als** 'than, as'. In this example, note how the change of case '**ich/mich**' affects the meaning.

Er kennt ihn viel besser als *ich/* **als** *mich.*	He knows him much better than *I do/*than *he knows me.*

2) With place names German often uses this construction where English has 'of'.

Ich bin auf der Insel Sylt geboren und in der Stadt Cuxhaven zur Schule gegangen. Jetzt studiere ich an der Universität Tübingen.	I was born on the island of Sylt and went to school in the town of Cuxhaven. Now I am studying at the University of Tübingen.

3d   Quantities, measurements and prices

(i)   Case usage

The use of case with measurement phrases varies greatly but depends mainly on how exact the measure is. [Plural forms: ➤(ii) below.]

(A) Container/standard measure (+ adjective) + noun: the whole phrase is in the same case.

In der Kohlenindustrie bleiben viele *Tonnen hochwertige Kohle* **unverkauft.**	In the coal industry many *tons of high-grade coal* remain unsold.

(B) Indefinite quantity (+ adjective) + noun: the quantity is followed by **von** plus the dative or, especially in writing, by a phrase in the genitive. If there is no adjective, then **von** can be left out; the whole phrase is then in the same case.

Eine *Anzahl unrentabler Bergwerke* **müssen mit der Stilllegung rechnen.** *Eine ganze Menge Bergleute* **würden dann ihre Arbeit verlieren.**	A *number of unprofitable mines* face closure. *A great many miners* would then lose their jobs.

(C) Nouns of number (**das Dutzend/Hundert/Tausend** and **die Million/Milliarde**) [➤30a(ii)] follow the usage of:

• (A) above if they are preceded by a number.

In unserer Region haben *zwei* ***Millionen Leute* keine Arbeit.**	In our region *two million people* are out of work.

• (B) above in the plural without a number.

In manchen Städten gibt es ***Tausende von jungen Arbeitslosen.***	In many towns there are *thousands of young unemployed.*

(ii) *Plural measures*

Masculine and neuter nouns of number, measurement or value do not use their plural forms when they follow a number or another expression of quantity. This also applies to **der Euro.** However, feminine nouns of measurement use their plural forms.

Sieben Glas Bier, vier Flaschen Wein und zwei Dutzend Bratwürste bitte!	Seven glasses of beer, four bottles of wine and two dozen grilled sausages please!
Bei -10 Grad Kälte braucht man mehrere Paar Handschuhe.	At -10 degrees you need several pairs of gloves.
Orangen - zehn Stück für drei Euro!	Oranges - ten (pieces) for three Euros!

B
PUTTING A SENTENCE TOGETHER: SYNTAX

4   *Recognizing sentences*

5   *Linking clauses together*

6   *Asking for information: direct questions*

Recognizing sentences

4a   What is a sentence?

A sentence is a spoken or written utterance which has a *subject* and a *predicate*. When talking, we often say things which are not sentences, for example, exclamations or isolated phrases which make perfect sense, because we know the context. In writing, however, we usually use complete sentences. The way a sentence is put together is known as its *syntax.*

4b   The subject of a sentence

(i)   Generally speaking, the subject is the word or phrase whose action or state the sentence is describing. In other words, it answers the question **Wer/Was ist ...?** 'Who/What is ...?' or **Wer/Was macht ...?** Who/What is ... doing?.

Die meisten deutschen Familien **besitzen ein Auto.**   *Most German families* own a car.

➤   *It* is obvious that you'll get wet. *It*'s raining: impersonal subjects ➤25e.

(ii)   Sometimes the verb is in the passive [➤ch.15]. This means that, instead of doing the action, the subject is at the receiving end.

Viele Leute **werden jeden Monat bei Autounfällen verletzt.**   *Many people* are injured each month in car accidents.

(iii)   In commands the assumed subject is 'you'. In German the familiar forms **du** and its plural **ihr** are usually omitted, but the more formal **Sie** is always retained [➤13b].

Passen *Sie*/**Passt auf, wenn** *Sie*/*ihr* **am Steuer sitzen/sitzt!**   Pay attention when you are sitting behind the wheel.

4c *The predicate of a sentence*

The predicate consists of the rest of the sentence, apart from the subject. Its essential element is the main verb, that is, a verb in one of the simple tenses [➤11b]. This verb agrees with the subject and its form changes to match the subject. Chapter 7 describes the various types of verb and what they do.

Ihr Taxi *wartet*. Ihre Eltern *warten*.	Your taxi *is waiting*. Your parents *are waiting*.

Most predicates consist of more than this minimum. For example, they may contain adverbial expressions[1] [➤ch.28], objects of the verb[2] [➤8d] or non-finite verbs[3] [➤ch.10].

Das Taxi musste *lange*[1] *auf Sie*[2] *warten*[3].	The taxi had to *wait*[3] *a long time*[1] *for you*[2].

4d *Sentences and clauses*

There are three types of complete sentence:

• statements, which are the basic form;
• direct questions [➤ch.6];
• commands [➤ch.13].

All three must have a main clause. They may also have any number of subordinate clauses.

(i) *Main clauses*

A main clause is a sentence which can stand by itself, though it may not make much sense unless you know what the speaker is talking about. [➤5a(i) for more examples.]

Es hat lange auf Sie gewartet. – Was? – Ihr Taxi!	*It waited a long time for you. –* What? – Your taxi!

(ii) *Subordinate clauses*

A subordinate clause is always dependent on another clause, whose meaning it completes or expands. It is linked to the main clause by one of three types of word:

• a subordinating conjunction [➤5a(ii), 5c(ii)];

SYNTAX

- a question word [➤5b];
- a relative pronoun [➤5d].

In the following example the subordinate clauses are in italics. [For further examples ➤paragraphs referred to above].

Ich konnte nicht länger bleiben, *da mein Taxi schon auf mich wartete. Nachdem ich mich von allen verabschiedet hatte,* **verließ ich das Haus.**	I could not stay any longer, *as my taxi was already waiting for me.* *After I had said goodbye to everybody,* I left the house.

Note Because the finite verb is sent to the end of subordinate clauses [➤4e(iv)], they tend to be clumsier than in English and French. Germans will therefore often avoid them by using two main clauses containing suitable adverbs. [Avoiding relative clauses: ➤25j(viii).]

Mein Taxi wartete schon auf mich, *also* **konnte ich nicht länger bleiben. Ich verabschiedete mich von allen,** *dann* **verließ ich das Haus.**	My taxi was already waiting for me, *so* I could not stay any longer. I said goodbye to everybody, *then* I left the house.

4e   *The order of words and phrases: syntax*

German syntax is a flexible system in which some elements are fixed and others movable. The main clause of any German statement consists of three *blocks* of information. (The German names are given here in case you come across them.)

- The *'opening block'* (**das Vorfeld**) contains just one item of information – this may be a single word, a phrase or a subordinate clause.
- The *'central block'* (**das Mittelfeld**) contains most of the information and always starts with the main verb. Hence the often quoted rule 'main verb second'.
- The '*final block*' (**das Nachfeld**) contains elements that complete the meaning of the main verb – verbal particles, or the infinitive or past participle of other verbs.

Opening block	*Central block*	*Final block*
Mein Sohn	*schläft* **immer wie ein Bär.**	
Wenn er Ferien hat,	*steht* **er morgens selten vor elf Uhr**	**auf.**
Dann	*will* **er immer gleich**	**frühstücken.**

Paragraphs (i) to (iii) below look at main clause statements in greater detail. Paragraph (iv) deals with the differences in subordinate clauses. Paragraph (v) lists things which may come before the opening block or after the final block.

Note 1) Questions have the same word order as statements except that they start either with the main verb (Yes/No questions [➤6b]) or with a question word [➤6d].

2) Commands have the same word order as statements except that they start with the main verb [➤ch.13].

(i) *The opening block in main clauses*

The opening block does not usually convey the main point of the statement. It often picks up and perhaps emphasizes something already mentioned or assumed to be known. The block may contain:

(A) the subject [➤4b]. This is naturally very common but, unlike in English or French, the subject has no more right to this position than any other element.

Ich	**habe einen Feinmechanikbetrieb**	**gegründet.**

In *I* founded a precision engineering firm.

(B) an adverb or adverbial phrase [➤28a]. Time phrases and short unemphatic adverbs like **da** or **also** often start the sentence, but almost any adverbial may do so, especially if it refers back in some way.

Damals	**hatten wir immer noch Hochkonjunktur.**	
In unserem Städtchen	**herrschte Mangel an Arbeitskräften.**	

In *those days* we were still in a boom.
In *our small town* there was a shortage of labor.

(C) a subordinate clause [➤4d(ii)]. These usually answer the same questions as adverbs.

Weil das Geschäft gut lief,	**konnte ich eine erfahrene Betriebsleiterin**	**anstellen.**

Because the business was running well, I was able to appoint an experienced plant manager.

21

SYNTAX

(D) an object of the verb. This could be direct (accusative) [➤8d(i)], indirect (dative) [➤8d(ii), 8e] or prepositional [➤8g]. [A genitive object would also be possible, but ➤8d(iii)].

Ihr *Auf sie*	vertraute ich die tägliche Organisation konnte ich mich ohne Bedenken	an. verlassen.

I entrusted the day-to-day organization *to her*. I could rely *on her* without hesitation.

(E) an infinitive or past participle [➤10a, 10b(iii)].

Bereut	habe ich es nie.	

I have never *regretted* it.

(F) a participle clause [➤10b(v)]. Apart from set phrases, this is uncommon in colloquial German.

Von ihr geleitet,	lief alles wie geölt.	

Managed by her, everything ran like clockwork.

(ii)   *The central block in main clauses*

The central block contains the main information of the statement, starting with the main verb. In general, information is given in increasing order of importance, so that elements which:

• give new information
• are emphasized or longer
• are closely linked to the verb

tend to come later than other elements.
This produces the following normal order after the verb, but remember that a particular emphasis or linking together of ideas may well change the order.

(A) Personal pronouns, if any, in the order subject – direct object – indirect object.

Schließlich	habe *ich es ihr* fast völlig	überlassen.

In the end *I* left *it* almost entirely *to her*.

(B) Other subjects (nouns or other pronouns such as **das, etwas, niemand**). If neither the subject nor the direct object shows the case, then the subject comes after the pronoun object.

Ab 1989	hat uns *die Rezession* immer mehr	geschadet.

From 1989 on *the recession* harmed us more and more.

(C) Indirect (dative) noun objects.

Ich	habe *dem Personal* die Situation	erklärt.

I explained the situation *to the staff.*

(D) Most adverbial expressions (but see F, G and H below), in the order:

- Short adverbs expressing the speaker's attitude [➤29c(iii)];
- Time (**Wann?**);
- Reason and cause (**Warum?**);
- Place (**Wo?**).

(In the following example the * sign shows where each adverbial starts.)

Wir	hatten *zwar *zu der Zeit *aus verschiedenen Gründen *in der Region wenig Konkurrenz.	

For various reasons we had *at that time admittedly* little competition *in the region.*

(E) Direct (accusative) noun objects.

Trotzdem	mussten wir von Zeit zu Zeit *Arbeiter*	entlassen.

All the same we had to lay off *workers* from time to time.

(F) Negatives which refer to the whole statement. If **nicht** refers only to one specific element, then it goes before that element.

Die Firma	konnte bei sinkender Nachfrage ihren Lohn *nicht* (mehr)	zahlen.

With the declining demand the firm could *not* (no longer) pay their wages.

(G) Adverbials of manner (**Wie?**).

| Das | haben wir immer *sehr ungern* | gemacht. |

We always did it *very unwillingly*.

(H) Complements of linking verbs [➤8c] and prepositional phrases which are closely linked to the verb. The latter include prepositional objects [➤8g] and phrases answering the questions **Wo?** 'Where?' after verbs of position and **Wohin?** 'Where to?' after verbs of motion.

Wir	haben das Arbeitsamt umsonst *um Hilfe*	gebeten.
Es	wurden immer mehr Leute *arbeitslos.*	
Man	sah sie Tag für Tag *vor dem Arbeitsamt*	stehen.

We asked the employment office in vain *for help*. More and more people were becoming *unemployed*. You could see them standing day after day *in front of the employment office*.

(iii)   *The final block in main clauses*

The final block contains elements which are directly linked to the main verb, whose meaning they complete. These are:

• verbal particles;
• past participles;
• infinitives.

The more complex the verb construction is, the more elements there are in the final block. If we start with a simple sentence and make it more complex in various ways, both the process and the order of elements become clear.

(A) Sentence with full verb in a simple tense (here the present). Final block empty.

| Mein Partner | *kommt* heute mit dem Intercityzug aus Berlin. | |

My partner *is coming* today on the Intercity train from Berlin.

(B) Verbal particle **an** added in final block. Also relevant to: all other verbal particles [➤16e(ii)].

Mein Partner	*kommt* bald mit dem Intercityzug aus Berlin	*an.*

My partner *is arriving* soon on the Intercity train from Berlin.

(C) Modal auxiliary **soll** introduced. Infinitive **ankommen** moved to end. Also relevant to: other modal verbs [➤ch.9]; compound future with auxiliary **werden** [➤12c].

Mein Partner *ankommen.*	*soll* bald mit dem Intercityzug	aus Berlin

My partner *is due to arrive* soon on the Intercity train from Berlin.

(D) Perfect tense with auxiliary **ist**. Past participle **angekommen** moved to end. Also relevant to: all perfect tenses with auxiliaries **haben** or **sein** [➤17c]; passive with auxiliary **werden** [➤ch.15].

Mein Partner	*ist* gerade mit dem Intercityzug aus Berlin	*angekommen.*

My partner *has* just *arrived* on the Intercity train from Berlin.

(E) Past conditional of modal auxiliary **können**. Infinitive-past participle **können** moved to end. Also relevant to: all perfect tenses of modal verbs [➤9b(i)].

Mit dem ICE	*hätte* er früher	ankommen *können.*

He *could have* arrived earlier on the Intercity train.

(F) Future perfect with auxiliary **wird** [➤12c]. Auxiliary infinitive **sein** moved to end. Also relevant to: modal verbs with perfect infinitives [➤9c(ii), (iv) and (v)].

Bis vier Uhr	*wird* er wohl trotzdem	angekommen *sein.*

All the same, he *will* no doubt *have* arrived by four o'clock.

(iv) *Word order in subordinate clauses*

Subordinate clause word order differs from main clauses in two important ways:

(A) The finite verb is moved from second position to the end of the final block. This is in effect simply an extension of the verb movements shown in paragraph (iii) above. [Position of **hätte** in second example below: ➤9b(iii)].

(B) The subject normally comes immediately after the conjunction. As in main clauses, a pronoun object (especially **sich**) may come before a noun subject. [Relative clauses: ➤5b].
The following examples, adapted from examples (iii) A, E and F above, show these changes in action.

Main clauses	Subordinate (center)	Subordinate (final)
Ich hoffe,	***dass* mein Partner heute zu uns**	***kommt.***
Ich glaube nicht,	***dass* er mit dem ICE**	***hätte* kommen *können.***
Ich weiß nicht,	***ob* er bis vier Uhr**	**angekommen *sein* wird.**

I hope *that* my partner *comes* to see us today.
I do not think *that* he *could have* come by Intercity train.
I don't know *whether* he *will have* arrived by four o'clock.

(v) Outside the blocks

(A) The following elements may come before the opening block without affecting the word order. They are separated by a comma:

• the name of the person being spoken to;
• interjections [➤26b], including **ja, nein** and their equivalents;
• clauses starting with 'whoever', 'however', 'whenever' etc. [➤5a(ii)F];
• certain words and phrases put in as an aside, for example:

Das heißt (d.h.), ...	That is (i.e.), ...
Im Gegenteil, ...	On the contrary, ...
Kurz, ...	In short, ...
Nun/Na, ...	Well, ...
Offen gestanden, ...	To be frank, ...
So, ...	Well now/Right, ...
Sehen Sie/Siehst du, ...	Well, you see, ...
Wie gesagt, ...	As I said, ...
Wissen Sie/Weißt du, ...	You know, ...

(B) The following elements normally go after the final block:

• subordinate clauses, including relative clauses if possible, separated by a comma. (Subordinate clauses may also fill the opening block.)
• **zu** + infinitive clauses;
• (usually) comparative phrases after **als** and **wie;**
• over-long phrases, and afterthoughts. The latter are naturally common in speech and in informal writing.

Wir haben gestern Siegfried gesehen, *der von dir gesprochen hat.* Er ist noch dicker geworden *als sein Bruder.*	We saw Siegfried yesterday, *who spoke of you.* He has gotten even heavier *than his brother.*
Wir haben vor, dich bald zu besuchen, *vielleicht nach Ostern.*	We plan to visit you soon, *perhaps after Easter.*

Linking clauses together

5a Clauses with conjunctions

'Conjunction' means 'joining'. There are two sorts of conjunctions: 'coordinating' and 'subordinating'. Their names reflect their function in the sentence.

(i) Joining equals: coordinating conjunctions

Coordinating conjunctions link clauses of equal status: main with main [➤4d(i)], subordinate with subordinate [➤4d(ii)]. They tell us something about how the clauses relate to each other (reinforcing, contrasting, etc.), but they do not affect the word order of the following clause. Almost all of them can also link words, phrases and parts of clauses.

(A) und 'and'.
Alternatives which link phrases but not clauses are **sowie** and **sowohl ... als/wie (auch) ...** 'both ... and ...'. These are more used in writing – in speech 'both X and Y' is normally rendered as **X und auch Y**.

Mein Geschäft wächst, *und* ich brauche dringend ein Darlehen.	My business is growing, *and* I urgently need a loan.

(B) oder 'or', **entweder ... oder ...** 'either ... or ...', **beziehungsweise** 'or alternatively'/'... respectively'.
oder cannot be used for English 'not ... or ...' [➤(C) below].

***Entweder* die Bank leiht mir das Geld, *oder* ich kann nicht expandieren. Ich brauche sofort eine halbe Million, *bzw.* 1,5 Millionen über vier Jahre.**	*Either* the bank lends me the money, *or* I can't expand. I need half a million immediately, *or alternatively,* 1.5 million over four years.

(C) weder ... noch ... 'neither ... nor ...'
Note that **weder** does not usually start a clause, but comes after the verb; **noch** starts the second clause, but the verb comes immediately after it. In speech, **und auch nicht/kein ...** is a common alternative; this is also used for 'not ... or ...' and for 'nor' without a preceding 'neither'.

Ich habe *weder* selber das Geld, *noch* kenne ich jemand, der es mir leihen kann.	I *neither* have the money myself, *nor* do I know anyone who can lend it to me.

(D) aber, allein, jedoch 'but, however'.
Of these **aber** is by far the most common. The others are mainly literary alternatives. Unlike English 'but', **aber** and **jedoch** can be used not just at the start of a sentence or clause, but also within it.

Mein Onkel ist reich, *aber* ich kann ihn nicht darum bitten. Er ist zwar Millionär, will *aber/ jedoch* sein Geld nicht riskieren.	My uncle is rich, *but* I can't ask him for it. He may be a millionaire, *but* he doesn't want to risk his money.

(E) nicht (nur) ... sondern (auch) ... 'not (only) ... but (also) ...'
sondern, not **aber**, must always be used when 'but' contrasts with an earlier 'not'. Thus *sie ist nicht groß, aber stark* means 'she is not big *but (she is)* strong'.

Er ist *nicht nur* alt, *sondern auch* sehr vorsichtig.	He is *not only* old *but also* very cautious.

(F) denn 'for, as, because'.
Now little used in speech. A useful alternative is to use the adverb **nämlich** 'you see' after the verb in the second main clause.

Er vertraut mir nicht, *denn* er erinnert sich noch an meine Jugend!	He doesn't trust me, *because* he still remembers my youth!
Er vertraut mir nicht - er erinnert sich *nämlich* noch an meine Jugend!	He doesn't trust me – *you see*, he still remembers my youth!

(ii) *Clauses dependent on other clauses: subordinating conjunctions*

Subordinating conjunctions link subordinate clauses [➤4d(ii)] to the rest of the sentence. Remember that the finite verb goes at the end. Usually these subordinate clauses are adverbial expressions [➤ch.28], and many of them answer one of the

29

questions listed in paragraphs 6d(v) to (ix). Only the more common conjunctions are listed here.

(A) dass 'that'.

This is a pure linking word, with no meaning of its own. It is common after verbs of speech, thought, etc. [e.g. in reported speech, ►14c(ii)]; here it is often left out, in which case the following clause has main clause word order. Do not use **dass** for other English uses of 'that', especially as in 'the person/thing *that* I saw' [►25j] or *'that's* wrong' [►25g].

Ich glaube wirklich, *dass* Fritz mich meidet. (**Ich glaube, Fritz meidet mich.**)	I really believe *(that)* Fritz is avoiding me.

(B) Time.

als	when	**sobald**	as soon as
bevor	before	**solange**	so as long as
bis	until	**während**	while
nachdem	after	**wenn**	when(ever)
seit(dem)	since	**wie**	as

Note 1) **als** 'when' is used only for single events in the past. In all other cases use **wenn**.

2) **sobald** and **solange** are spelled as one word and are not followed by **wie**.

***Wenn* er mich sieht, haut er ab. *Als* ich neulich Einkäufe machte, bin ich ihm begegnet. *Sobald* er mich gesehen hat, ist er weggerannt!**	*When(ever)* he sees me he takes off. Recently, *when* I was doing some shopping, I ran into him. *As soon as* he caught sight of me, he ran off!

(C) Reasons and causes.

da	as, since	**weil**	because
nun da	now that, seeing that	**zumal**	especially as

***Da* ich ihn dringend sprechen wollte, bin ich ihm nachgelaufen. Ich habe ihn aber aus den Augen verloren, *weil* er mir zu schnell war.**	*As* I urgently wanted to speak to him, I ran after him. But I lost sight of him, *because* he was too quick for me.

(D) Purpose and result.
Be careful to distinguish the two meanings of the English 'so that', as shown in the examples.

damit	so that, in order that	**sodass**	so that, with the result that

Ich habe Tempo zugelegt, *damit* er mir nicht entwischen konnte. Es wurde dunkel, *sodass* ich nicht gut sehen konnte.	I got moving, *so that* he couldn't give me the slip. It was getting dark, *so that* I couldn't see well.

(E) Manner and degree.
After **als ob** the conditional is normal. In formal writing the **ob** in **als ob** may be left out; the verb then comes immediately after **als**. [(an)statt/außer/ohne dass: ➤27c]

als ob	as if, as though	**sofern**	provided that
dadurch dass	by ...ing	**soweit**	as, so far as
indem	by ...ing	**wie**	as, like

Ich holte ihn endlich ein, *indem* ich mich durch den Verkehr schlängelte. Er tat, *als ob* er froh wäre, /*als* wäre er froh, mich zu sehen.	I finally caught up with him *by* dodg*ing* through the traffic. He pretended to be (acted *as though* he were) glad to see me.

(F) Conditions and concessions
falls is sometimes used for 'if' where **wenn** could mean 'when(ever)' [➤(B) above]. **trotzdem** is not strictly correct here, but it is increasingly used.

es sei denn	unless	**trotzdem**	even though
falls	if	**wenn**	if [➤14d]
obwohl	although		

***Obwohl* ich ziemlich böse war, habe ich nichts gesagt. *Wenn* ich nur wüsste, was mit ihm los ist – *es sei denn*, er schuldet meinem Vater Geld!**	*Although* I was pretty annoyed, I said nothing. *If* only I knew what was the matter with him – *unless* he owes my father money!

Note   Any of the question words **wer, wie, wo** etc. [➤6d] can be used with **auch (immer)** to mean 'who*ever*', 'how*ever*', 'wher*ever*', etc. 'How*ever*' + adjective or adverb is **so ... auch**. Notice that these clauses do not usually affect the word order in the following sentence.

***Was** er **auch immer** gemacht hat, er braucht mir nicht aus dem Weg zu gehen. **So** seltsam er **auch** sein mag/ist, ich mag ihn gern.*	*Whatever* he has done, he doesn't have to avoid me. *However* strange he may be, I like him.

5b   Relative clauses

Relative clauses are introduced by relative pronouns [➤25j for fuller treatment]. They describe or define a noun and thus do much the same job as an adjective [➤ch.24]. The relative clause comes very soon (usually immediately) after the noun it refers to. For this reason the noun is known as the *antecedent*. [Avoiding relative clauses: ➤25j(viii).]

Es gibt ebenso viele Leute, *die* das Unglaubliche glauben, wie Leute, *die* das Unzweifelhafte bezweifeln.	There are just as many people *who* believe the incredible as people *who* doubt the indubitable.
Mein Cousin Alfons, *der* Philosoph ist, hat ein Auto gekauft, das einen Motorschaden hat.	My cousin Alfons, *who* is a philosopher, has bought a car which has an engine problem.

   'The firm (*that*) I work *for* makes bottles': German cannot leave out the relative pronoun or place a preposition at the end of the relative clause in this way [➤25j(i)].

5c   Indirect speech

There are two ways of reporting what people have said (or perhaps thought). Both are introduced by verbs like **sagen** 'say', **antworten** 'answer', **fragen** 'ask', **denken/glauben** 'think'.

(i)   Repetition of direct speech

The first way is simply to repeat what was said or thought, the *direct speech*. In writing we would then use quotation marks.

„Ich gehe um halb zehn zu einer Konferenz," sagte mein Chef.	"I am going to a meeting at half past nine," my boss said.
Ich dachte: „Sie werden zu spät kommen."	I thought, "You'll be late."
Ich fragte ihn: „Wo findet sie statt?"	I asked him: "Where is it taking place?"

(ii) Indirect speech

The second way is known as *indirect speech* or *reported speech*. You rephrase what was said in a clause, which may start with the conjunction **dass** 'that' [➤5a] or a question-word [➤5d]. [Omission of **dass**: ➤5a(ii).]

Er sagte, er gehe um halb zehn zu einer Konferenz.	He said that he was going to a meeting at half past nine.
Ich dachte, *dass* er zu spät kommen würde.	I thought that he would be late.
Ich fragte ihn, *wo sie stattfände*.	I asked him where it was taking place.

(iii) The effects of using indirect speech

As you can see, direct speech is changed in several ways when it is reported in the second way:

(A) Pronouns are changed if necessary so that they still refer to the right person. If a pronoun is the subject, the main verb is changed to match it.

(B) The changes in verb tenses are dealt with in paragraph 14c(i).

(C) If the reported speech starts with **dass** or a question-word, then subordinate clause word order is used [➤4e(iv)]. Otherwise, normal main clause order applies.

5d Indirect questions

Indirect questions are a form of indirect speech [➤5c]. They are introduced by the same types of verb, followed by the relevant question-word [➤6d]. Indirect Yes/No questions [➤6b] and tag questions [➤6c], which have no question-word, are introduced by **ob** 'whether'. Indirect questions are used for various purposes:

SYNTAX

(i)   Reporting

To report that a direct question [➤6a] has been or is going to be asked:

Ich fragte ihn, *ob* **er beschäftigt sei/wäre.**	I asked him *whether* he was busy.

(ii)   Politeness

To ask more courteously:

Könnten Sie mir sagen, *wann* **die Konferenz anfängt?**	Could you tell me *when* the meeting starts?

(iii)   Answering

To say whether we know the answer:

Ich weiß nicht, *wer* **den Vorsitz führt.**	I don't know *who* is chairing it.

5e   Indirect requests and commands [➤ch.13]

These are usually reported using **sollte(n)** + the infinitive [➤8h(ii)]. **müsste(n)/dürfte(n)** indicate a more forceful command.

Der Chef sagte mir, ich *sollte* **die Tagesordnung vorbereiten. Ich** *dürfte* **auf keinen Fall den Kaffee wieder vergessen.**	The boss told me I *should* prepare the agenda. On no account *was* I to forget the coffee again.

Asking for information: direct questions

6a *What is a direct question?*

A *direct question* is a form of direct speech. It tells us word for word what the person said or thought. The questions in the examples below are all direct questions – these are the actual words used, expecting a direct answer. But we often also talk about questions which have been or are going to be asked. These are indirect questions [➤5d].

6b *True or false: Yes/No questions*

In this type of question we are asking whether something is true or not, so it is always possible to answer 'Yes' or 'No'. A German Yes/No question normally starts with the main verb, followed immediately by the subject.

Fahren Sie in die Stadt? – Ja.	Are you going into town? – Yes.
Können Sie mich mitnehmen? – Nein!	Can you give me a lift? – No!

6c *Checking up: tag questions*

Tag questions are statements with a questioning 'tag' added to the end which asks for confirmation of the statement. English uses an enormous number of tags. German has one standard tag, **nicht wahr?** 'not true?'. Particularly in speech, people often just say **nicht?** or use some colloquial expression like the South German **gelt?**

Sie haben einen Hund, *nicht wahr? –* Ja.	You have a dog, *don't you?* – Yes.

6d *Asking for details: question-word questions*

We use these questions when we want to find out more about something we already know. They always start with a question-word such as those listed below and then continue like a

Yes/No question. As you can see, German question-words always begin with the letter **w**.

 Many of these question-words are the same as or closely related to relative pronouns [➤25j] or conjunctions [➤5a]. Do not confuse them!

➤ The questions in paragraphs 6d(i) to 6d(iv) are answered by a noun phrase [➤19b].

(i)   People: **Wer? Wen? Wem? Wessen?** *'Who(m)? Whose?'*

Wer fährt mit Ihnen? – Niemand. **Wessen Gepäck ist denn das? – Meins.**	*Who* is going with you? – Nobody. *Whose* luggage is that? – Mine.

(ii)   Things: **Was?** *'What'?*

Was wollen Sie in der Stadt machen? – Nichts Besonderes.	*What* are you going to do in town? – Nothing special.

(iii) Selection: **Welcher? Welche? Welches?** *'Which ...? (What ...?)'*

Welche Straße nehmen Sie? – Die Autobahn.	*Which* road are you taking? – The highway/motorway.

(iv) Definition: **Was für (ein) ...?** *'What sort of ...?'*

Was für einen Wagen haben Sie? – Einen sehr alten!	*What kind of* car do you have? – A very old one!

➤ The questions in paragraphs 6d(v) to 6d(ix) are answered by adverbial expressions [➤ch.28].

(v)   Time: **Wann?** *'When?'*

Wann fahren Sie los? – In einer halben Stunde.	*When* are you leaving? – In half an hour.

(vi)   *Place:* **Wo? Wohin? Woher?** *'Where? Where to? Where from?'*

Wo haben Sie Ihren Wagen geparkt? – Auf dem Parkplatz.	*Where* did you park your car? – In the parking lot.

(vii)   *Manner (methods and means):* **Wie?** *'How?'*

Wie kommen Sie nach Hamburg? – Ich werde den Zug nehmen.	*How* are you getting to Hamburg? – I'll take the train.

(viii)   *Quantity, quality and degree:* **Wie viel? Wie viele? Wie ...?** *'How much? How many? How ...?'*

Wie viel Gepäck haben Sie denn? – Sehr viel. – Wie groß ist Ihr Wagen? – Ziemlich klein.	*How much* luggage do you have? – A lot. – *How* big is your car? – Fairly small.

(ix)   *Reasons:* **Warum?** *'Why?'*

Warum können Sie mich nicht mitnehmen? – Sie haben einen sehr großen Koffer, und ich habe nicht genug Platz.	*Why* can't you take me? – You have a very large suitcase, and I don't have enough room.

C
ACTIONS AND STATES: VERBS AND THEIR USES

7	What verbs do
8	What verbs govern: their role in the sentence
9	Attitudes to action: modal verbs
10	Verb forms not related to time: non-finite forms
11	The passage of time: the use of tenses
12	Statements of fact: past, present and future
13	Requests and commands: the imperative
14	Areas of uncertainty: der Konjunktiv
15	Things done to you: the passive
16	Types of German verbs
17	The formation of tenses: how are verbs conjugated?
18	Verb tables

What verbs do

7a Full verbs

The very great majority of verbs tell us about the actions, state of mind or situation of the subject of the sentence. These we call *full* verbs.

Dieses Jahr *fahren* wir mit meinen Eltern in Urlaub. Sie *wohnen* weit von uns, und wir *sehen* uns nicht oft.	This year we *are going* on vacation with my parents. They *live* far from us, and we *don*'t *see* each other often.

7b Auxiliary verbs

A much smaller group of verbs is used in combination with full verbs. For example, they may make a compound tense or give a certain slant to an action. These are called *auxiliary* (i.e. helping) verbs. Note that most German auxiliaries also have a full meaning.

The main auxiliary verbs are:

(A) haben, **sein**.
These form the compound past tenses [➤17c].

(B) werden.
This forms the compound future [➤12c] and the passive [➤ch.15].

(C) dürfen, können, mögen, müssen, sollen, wollen.
These are the modal verbs, which show the subject's attitude to an action [➤ch.9].

(D) lassen.
This means 'to have something done' [➤9c(vii)].

Ich *habe* eine Pauschalreise nach Thailand gebucht. Wir *sind* noch nie dort gewesen. Wir *wollten* letztes Jahr da Urlaub machen, aber wir *konnten* keinen Flug bekommen. Meine Eltern *werden* zu uns kommen, und dann fliegen wir zusammen nach Bangkok.	I *have* booked a package vacation to Thailand. We *have* never been there. We *wanted* to go there on vacation last year, but we *couldn't* get a flight. My parents *will* come to our house, and then we are going to fly together to Bangkok.

8 What verbs govern: their role in the sentence

8a What does a verb govern?

A sentence can contain many items of information besides that given by the subject and main verb. Some of these are optional extras, but others depend directly on the main verb and cannot be removed without leaving the sentence incomplete. These are said to be 'governed' by the verb.

Note The groupings used in the following paragraphs are not the only possible ones, but differences of classification really do not matter. What is important is to know how a particular verb functions in a particular context.

8b Self–sufficient verbs

Any verb which does not govern a direct (accusative) object is *intransitive* [➤8d(i)]. Some of these verbs do not take any object at all.

Wir *schliefen* (immer noch) (fest), als meine Eltern (mit dem Taxi) *ankamen.*	We *were* (still) *sleeping* (soundly) when my parents *arrived* (by taxi).

8c Verbs linking equals: the complement

A small number of verbs simply act as a link between the subject and another word or phrase, which is called the *complement* of the verb. Because it refers to the same person or thing as the subject, the complement is always in the nominative case [➤22c].

Meine Eltern *sind* beide ausgezeichnete Musiker. Mein Vater ist Amateur *geblieben*, aber meine Mutter ist Konzertpianistin *geworden.*	Both my parents *are* excellent musicians. My father has *remained* an amateur, but my mother has *become* a concert pianist.

VERBS AND THEIR USES

8d   Verbs with one object

A very large number of verbs normally govern a noun phrase [➤19b] which is affected by the action of the verb. This noun phrase is the object of the verb. In German it may be in one of three cases.

(i)   Verbs with an object in the accusative [➤22d]

These verbs are *transitive*, and the noun phrase is the direct object. Any verb which does not govern a direct object is *intransitive*.

Ich *höre* gern Musik, aber ich *spiele* kein Instrument. Stattdessen *besitze* ich einen CD-Spieler.	I like *listening* to music but I *don*'t *play* any instrument. I *own* a CD player instead.

Note   German cannot use the same verb both transitively and intransitively as easily as English can. Very often, some other construction is used to distinguish between the two usages:

(A) When the English intransitive is really an action done to the subject, German is likely to use the transitive verb with a reflexive pronoun as its object [➤8f].

In aller Eile haben wir *uns gewaschen* und *angezogen*.	We *washed* and *dressed* very hurriedly.

(B) Sometimes two different verbs are used, which may well be related to each other.

Die Kinder waren schon um halb sieben *aufgewacht,* aber sie hatten uns nicht *geweckt*.	The children had *woken up* at half past six, but they had not *woken* us.

Other examples of similar pairs are:

Ich besteige ihn.	I climb it (a mountain).	**Ich steige.**	I climb.
Ich betrete es.	I enter it (a room).	**Ich trete ... ein.**	I enter.
Ich ertränke ihn.	I drown him.	**Er ertrinkt.**	He drowns.
Ich lege mich ... hin.	I lie down.	**Ich liege.**	I am lying (there).
Ich setze mich.	I sit down.	**Ich sitze.**	I am sitting.

Ich stelle es ...	I stand it (somewhere).	**Es steht.**	It stands.
Ich verlasse es.	I leave it (a place).	**Ich gehe weg.**	I leave (go away).
Ich versenke es.	I sink it (a ship)	**Es sinkt.**	It sinks.

(C) Sometimes **lassen** 'let' [➤9c(vii)] + an intransitive verb may express a transitive meaning.

Mein Sohn hat das Fenster aufgemacht und seine Wollmütze *fallen lassen*.	My son opened the window and *dropped* his wool hat.

(D) Conversely, **sich lassen** 'can be done' [➤15f(v)] + a transitive verb can translate into an intransitive verb in English.

Sie ist auf die Straße gefallen – das Fenster *lässt sich* wirklich zu leicht *aufmachen*.	It fell onto the street – the window really *opens* too easily.

(ii) *Verbs with an object in the dative [➤22f]*

Though smaller, this group is still large, and some very common verbs belong to it. As many of these verbs take a direct object in other languages (e.g. in French or English), it is important to learn them with an object in the dative, as shown in the following examples. Some of these examples are given in the perfect tense, to show the use of **sein.**

(A) Some common verbs.

Ich habe ihnen ... geantwortet.	I answered them.
Ich bin ihnen ... begegnet.	I met them (by chance).
Ich werde ihnen ... danken.	I shall thank them.
Ich habe ihnen ... gedient.	I served them (as a servant).
Ich habe ihnen ... gedroht.	I threatened them.
Ich bin ihnen ... gefolgt.	I followed them.
Ich gehorchte ihnen nicht.	I did not obey them.
Gilt das mir?	Does that go for me? Are you referring to me?
Das gehört mir.	That belongs to me/That's mine.
Die kleine Wohnung genügt uns nicht mehr.	The little apartment is no longer sufficient for us.
Die Kinder gleichen mir.	The children resemble/are like me.
Ich habe ihnen ... gratuliert.	I congratulated them.

VERBS AND THEIR USES

Ich habe ihnen ... geholfen.	I helped them.
Das passt mir nicht.	That doesn't suit/fit me.
Was ist Ihnen passiert/geschehen?	What happened to you?
Mein Knie tut mir weh.	My knee is hurting (me).

➤ *I was followed* by two men: dative verbs used in the passive ➤15d.

(B) Verbs with the separable particles **bei-, entgegen-, nach-** and **zu-**, and with the prefixes **ent-** meaning 'escaping' and **wider-** meaning 'opposition'.

Ich bin meinem Partner *entgegengefahren.* **Normalerweise** *steht* **er mir** *bei,* **aber diesmal hat er mir** *widersprochen.* **Er hat mir** *zugenickt* **und ist weggegangen. Ich bin ihm** *nachgelaufen* **– er sollte mir nicht** *entkommen.*	I *drove to meet* my partner. Normally he *supports* me, but this time he *contradicted* me. He *nodded to* me and left. I *ran after* him – he wasn't going to *get away from* me.

(C) A number of verbs which are often used impersonally [feelings and sensations: ➤8j].

Es ist mir ... aufgefallen/eingefallen.	It struck/occurred to me.
Was fehlt Ihnen?	What's the matter with you?
Das hat mir nicht ... gefallen.	I didn't like it (it didn't please me).
Es ist ihnen ... gelungen (etwas zu tun).	They succeeded (in doing something).
Hat's (Ihnen) geschmeckt?	Did you like it (food)?
Es tut mir sehr leid (, dass ...)	I am very sorry (that ...).

(iii)   *Verbs with an object in the genitive [➤22e]*

Only a few verbs take a genitive object. They are only used in elevated written style. Many of them are reflexive. The first German text shows two of them. Their more usual alternatives appear in the second text.

H. *gedachte* **nie der Leiden anderer Leute. Er** *bedurfte* **ihres Wohlwollens nicht.**	H. never *thought* of the sufferings of other people. He did not *need* their goodwill.
H. *dachte* **nie an die Leiden anderer Leute. Er** *brauchte* **ihr Wohlwollen nicht.**	

Genitive objects are also used in a few set phrases, though these too have a very literary ring.

Die Hitze des Brandes *spottete jeder Beschreibung,* **aber der Feuermann** *achtete nicht der Gefahr.* **Erst im letzten Augenblick** *besann er sich eines Besseren* **und zog sich etwas zurück.**	The heat of the fire *beggared description,* but the fireman *paid no heed to the danger.* Only at the last moment did he *think better of it* and drew back a little.

8e Verbs with two objects: direct and indirect objects

Some transitive verbs have not only a direct object in the accusative but also an indirect object in the dative case. (For the order in which these objects come in the sentence ►4e.) The indirect object refers to a person (or a thing) involved in some way in the action of the verb.

(i) Indirect objects: to whom, from whom

Indirect objects refer to people to whom something is said, given, sent, shown, etc., or from whom it is taken.

Mein Sohn hat *meinem Mann* **ein neues Computerprogramm** *gegeben.* **Er hat** *mir gesagt,* **es wäre leicht zu verstehen, aber er musste** *ihm zeigen,* **wie es funktionierte!**	My son *gave my husband* a new computer program. He *told me* that it was easy to understand, but he had to *show him* how it worked!

Other examples include:

Ich beschreibe es ihnen.	I describe it to them.
Ich erkläre es ihnen.	I explain it to them.
Ich erzähle es ihnen.	I tell them about it.
Ich teile es ihnen mit.	I inform them of it.
Ich bringe es ihnen.	I bring it to them.
Ich bringe es ihnen bei.	I teach it to them.
Ich schicke es ihnen.	I send it to them.
Ich leihe es ihnen.	I lend it to them.
Ich nehme es ihnen.	I take it from them.

VERBS AND THEIR USES

Note also:

Es nutzt mir nichts.	It is of no benefit to me.
Es schadet mir nichts.	It does me no harm.

Note   **bitten** 'ask, request', **fragen** 'ask, inquire' and **sprechen** 'speak to' take a direct (i.e. accusative) object.

Ich habe *ihn gefragt,* wie es funktionierte, aber er hat *mich gebeten, ihn* später dazu *zu sprechen.*	I *asked him* how it worked, but he *asked me* to *speak to him* about it later.

➤   *She was given* a dictionary: indirect objects with passive verbs ➤15a, 15f(ii).

(ii)   *Indirect objects: for whom*

Sometimes indirect objects refer to people for whom something is done.

Ich *kaufe dir* ein Bier, wenn du *mir* einen Sitzplatz *findest.*	I'll *buy you* a beer if you *find me* a seat.

(iii)   *Possessive dative*

When referring to parts of the body and articles of clothing, German often uses the definite article **der**, etc. 'the' where English uses 'my, your' etc. [➤23h(iii)]. An indirect object (known as a *possessive dative*) is added to emphasize the event, or for clarification if you would not otherwise know whose body or clothing it is. It *must* be added if the direct object does not belong to the subject of the sentence.

Kannst du *mir* die Brieftasche herausholen? Ich habe *mir* das Handgelenk verstaucht.	Can you get *my* wallet out (for me)? I have sprained *my* wrist.

Note   A very few verbs take two objects in the accusative, the commonest being **kosten** 'cost', **lehren** 'teach', **angehen** 'concern', **nennen/heißen** 'call/name'.

Dein verflixtes Spezialbier hat *mich ein Heidengeld* **gekostet! –** *Was* **geht** *mich* **das an?**	Your blasted special beer cost *me a fortune*! – Of *what* concern is that to *me*?

8f *Objects which refer to the subject: reflexive verbs*

In a reflexive verb the action is turned back on the subject. The object is a *reflexive pronoun* [➤25c], which refers to the same person or thing as the subject. The rules for reflexive verbs are exactly the same as for any other verb, for example, in the order of objects [➤4e] or in the use of **haben** to form compound past tenses [➤17c(i)].

There are various types of reflexive verbs.

(i) A limited number of verbs can only be used with a reflexive pronoun, which often has little independent meaning. For example:

Am Ende des Abends *bedankten* **wir** *uns* **alle bei der Gastgeberin und** *verabschiedeten uns*. **Stefan** *benahm sich* **sehr eigenartig, weil er** *sich* **in sie** *verliebt* **hatte. Meine Wohnung** *befindet sich* **außerhalb der Stadt. Ich** *beeilte mich*, **ein Taxi zu finden.**	At the end of the evening we all *said thank you* to the hostess and *said goodbye*. Stefan *behaved* very strangely, because he had *fallen in love* with her. My apartment *is (situated)* outside the town. I *hurried* to find a taxi.

(ii) There are some verbs which do not have to be used with a reflexive pronoun but which alter their meaning, sometimes entirely, when they are. For example:

Leider *verlief* **ich** *mich* **sofort. Ich hatte** *mich* **auf mein Gedächtnis** *verlassen*, **aber ich konnte** *mir* **nicht** *vorstellen*, **wo ich war. Endlich** *stellte* **es** *sich heraus*, **dass ich nicht weit von zu Hause war. Es** *lohnte sich* **nicht mehr, ein Taxi zu nehmen.**	Unfortunately I *lost my way* immediately. I had *relied* on my memory, but I could not *imagine* where I was. Finally it *turned out* that I was not far from home. It *was* no longer *worth* taking a taxi.

(iii)   Finally, so long as it makes sense, any verb with an object in the accusative [➤8d(i)] or dative [➤8d(ii), 8e] can have a reflexive pronoun as an object, showing that in this case the action relates back to the subject.

Erschöpft *goss* ich *mir* einen kleinen Schlummertrunk *ein*, *zog mich* schnell *aus* und *warf mich* ungewaschen ins Bett.	Exhausted, I *poured myself* a small nightcap, *got undressed* quickly and *threw myself* unwashed into bed.

8g   Verbs + preposition + noun phrase: prepositional objects

Many German verbs can be linked to a noun phrase by a preposition. These verb–preposition combinations are fixed: you could not use a different preposition without at least changing the meaning and probably making nonsense. Some are similar to English but many are not. It is important to learn each combination as you come to it.

Most German prepositions can be associated with a verb in this way. The following paragraphs list some of the more common combinations. [For the basic meanings of prepositions, and the cases that follow them, ➤ch.27.]

Note   When the preposition is followed by a pronoun referring to a thing or things, the two combine to form a compound consisting of **da(r)-** + the preposition. (The **-r-** is used before a vowel.) [➤25b(iv)A]

Sind das Ihre Papiere? – Ja, ich arbeite heute *daran*. Aber wo ist mein Rotstift? Ich habe eben *damit* geschrieben.	Are these your papers? – Yes, I'm working *on them* today. But where's my red pencil? I was just writing *with it*.

➤   I am relying on (your) seeing him today: use of **da(r)–** + preposition to introduce a clause ➤8h(ii)D, 8i.

(i)   *+ an*

Almost always + a dative noun phrase, which very often has the sense of 'main cause or focus of the action'. For example:

Ich arbeite an ...	I work at ...
Ich erkenne sie an ...	I recognize her by ...
Ich freue mich an ...	I get pleasure from ...

Ich hindere ihn an ...	I prevent him from ...
Ich leide an ...	I suffer from ...
Ich nehme an ... teil.	I take part in ...
Ich rieche an ...	I sniff at ...
Er ist an ... gestorben.	He died of ...
Es fehlt mir an ...	I have no ...
Es liegt mir viel an ...	... is important to me.

There are a few common verbs with **an** + an accusative noun phrase, mostly referring to mental processes. For example:

Ich denke an ...	I think about ...
Ich erinnere dich an ...	I remind you of ...
Ich erinnere mich an ...	I remember ...
Ich glaube an ...	I believe in ...
Ich gewöhne mich an ...	I get used to ...

(ii)   + auf

Almost always + an accusative noun phrase. This is the most common linking preposition, with a wide range of meanings, especially 'aim or direction of the action'. For example:

Ich achte auf ...	I pay attention to ...
Ich antworte auf ...	I reply to ...
Das bezieht sich auf ...	That refers to ...
Das folgt auf ...	That follows (on from) ...
Ich freue mich auf ...	I look forward to ...
Ich hoffe auf ...	I hope for ...
Es kommt auf ... an.	It depends on ...
Ich passe auf ... auf.	I keep an eye on ...
Ich schimpfe auf ...	I curse at ...
Ich verlasse mich auf ...	I rely on ...
Ich verzichte auf ...	I do/go without ...
Ich warte auf ...	I wait for ...
Ich zähle auf ...	I count/rely on ...
Ich zeige auf ...	I point at ...
Ich ziele/schieße auf ...	I aim/shoot at ...

There are very few verbs with **auf** plus a dative noun phrase. They mostly have the sense of 'based on, resting on'. For example:

Ich bestehe auf ...	I insist on ...
Das beruht auf ...	That is based on ...

[but **das gründet sich auf** + accusative]

(iii)   + aus

Always + a dative noun phrase, mostly with the sense of '(out) of, from'. For example:

Es besteht aus ...	It consists of ...
Ich stelle es aus ... her.	I make it out of ...

(iv)   + für

Always + an accusative noun phrase, mostly with the sense of 'for, concerning'. For example:

Ich bedanke mich bei ihnen für ...	I thank them (formally) for ...
Ich danke dir für ...	I thank you for ...
Ich halte ihn für ...	I think he is ...
Ich interessiere mich für ...	I am interested in ...

(v)   + in

Usually + an accusative noun phrase, mostly with the sense of 'focus of the action'. For example:

Ich verliebe mich in ...	I fall in love with ...
Ich mische mich in ... ein	I stick my nose into ...

There are very few verbs with **in** + a dative noun phrase, the most common being:

Es besteht in ...	It consists in ...

(vi)   + mit

Always + a dative noun phrase, mostly with the sense of 'matter in hand' or 'person concerned'. For example:

Ich befasse mich mit ...	I deal with ...
Ich beschäftige mich mit ...	I occupy myself with ...
Ich fange mit ... an.	I start with ...
Ich höre mit ... auf.	I stop (doing) ...
Ich finde mich mit ... ab.	I come to accept ...
Ich rechne mit ...	I count on (doing) ...
Ich telefoniere mit ...	I talk to ... on the phone.
Ich stimme mit ... überein.	I agree with ...
Ich unterhalte mich mit ...	I talk to ...
Ich versehe ihn mit ...	I provide him with ...

(vii) + *nach*

Always + a dative noun phrase, usually meaning 'thing desired or sought'. For example :

Ich frage nach ...	I ask/inquire about ...
Ich greife nach ...	I grab for ...
Ich rufe nach ...	I call (out) for ...
Ich sehne mich nach ...	I long for ...
Ich strebe nach ...	I strive for ...
Ich suche nach ...	I search for ...

After verbs of the senses, **nach** + the noun phrase refers to the thing sensed. For example:

Es duftet/riecht/stinkt nach ...	It smells of ... (in increasing order of unpleasantness!)
Es schmeckt nach ...	It tastes of ...
Es sieht nach ... aus.	It looks like ... (weather)

(viii) + *über*

Always + an accusative noun phrase, used with a large number of verbs, almost always in the sense of 'about, concerning'. For example :

Ich ärgere mich über ...	I am/get annoyed at ...
Ich denke über ... nach.	I think about... or ... over.
Ich täusche mich über ...	I am wrong about ...
Ich freue mich über ...	I am pleased about ...
Ich spotte über ...	I make fun of ...

Verbs of 'talking, reading, writing, knowing' can often be used with either **über** + accusative or **von** + dative. **über** normally implies a longer, more thorough process than **von**. For example:

Sie weiß viel *über* Eheberatung.	She knows a lot *about* marriage counseling.
Er wusste nicht *von* meiner Heirat.	He did not *know* about my marriage.

(ix) + *um*

Always + an accusative noun phrase, mostly in the sense of 'concerning'. For example :

Ich bitte sie um ...	I ask her for ...
Ich bringe ihn um ...	I take ... away from him.

VERBS AND THEIR USES

Es geht um ...	It concerns ...
Es handelt sich um ...	We are talking about ...
Ich kämpfe um ...	I fight for ...
Ich kümmere mich um ...	I take care of ...

(x) + von

Always + a dative noun phrase, mostly in the sense of 'away from' or 'about'. For example:

Ich erhole mich von ...	I recover from ...
Es hängt von ... ab.	It depends on ...
Ich rate ihm von ... ab.	I advise him against ...
Ich träume von ...	I dream of ...

(xi) + vor

Always + a dative noun phrase, mostly in the sense of 'danger, risk'. For example:

Ich (be)schütze ihn vor ...	I protect him from ...
Ich fürchte mich vor ...	I am afraid of ...
Ich habe Angst vor ...	I am afraid of ...
Ich scheue mich vor ...	I am frightened of ...
Ich rette ihn vor ...	I save him from ...
Ich verberge ihn vor ...	I hide him from ...
Ich warne ihn vor ...	I warn him against ...

(xii) + zu

Always + a dative noun phrase, mostly conveying 'belonging together' or 'inviting, persuading, forcing'. For example :

Das dient zu ...	That is used for ...
Das eignet sich zu ...	That is suitable for ...
Ich gehöre zu ...	I am one of ...
Ich lade Sie zu ... ein.	I invite you to ...
Das passt zu ...	That matches ...
Ich trage zu ... bei.	I contribute to ...
Ich überrede sie zu ...	I talk her/them into ...
Ich zwinge ihn zu ...	I force him into ...

8h Verbs + infinitives of other verbs

There are only two ways in which a German verb can be linked to the infinitive of another verb. With the exceptions noted below, the person performing the action must be the same for both verbs.

➤ Notes on forms of the infinitive and cross–references to its uses: ➤10a.

(i) *The bare infinitive*

A *bare* infinitive is one which is not introduced by **zu** 'to' [➤8h(ii)], as in English 'I must go'. Only certain groups of verbs govern bare infinitives, but many of them are very common. Some have alternative constructions which are indicated below.

Note These are the main points to remember about the use of the bare infinitive. See A to G below for examples.

1) The infinitive is part of the same clause as the verb governing it and is therefore not separated from it by a comma.

2) In a main clause, the infinitive usually goes at the end, but especially with modals or **tun** it can be put at or very near the beginning for emphasis. [Infinitives in subordinate clauses: ➤4e(iv).]

The main groups of verbs which govern bare infinitives are:

(A) The modal verbs (**dürfen, können, mögen, müssen, sollen, wollen**) and **lassen**. As these are by far the most important verbs of this type they are discussed separately in Chapter 9.

(B) Certain verbs of motion: **fahren** 'go (in a vehicle)', **gehen** 'go (on foot or generally)', **kommen** 'come', **schicken** 'send'. With **schicken** the direct object carries out the action of the infinitive. If the reason is emphasized or the clause is long, the infinitive may be introduced by **um ... zu** 'in order to'. [**spazieren gehen/ spazieren fahren** 'go for a walk/drive': ➤16e(ii)].

Kommst du heute *schwimmen?*	Are you *coming swimming* today?
– Hast du denn vergessen?	– Have you forgotten then?
Ich bin extra *gekommen, um*	I *came* specially *to discuss* our
unser Projekt *zu besprechen!*	project!

(C) A few verbs of the senses: **fühlen** 'feel', **hören** 'hear', **sehen** 'see', **spüren** 'sense'. The direct object of these verbs carries out the action of the infinitive. With longer sentences, a clause with **wie** is often preferred. Notice how English often uses the '-ing' form of the verb instead of the infinitive.

Ich *sah* den Dieb durchs Fenster *steigen* und *hörte, wie* er alle Schubladen *aufmachte.*	I *saw* the thief *climb(ing)* through the window and *heard* him *opening* all the drawers.

(D) bleiben 'remain', **finden** 'find', **haben** 'have', when followed by a verb of position. With **finden** and **haben** the direct object carries out the action of the infinitive. Here English always uses the '-ing' form. [**stehen bleiben** 'stop', **sitzen bleiben** 'stay back (in school)' : ►16e(ii)].

Ich *blieb* voller Angst auf dem Bett *sitzen* – ich *hatte* ja einen Revolver in einer der Schubladen *liegen!*	I *stayed sitting* on the bed, very frightened – after all, I *had* a revolver *lying* in one of the drawers!

(E) brauchen 'need', **heißen** 'command', **helfen** 'help', **lehren** 'teach', **lernen** 'learn'. These verbs may also be used with **zu** + infinitive, especially if the clause is complex. Except with **brauchen**, a comma goes before the **zu** + infinitive clause. With **heißen**, **helfen** and **lehren**, the object carries out the action of the infinitive. [**heißen** 'mean': ►(G) below. **kennen lernen** 'meet': ►16e(ii).]

Mein Onkel *lehrt* mich *kochen* – ich *lerne* alles *machen.* Dafür *helfe* ich ihm, seine Kochbücher in Ordnung *zu bringen*, aber er *heißt* mich immer wieder von vorne *anfangen*. Das *brauche* ich wirklich nicht (zu) *machen.*	My uncle is *teaching* me to *cook* – I am *learning* to *do* everything. In exchange, I am *helping* him (to) *tidy up* his cookbooks, but he keeps *telling* me to *start* again. I really don't *have/need* to *do* that.

(F) tun (do) – often used in colloquial German to emphasize the action of the infinitive [►8h(i)Note 2].

Arbeitet er gerne? – Und wie! Er *tut* doch nichts als *arbeiten.* Sogar *schlafen tut* er wenig!	Does he like working? – And how! He *does* nothing but *work (and work).* He *does*n't even *sleep* much!

(G) A few other verbs in certain idiomatic expressions only. For example:

Mit diesem Gebrauchtwagen *bist* **du aber nicht** *gut* **beraten!**	This car will not *serve* you *well*.
Du *hast* **gut** *reden*!	That's easy for you to *say*!

(ii)   *zu + infinitive*

A large number of verbs can be followed by a clause with **zu** + infinitive. An English equivalent would be '*I refuse to go*'.

Note   1) The **zu** + infinitive clause is normally separated from the main clause by a comma.

2) **zu** + infinitive is always placed at the end of the infinitive clause. [Other uses of **zu** + infinitive: ➤10a(iv).]

3) There are three cases when no comma is used before **zu** + infinitive.

• Often, when the main clause consists only of a verb and its subject:

Wir hofften **(,) am Nachmittag ein Picknick zu machen,** ...	*We hoped* to have a picnic in the afternoon, ...

• When the infinitive clause consists only of **zu** + infinitive:

... aber gegen halb zwei hat es angefangen *zu regnen*.	... but at about half past one it began *to rain*.

• When the main verb is one of those in group (A) below.

Verbs which may be followed by a clause with **zu** + infinitive can be grouped into loose categories:

(A) Verbs with a close link to the infinitive, whose meaning they modify in some way. (Note: no comma.) For example:

In der Reparaturwerkstatt *haben* **wir/***gibt es* **viel zu tun. Es** *scheint* **uns immer an Personal zu fehlen.**	In the repair shop we *have*/there *is* a lot to do. We always *seem* to be short of staff.

VERBS AND THEIR USES

Ich *bekomme* die schwierigen Apparate zu reparieren, weil sonst keiner es zu machen *weiß*. Darum *hoffe* ich eine andere Stelle zu kriegen.	I *get* the difficult equipment to repair, because no one else *knows* how to do it. That is why I *hope* to get another job.

(B) A fairly small number of verbs with an object (usually dative) which carries out the action of the infinitive. For example:

Erlauben Sie mir, Ihnen einen Rat zu geben. Ich *bitte* Sie, mich anzuhören. Ich kann Ihnen nicht *verbieten*, uns zu verlassen, aber ich *rate/empfehle* Ihnen, bei uns zu bleiben. Es *täte* mir *leid*, Sie zu verlieren.	*Allow* me to give you some advice. Please (I *ask* you to) listen to me. I cannot *forbid* you to leave us, but I *advise/recommend* you to stay with us. I would *be sorry* to lose you.

(C) Other verbs include **anfangen** 'begin', **aufhören** 'stop, cease', **beschließen** 'decide', **fürchten** 'fear', **hoffen** 'hope', **vergessen** 'forget', **versprechen** 'promise', **versuchen** 'try', **vorhaben** 'plan', **wagen** 'dare', **zögern** 'hesitate'.

Bei meiner Arbeitslast *zögere* ich, hier zu bleiben. Ich habe *beschlossen,/Ich habe* vor, eine leichtere Arbeit zu suchen. Ich werde nicht *vergessen*, Sie auf dem Laufenden zu halten.	With my work load I *hesitate* to stay here. I have *decided/I plan* to look for easier work. I shall not *forget* to keep you informed.

(D) Verbs with prepositional objects [►8g]. Here the infinitive clause is normally introduced by an adverb formed from **da(r)-** plus the preposition, though this may be left out with some verbs. For example:

Ich *erinnere mich* (daran), dieses Thema schon mal besprochen zu haben. Ich *freue mich* darauf, Sie noch eine Weile bei uns zu haben!	I *remember* discussing this subject before. I *look forward* to having you with us a little while yet!

8i Wanting someone else to do it: verbs + subordinate clauses

English frequently uses an object followed by an infinitive in constructions such as 'they told/wanted *me to leave*.' Some German verbs can also govern this construction, but usually the other person's action is put into a subordinate clause [➤-4d(ii)].

Ich will, *dass Sie* mich fair behandeln. Ich habe nicht vergessen, *wie/dass Sie* mich letztes Jahr heruntergestuft haben. Sie erwarten immer, *dass ich* zu viel für zu wenig mache.	I want *you to* treat me fairly. I have not forgotten *your* downgrading me last year. You always expect *me to* do too much for too little.
Ich erinnere mich (daran), *dass wir* auch davon gesprochen haben. Ich bestehe darauf, *dass Sie* sich endlich entschließen!	I remember *our* talking about that as well. I insist on *your* finally making up your mind!

8j Impersonal verbs

Impersonal verbs have the general pronoun **es** 'it' as their subject. [For full details ➤25e.]

8k Feelings and sensations: idioms with haben and sein

German has two sets of idioms which are different from English. Some have alternatives which are more like English.

(i) *ich habe* etc. + noun

Ich habe Hunger/Durst (bin hungrig/durstig).	I am hungry/thirsty.
Ich habe Angst (fürchte mich) vor ...	I am afraid of ...
Ich habe Sorgen (bin besorgt).	I am worried.
Ich habe Fieber.	I have a fever.

(ii) *mir ist* etc., alone or + adjective

Note that **ich bin kalt** means 'I am a cold person', and **es ist kalt** refers to the weather.

VERBS AND THEIR USES

Mir ist, als hätte ich ihn schon einmal gesehen.	I have a feeling that I have seen him before.
Mir ist kalt/warm/heiß.	I am cold/warm/hot.
Mir ist schlecht/übel.	I feel ill/nauseous.

Attitudes to action: modal verbs

9a The function of modal verbs

The verbs listed in paragraphs 9c(i) to (vii) are known as *modal auxiliaries* or *modals* for short. (**lassen** is not generally classed as a modal, but it shares many of their characteristics.) These verbs can occasionally carry a full meaning, as in **Kaffee mag ich nicht** 'I don't like coffee', but usually they are used with the infinitive of another verb [without **zu**, ►8h(i)]. This chapter deals with the way modals are used in main and subordinate clauses. [For details on the formation of the tenses ►16c(ii).]

9b Modal verbs in action

Unlike their English equivalents ('can', 'must' etc.) German modals have a full range of tenses, though they avoid the longer forms. The tenses of **müssen** (taken as an example) are listed overleaf [►9b(v)].

These are the main points to remember about modals and (unless specifically excluded) **lassen.**

(i) When any of the perfect tenses are used with an infinitive placed at the end of the clause (as is normal), the infinitive of the modal is used instead of the past participle. This creates a very characteristic rhythm of **-en -en**, which is the best way to remember this construction.

Warum habt ihr meinen Wagen nicht gleich reparieren *lassen?* **– Wir haben keinen Mechaniker finden** *können.*	Why didn't you *have* my car repaired at once? – We *could*n't find a mechanic.

(ii) The simple conditionals **könnte**, **möchte**, etc. are always used rather than the compound conditional with **würde**. With **lassen**, the simple conditional **ließe** is used more in **wenn** clauses and the compound conditional **würde ... lassen** more in the main clause [►14d(ii)Note].

VERBS AND THEIR USES

> **Wenn ich einen Mechaniker finden *könnte, würde* ich den Wagen sofort reparieren *lassen.***
>
> If I *could* find a mechanic, I *would have* the car repaired immediately.

(iii) When the perfect tenses are used in subordinate clauses, the auxiliary **haben** comes first in the final block [➤4e(iii), (iv)], not at the very end.

> **Es tut mir leid, dass ich nicht zu deiner Abschiedsparty *habe* kommen *können.***
>
> I'm sorry that I *could*n't *come* to your farewell party.

(iv) In certain cases the infinitive that follows may be left out, because it is 'understood' what it is. The modal verb then takes over any associated verbal particle [e.g. **zurück**, ➤16e(ii)], and perfect tenses use the past participles in **ge-**, not the infinitive. Apart from some set phrases, this happens mainly when the verb in question

- has just been mentioned;
- is **tun/machen** 'do' or a verb of motion. [➤also 9c(ii).]

> **Warum bist du nicht gekommen?**
> **— Ich *konnte* (es) nicht. Ich *musste* zur Garage zurück, um deinen Wagen zu holen.**
>
> Why didn't you come?
> — I *could*n't. I *had to go* back to the garage to get your car.

(v) In the following list the terms 'simple' and 'compound' refer to the forms of **müssen**, not to the whole construction.

Present/simple future	**Es muss ... warten.**	It must/has to wait.
Simple past	**Es musste ... warten.**	It had to wait.
Perfect	**Es hat ... warten müssen.**	It (has) had to wait.
Pluperfect	**Es hatte ... warten müssen.**	It had had to wait.
Compound future	**Es wird ... warten müssen.**	It will have to wait.
Conditional	**Es müsste ... warten.**	It would have to wait.
Past conditional	**Es hätte warten müssen.**	It would have had to wait.
Konjunktiv I simple	**Es müsse warten.**	(They said that) it had to wait.
Konjunktiv I perfect	**Es habe ... warten müssen.**	(They said that) it had had to wait.

9c *The parts and meanings of modal verbs*

The headings for each verb give the infinitive, the **er/sie/es** form of the present and of the simple past, and finally the past participle.

(i) **dürfen, darf, durfte, gedurft**: *'may, am allowed to; might'* **nicht dürfen**: *'must not'*

(**A**) Permission (the basic meaning).
As in English, **kann** 'can' is often felt to be less formal than **darf** 'may', but the latter is not at all uncommon, even in colloquial speech.

Darf/Kann ich ohne weiteres ein **Buch aus der Stadtbücherei entleihen?**	*May*/Can I take a book out of the public library just like that?

(**B**) Prohibition (in the negative).
This is often equivalent to the English 'must not' and thus both the opposite of A above and one of the opposites of **muss.** The conditional **dürfte** can also express a strong 'should not'.

Ohne Leserkarte *darf*/kann man **keine Bücher entleihen – Meine Freundin benutzt immer die Karte ihrer Schwester. Ich finde, das** *dürfte nicht* **erlaubt sein.**	Without a reader's card you *may* not/cannot take any books out – My girlfriend always uses her sister's card. I believe that *shouldn't* be allowed.

(**C**) Polite suggestions or requests.

Darf/Dürfte ich fragen, ob Sie **hier in der Stadt wohnen oder arbeiten?**	*May/Might* I ask whether you live or work here in town?

(**D**) Likelihood (in the conditional).

Sie arbeiten hier? Gut, dann *dürfte* **es keine Probleme geben.**	You work here? Good, then there *should*n't be any problems.

(ii) **können, kann, konnte, gekonnt**: *'can, am able to; could'*

(**A**) Ability or opportunity.

VERBS AND THEIR USES

Können Sie mir sagen, was dieser schwedische Text bedeutet? – *Könnten* Sie Montag wiederkommen? Ich *kann* Ihnen leider nicht helfen. Ich habe dich kommen hören, aber ich *konnte* dich nicht sehen.

Can you tell me what this Swedish text means? – *Could* you come back on Monday? I'm afraid I *can't* help you.

I heard you coming, but I *couldn't* see you.

(B) Possibility, especially with **könnte.**

To avoid confusion with meaning (A) above, an adverb such as **vielleicht** 'perhaps' or **möglicherweise** 'possibly' can be used.

Ich *kann* mich irren, aber ich glaube, Montag *könnte* ein Kollege von der Universitätsbibliothek da sein.

I *may* be wrong, but I believe that a colleague from the university library *may* be here on Monday.

(C) Knowledge of something learned.

Here **kann** is often used without any other verb, that is, the thing learned is its direct object.

Der *kann* Schwedisch – ich *kann* es leider nicht.

He *can speak* Swedish – I'm afraid I *can't.*

(D) Permission.

Sie *können* aber gerne die schwedisch–deutschen Wörterbücher benutzen.

But you're welcome to (*can* by all means) use the Swedish–German dictionaries.

1) Do not confuse the two meanings of the English 'could':

• **Ich konnte ihn sprechen/ habe ihn sprechen können** means 'I *was able* to speak to him'.

• **Ich könnte ihn sprechen** means 'I *would be able* to speak to him'.

2) Do not confuse the two meanings of the English 'They *could have spoken* to him yesterday', which correspond to (A) and (B) above:

• **Sie** *hätten* **ihn gestern** *sprechen können.* (missed opportunity (A): '... but they didn't').
• *Sie* *könnten* **ihn gestern** *gesprochen haben.* (possibility (B): '...and perhaps they did').

(iii) *mögen, mag, mochte, gemocht: '(would) like; may'.*

(A) Likes and dislikes.
The present/past tenses **mag/mochte** and the conditional **möchte** correspond fairly closely to English 'like(d)' and 'would like':
• **mag** and **mochte** are most often used without any other verb, that is, the person or thing (dis)liked is their direct object. The English 'I like swimming' etc. is usually best expressed by **ich schwimme gern** (literally 'I swim willingly'). Note also the use of **gefallen** 'please', as in **Bremen gefällt mir sehr** 'I like Bremen very much'.

Möchten Sie eine Zigarre? – Nein, danke! Zigaretten *mag* ich auch nicht.	*Would* you *like* a cigar? – No thank you! I *don't like* cigarettes either.

• **möchte**, on the other hand, *is* used with an infinitive or, if there is a change of subject, with a **dass** clause [➤8i]. **gern** is often used as well; the comparative **lieber** means 'would prefer'.

Ich *möchte gern/lieber* ein bisschen frische Luft schnappen.	I *would like/prefer* to get a bit of fresh air.

Note   **möchte** cannot be used for the English 'I *would have liked/preferred* to do it'. The German for this is **ich *hätte* es *gern/lieber* gemacht.**

Ich *hätte lieber* eine Tasse Kaffee getrunken, aber wir hatten nur noch Tee im Haus.	I *would have preferred* to drink a cup of coffee, but we only had tea in the house.

(B) Possibility.
Apart from some set phrases, **mag/mochte** are little used in this sense in colloquial German. [**mag** after 'however, whatever, whoever' etc. : ➤5a(ii).]

Das *mag* meinen Freunden seltsam erscheinen. – Ja, das *mag* wohl sein.	That *may* seem strange to my friends. – Yes, that *may* well be.

(iv) **müssen, muss, musste, gemusst**: *'must, have to, need to; ought'*

(A) Necessity, obligation, compulsion.
Note that the negative **Sie *müssen* es nicht machen** means 'you don't *have to/need to* do it'. In fact, the alternative **Sie *brauchen* es nicht (zu) machen** is probably more common. The English phrase 'you *must* not do that' is **Sie *dürfen* das nicht machen** [➤9c(i)B].

Dieses Buch ist überfällig – Sie *müssen* drei Euro Gebühr zahlen. Die anderen Bücher *müssen/brauchen* Sie noch nicht zurückbringen.	This book is overdue – you'll *have to* pay a fine of 3 euros. You don't *have/need to* return the other books yet.

(B) Logical deduction, supposition.

Entschuldigung, ich *muss* es vergessen haben. – Na ja, Sie *müssen* ja viel zu tun haben.	Sorry, I *must* have forgotten it. – Well, you *must* have a lot to do.

(C) The conditional **müsste.**
This adds the idea of 'ought to' or 'possibly' to (A) and (B) above [➤**sollte** overleaf].

Stimmt, aber mein Gedächtnis ist nicht so gut, wie es sein *müsste.*	True, but still, my memory is not as good as it *ought to* be.

 Do not confuse the two meanings of the English 'They *ought to/should have spoken* to him yesterday', which correspond to (A) and (B) above:

• **Sie *hätten* ihn gestern *sprechen müssen*** (obligation (A): '... but they didn't', with the added implication that it is now too late [➤9c(v)C Note].)

• **Sie *müssten* ihn gestern *gesprochen haben*** (supposition (B): '... and no doubt they did').

(v) ***sollen, soll, sollte, gesollt****: 'am meant to, supposed to; should, ought to'*

(A) (In the present and past tenses) Somebody else's intention or requirement.
***Soll ich* das machen?** is often the neatest way of saying '*Do you want me* to do that?'

Ich kann nicht mitkommen, ich *soll* hier auf Monika warten. – *Soll* ich Ihnen etwas kaufen?	I can't come with you, I *am supposed* to wait for Monika here. – *Do you want me* to buy anything for you?

(B) (In the conditional) Obligation, duty.

Zigaretten bitte. Ja, ich weiß, ich *sollte* nicht so viel rauchen.	Cigarettes, please. Yes, I know *I should*n't smoke so much.

(C) (In the present and past tenses) Report, hearsay, rumor.

'Nikostopp' *soll* einem das Rauchen abgewöhnen. Monika *soll* aber jetzt Nikostopp-süchtig sein!	'Nikostopp' *is supposed to* cure you of smoking, but Monika *is said to* be addicted to Nikostopp now!

(D) Commands, especially in indirect speech [➤5e].

Der Arzt hat mir auch gesagt, ich *soll(te)* Pralinen aufgeben. Na! „Du *sollst* nicht ertappt werden!" lautet das elfte Gebot.	The doctor also told me to give up (I *should* give up) chocolates. Hm! "Thou *shalt* not be found out!" says the eleventh commandment.

When talking about the past, be careful to distinguish between 'They *ought* to have spoken to him yesterday' ((B) above) and 'They are said to have spoken to him yesterday' ((C) above):

• **Sie *hätten* ihn gestern *sprechen sollen*** (duty (B): '.. but they didn't' [➤9c(iv)B Note])
• **Sie *sollen* ihn gestern *gesprochen haben*** (hearsay (C): '... I don't know whether they did'.)

65

VERBS AND THEIR USES

(vi)   *wollen, will, wollte, gewollt*: 'want to, will'

(A) Wish, desire.
In this meaning **wollen** can be used without another verb.

Ich *will* dich nicht hetzen, aber wir *wollen* bald losfahren. – Moment mal, ich *will* nur diesen Artikel lesen. Oder *willst* du die Zeitung?	I don't *want to* rush you, but we *want to* leave soon. – One moment, I just *want to* read this article. Or do you *want* the paper?

(B) Willingness, intention.
Note the use of **will nicht** 'refuses to' even with things.

Willst du mir wenigstens mit diesem Koffer helfen? Er *will* nicht zugehen. – Na, du *willst* nicht einsehen, dass er einfach zu voll ist.	*Will* you at least help me with this suitcase? It *will* not shut. – Well, you *refuse to* recognize that it is simply too full.

(C) Claim, assertion (often false).
Usually followed by a perfect infinitive (past participle + **haben/sein**).

Papa *will* letztes Jahr noch mehr hineingekriegt haben. – So? Na gut, ich *will* nichts gesagt haben.	Dad *claims* to have archived even more in last year. – Really? OK, *pretend* I didn't say anything.

(vii)   *lassen, lasse/lässt, ließ, gelassen*:
'let, allow to; have/get ... done; can be done'

(A) Allowing something to happen.

Vorsicht! Du *lässt* noch den ganzen Koffer fallen. *Lass* mich versuchen! – Ach, *lass* mich in Ruhe!	Careful! You'll drop (*let* fall) the whole suitcase. *Let* me try! – Oh, *leave* me in peace!

➤   **fallen lassen** 'drop (a plan)', **stehen lassen/liegen lassen** 'leave behind': infinitives as particles ➤16e(ii).

(B) Causing something to happen.

Gut, ich *lasse* es deinen Vater machen – der ist stark genug! Ich *lasse* ihn gleich holen.	OK, I'll *get* your father to do it – he is strong enough! I'll *get* them to fetch him.

(C) Possibility (**sich lassen**).
This is a useful replacement for 'can be done' [➤15f(v)].

Solche Koffer *lassen sich* nicht ohne Gewalt zumachen.	Suitcases like this *cannot be* shut without brute force.

10 Verb forms not related to time: non-finite forms

The *non-finite* verb forms are so called, because they do not by themselves define when the activity referred to happens. The three non-finite forms in German are the infinitive and the two participles.

10a The infinitive

The *infinitive* is the part of the verb most commonly listed in dictionaries. It 'names' a certain activity or state without saying when it happens, and it usually completes the meaning of the main verb.

(i) Formation of the infinitive

(A) All infinitives end in **-(e)n**; the **-e-** is dropped in **sein** 'be', **tun** 'do' and any verb ending in **-eln** or **-ern**.

(B) With the single exception of **sein** (which has **wir/sie *sind*** 'we/they *are*'), the infinitive of all German verbs is identical to the **wir/sie** forms (first/third person plural) of the present tense.

Wir fahren jedes Wochenende ins Grüne. Heute wollen wir nach Beck *fahren. Fahren Sie* mit?	*We drive* to the country every weekend. Today we want to *drive* to Beck. *Are you coming* along?

(B) Verbal particles (e.g. **auf, beiseite, zurück** [➤16e(ii)]) and infinitives are written as one word, in the order particle **(+zu)** + infinitive.

Ich würde gerne *mitfahren*, aber ich habe versprochen, mit Andrea nach Frön *mitzufahren*.	I would like to *come with you,* but I have promised to *go with* Andrea to Frön.

(ii) Uses of the infinitive

Paragraph 10a(iii) discusses infinitive-nouns and paragraph 10a(iv) infinitive clauses. Many of the equivalents for English '-ing' listed in paragraph 10b(ii) use the infinitive in German. Other usages involving the infinitive are described in the following paragraphs:

➤ I heard him *shout*: verbs + bare infinitives ➤8h.
He started *to run*: verbs + **zu** + infinitive ➤8h(ii).
I could not *help* him: modal verbs + infinitive ➤9b.
His *efforts to find* his car were in vain: nouns + **zu** + infinitive ➤19h.
I was *ready to call* the police: adjectives + **zu** + infinitive ➤24g(ii).
Without hesitating he jumped into the river: prepositions + **zu** + infinitive ➤27c.

(iii) *Infinitive-nouns*

Because they are 'names', German infinitives are frequently made into nouns which refer to the activity in question. The English equivalent often uses the '-ing' form of the verb. German *infinitive-nouns* are neuter, they are spelled with a capital and they function just like any other noun. In fact, some nouns have lost most of their active verbal sense, e.g.: **das Andenken** 'souvenir', **das Essen** 'meal', **das Verbrechen** 'crime', **das Vergnügen** 'pleasure'. In most instances, however, the basic verbal meaning is strongly preserved.

Ach, die ländliche Ruhe! Das *Bellen* **der Hunde, das** *Zwitschern* **der Vögel, das** *Blöken* **der Schafe – nur das** *Schlafen* **ist schwierig!**	Ah, rural peace! The *barking* of the dogs, the *twittering* of the birds, the *bleating* of the sheep – only *sleeping* is difficult!

(A) Infinitive-nouns are used after some prepositions to form useful constructions:

• **beim** + noun meaning 'while/on doing something';
• **zum** + noun expressing purpose, 'for doing something';
• **geraten/kommen** + **ins** + noun, indicating the start of an action.

Das mittlere Pedal dient *zum* **Bremsen. Vorsicht aber** *beim* **Fahren – bei zu starkem Bremsen** **gerät/kommt man leicht** *ins Schleudern***.**	The middle pedal is *for braking*. Take care though *when driving – if you brake too hard* you'll easily get *into a skid*.

(B) Especially in written German, the object of the verb or other parts of the sentence may be included in the noun. Long compounds can be very clumsy, and it is often better to use a clause [➤10a(iv)].

Das ständige *Miteinanderplaudern* **ist beim Fahren nicht zu empfehlen, das** *Zeitunglesen* **noch weniger.**	Constant *chatting among yourselves* while driving is not to be recommended, still less *reading the newspaper.*

(iv)   Infinitive clauses

These are normally governed by **zu** + infinitive, which comes at the end. The English equivalent may use either 'to' + infinitive or the '-ing' form of the verb. Paragraph 8h(ii) deals with verbs with **zu** + infinitive. Infinitive clauses may also be the subject of the sentence. If the clause comes first there is no comma between it and the verb:

Einen guten Gebrauchtwagen mit niedrigem Kilometerstand *zu finden* **ist nicht leicht.**	*Finding/To find* a good used car with low mileage is not easy.

Note   1) If the infinitive clause is short the **zu** may be left out, especially when the main verb is a part of **sein.**

Hier Auto *(zu) fahren* **ist kein Vergnügen.**	*Driving* here is no pleasure.

2) If the clause comes after the main verb, it is often preceded by the *caretaker* subject **es.**

***Es* macht viel mehr Spaß, von anderen** *gefahren zu werden.*	*It* is much more fun *being driven* by others.

10b   The present and past participles

Despite their traditional names, the two participles do not by themselves refer to any particular time.

(i)   The formation and use of present participles: -end

(A) All *present participles* are formed in the same way, by adding **-d** to the infinitive, e.g. **warten***d* *'waiting'*, **wandern***d* *'hiking'*, **studieren***d* *'studying'*, **laufen***d*. *'running'*. The verbs **sein** and **tun** insert **-e-** before the **-n** to form **seiend** 'being' and **tuend** 'doing'.

(B) Verbal particles (e.g. **auf, beiseite, zurück** [➤16e(ii)]) and present participles are written as one word, in the order particle + participle, e.g. **anstehend, weiterwandernd, zurücklaufend** [➤also 10b(iv); note that compounds of **sein** use **-wesend**].

(ii) *German equivalents for English '-ing'*

Apart from the usages listed in 10b(iv) and (v), the present participle cannot be used in German in the same way as it is in English. German equivalents of English '-ing' are described in the following paragraphs:

➤ *After seeing* her I caught the train home: conjunction + subordinate clause ➤5a(ii).
Stop doing that!: verb + **zu** + infinitive ➤8h(ii).
He *insisted on coming* too: verb + preposition + **zu** + infinitive ➤8h(ii).
Hang-gliding is marvellous: infinitive-nouns ➤10a(iii).
Hanging upside down by your heels is good for the brain: infinitive clauses as subjects ➤10a(iv).
I *am writing* a letter: present continuous tense ➤12a(i).
Instead of mailing it I phoned home: prepositions + **zu** + infinitive ➤27c.

(iii) *The formation and use of past participles: (ge)-t or (ge)-en*

With minor exceptions (for example their use as sharp commands [➤13c(ii)]) German *past participles* are used in the same ways as in English, mainly as part of the compound past tenses [➤12b] and of the passive [➤ch.15].

(A) Regular weak participles are formed by adding **-(e)t** to the verb stem (the infinitive minus **-en**). English equivalents are 'walk-walked' and 'burn-burnt'. The **-e-** is used after **t** and **d**, and after **m** or **n** when preceded by any consonant except **l** or **r**. For example, **gemach*t*** 'did', **gelächel*t*** 'smiled', **gewarn*t*** 'warned', but **gerett*et*** 'saved', **gebad*et*** 'bathed', **geatm*et*** 'breathed', **geregn*et*** 'rained'. [Irregular weak verbs: ➤16c(ii)].

(B) Strong past participles have the same **-en** ending as the infinitive. Very often the stem vowel changes; in some irregular strong verbs there are also consonant changes, generally minor. English equivalents here are 'give-given' and 'break-broken'. For example, **gebissen** 'bitten', **geflogen** 'flown', **gesungen** 'sung', **vergessen** 'forgotten', **getragen** 'carried'. [Summary of strong verb classes: ➤16d(v). List of strong verbs: ➤18e.]

(C) Both weak and strong past participles have the prefix **ge-** before the verb stem unless the verb:

• already starts with a fixed prefix (e.g. **be-, ent-, er-, ge-, ver-, zer-** [➤16e(i)]). For example, **gestört** 'disturbed' but **zerstört** 'destroyed', **gestanden** 'stood' but **verstanden** 'understood'.

• is a weak verb ending in **-ieren**. For example, **gepasst** 'suited' but **pass*iert*** 'happened'. Note also **interviewt** 'interviewed' and **miaut** 'meowed'.

(D) Verbal particles (e.g. **auf, beiseite, zurück** [➤16e(ii)]) and past participles are written as one word, in the order particle (+**ge–**) + participle. For example, **an*gestanden*** 'queued', ***auf*gepasst** 'paid attention', ***bei*behalten** 'retained', ***aus*verkauft** 'sold out' [➤also 10b(iv)].

The following paragraphs deal with constructions involving the past participle:

➤ They *have invited* us to dinner: compound past tenses formed with **haben** ➤17c(i).

We *have been* there once before: compound past tenses formed with **sein** ➤17c(i).

The stairs to their apartment *had* just *been repaired*: the passive (formed with **werden**) ➤ch.15.

Look out!: abrupt commands ➤13c.

(iv) *Participles as adjectives*

Provided it makes sense, any present or past participle can be used as an adjective. *Participle adjectives* obey the same rules as all other adjectives [➤ch.24], that is:

• they take normal adjective endings when they are part of a noun phrase [➤24b(ii)]:

Mit *zunehmendem* Interesse gingen wir zum *vereinbarten* Treffpunkt.	With *increasing* interest we went to the *agreed* rendezvous.

• they can be used as nouns [➤24d]:

Der *Vorsitzende* war ein alter *Bekannter* von mir.	The *chairman* was an old *acquaintance* of mine.

• they can be used as adverbs [➤28b(i)]:

Er redete *erregt*, aber *treffend*.	He spoke *agitatedly* but *to the point*.

Many participles have developed distinct meanings of their own and are thought of as adjectives in their own right rather than as parts of the verb. For example:

(A) Present participles:

abwesend	absent	**empörend**	outrageous
ansteckend	infectious	**reizend**	charming
anwesend	present	**rührend**	touching
aufregend	exciting	**spannend**	exciting
bedeutend	important	**umfassend**	extensive
dringend	urgent	**wütend**	furious

(B) Past participles:

angesehen	respected	**erfahren**	experienced
aufgebracht	indignant	**geschickt**	skilled
aufgeregt	excited	**verliebt**	in love
ausgezeichnet	excellent	**verrückt**	crazy, insane
bekannt	famous		

(v) *Participle clauses*

Both present and past participles can be used to make free-standing clauses.

• The participle normally comes last within its own clause, which is separated by commas.
• A few past participle clauses have become frequently used set phrases, for example, **offen gestanden** 'frankly speaking' or **nebenbei gesagt** 'incidentally'.
• Otherwise, participle clauses tend to be used only in very formal German; this is especially true of those with present participles, which are nowhere near as common as their English equivalents.

(A) Present participle clauses:

Dem Vorsitzenden in die Augen *sehend*, sagte ich: „Sie irren sich."	*Looking* the chairman in the eye I said, "You're wrong."

(B) Past participle clauses:

Vom Beistand der anderen _ermutigt_, fuhr ich fort: „Das wissen Sie wohl selber."	_Encouraged_ by the support of the others I continued, "No doubt you know that yourself."

11 The passage of time: the use of tenses

11a   What do tenses tell us?

'Tense' is not the same thing as 'time', though the same words are often used to refer to both. Time is a fact of life, in which there are only three time zones (past, present and future). Tenses, on the other hand, are grammatical structures which often reflect a way of looking at an event as well as just record-ing when it happened. Both the number of tenses, the names given to them and their uses vary greatly from one language to another.

11b   One word or two? Simple and compound tenses

In the language of grammar a *simple* tense is a one-word form, while a *compound* tense uses two or more words (an auxiliary verb + one or more non-finite forms). German has four simple tenses: the present, the simple past, the present subjunctive and the simple conditional. For the compound tenses it uses these auxiliary verbs [➤7b]:

• **haben** 'have' or **sein** 'be' + past participle forms the com-pound past tenses [➤17c(i)];
• **werden** 'will' + infinitive forms the compound future [➤17c(ii)] and conditional [➤17c(iii)];
• **werden** 'become' + past participle forms the passive [➤ch.15].

11c   Doing or done to? The active and the passive

The majority of statements are about something done or to be done *by* the subject of the sentence: the verb is then said to be *active*. However, some statements relate what is being done *to* the subject: here the verb is in the *passive*. Chapters 12 to 14 discuss the active tenses, and Chapter 15 deals with the passive.

11d   The active tenses

Chapter 17 deals with the formation of tenses. The following list of active tenses is given for reference, using **warten** as an example of a *weak* verb and **bleiben** for the *strong* verbs [➤16b]. (The tenses of **Konjunktiv** I and the conditional [**Konjunktiv** II] are listed in paragraph 14b.) **Warten** uses **haben** in compound past tenses and **bleiben** uses **sein**, but this has nothing to do with being weak or strong.

Present/simple future	**Es wartet/bleibt.**	It waits/stays, is waiting/staying.
Simple past	**Es wartete/blieb.**	It waited/stayed, was waiting/staying.
Perfect	**Es hat ... gewartet/ ist ... geblieben.**	It has waited/stayed.
Pluperfect	**Es hatte ... gewartet/ war ... geblieben.**	It had waited/stayed.
Compound future	**Es wird ... warten/ bleiben.**	It will wait/stay.
Future perfect	**Es wird ... gewartet haben/geblieben sein.**	It will have waited/ stayed.

12 Statements of fact: past, present and future

The most used tenses are those which indicate that something is true or at least probable. For this reason they are known as the *indicative* tenses. This chapter discusses how they are used in German.

➤ Formation (conjugation) of tenses: ➤ch.17.
Word order in questions and commands: ➤4e Note.
Adding emphasis (I do/did do it): ➤29c(iii).

12a The present tense

German verbs have only one present tense. It is a simple tense whose main functions span several English constructions. Normally it is clear which meaning is intended, but any ambiguity can always be cured by adding an adverb such as **jetzt** 'now', **gewöhnlich** 'usually', **bald** 'soon'. More explicit constructions can also be used, but normally only for emphasis [➤(i) to (iii) below].

(i) What is happening now

Was *machst* du nur da oben?	What *are* you *doing* up there?
– Ich *rasiere* mich.	– I *am shaving*.

A more emphatic alternative is **ich bin *eben dabei, etwas zu machen*** 'I'm just doing something' [➤also10a(iii) **beim** + infinitive-noun].

(ii) What happens sometimes, usually or always

Bei dir *dauert's* immer so lange!	You always *take* so long!
– Du weißt, am Wochenende *stehe* ich später *auf*.	– You know I *get up* later on weekends.

The habitual nature of the activity can be stressed using **ich pflege es *zu machen*** 'I am in the habit of doing it', though this sounds rather stilted.

(iii)   *What is going to happen, often fairly soon*

This is the normal way of talking about the future, without any particular emphasis, and is used in German even in contexts where English would normally say 'I'*ll do* it' or 'I *am going to do* it'.

Wir *fahren* in zehn Minuten los! – Schon gut, ich *komme* gleich.	We *are leaving/are going to leave* in ten minutes! – All right, I'*m coming* right now.

The compound future with **werden** + infinitive either strengthens the assertion or adds some other emphasis [▶12c(i) and (ii)].

(iv)   *What has been happening up to now and may continue.*

This is a different way of looking at it from English. German sees the action as still going on (therefore present tense) and asks **Wie lange?** 'How long?' or **Seit wann?** 'Since when?'. However, German, like English, uses the *perfect* tense to refer to single events which either did not happen or came in a series [▶12b(vi)].

Ich *warte* schon eine Ewigkeit auf dich! – Ich war müde. Seitdem wir hier *wohnen*,/Seit dem Umzug *schlafe* ich nicht mehr gut.	I'*ve been waiting* for you for ages already! – I was tired. Since we *have been living* here/Since the move I *have* not *been sleeping* well.

(v)   *What happened in the (usually recent) past and is still fresh in the memory*

This usage, the so-called *narrative present*, is much more common in educated German, especially in speech, than in English. It may be used to stress the personal involvement of the narrator or simply to add a vivid or emphatic touch to the narration.

Ich *komme* ins Zimmer, und was *sehe* ich? Du *bist* immer noch im Bett!	I *come* (came) into the room and what *do* (did) I see? You *are* (were) still in bed!

12b   *The past tenses*

German has three active tenses which make statements about the past: one *simple* tense, **ich *machte* es** 'I *did* it' and two compound tenses: the *perfect,* **ich *habe* es *gemacht*** '*I have done* it' and the *past perfect* (or *pluperfect*), **ich *hatte* es *gemacht*** '*I had done it*'.

Note 1) Naturally, many past tense usages mirror those of the present tense, but transferred back in time.

2) German distinguishes between the simple past and the perfect in ways which are often very different from English and a good deal less clear-cut. Two important features are:

• in South Germany the simple past is not used very often;

• throughout Germany the simple past is much less common in speech than in writing, where it is more concise and avoids relegating of the full verb (i.e. the past participle) to the end of the sentence. However, the simple past of **haben** (**hatte** 'had', **sein** (**war** 'was') and the modals [➤ch.9] is common in both speech and writing.

In all cases, at least in speech and personal writing, the foreign learner should get used to using the perfect.

3) The German use of the pluperfect (the 'past in the past') is generally similar to English, though it is also used colloquially instead of the perfect.

(i)   Past events which are over and done with

Use perfect or simple past, as indicated in 2) above.

Vor zwei Jahren *haben* wir meine Eltern auf dem Land *besucht*. Unsere älteste Tochter *ist* nicht *mitgekommen*.	Two years ago we *visited* my parents in the country. Our eldest daughter *didn't come.*

(ii)   Past events accompanying the main narrative

The simple past is normal, at least in writing, but the perfect is possible. This is the parallel of the past to the present tense usage in paragraph 12a(i).

Während wir eine kleinere Landstraße entlang *fuhren* (*gefahren sind*), sind wir plötzlich auf eine Herde schwarzer Schafe gestoßen.	While we *were driving* along a small country road, we suddenly came on a flock of black sheep.

(iii) Past habits, generally assumed to be finished with

VERBS AND THEIR USES

Use perfect or simple past, as indicated in 2) above. This is the parallel of the present usage in paragraph 12a(ii); similarly, **ich *pflegte* es zu machen** 'I used to do it' is sometimes used to stress the habitual nature of the action.

In meiner Jugend *arbeitete* ich oft auf dem Bauernhof und *kannte* jede Schafsgattung.	In my youth I often *worked* on the farm and *knew* every breed of sheep.

(iv) *A state or activity which began before the events being narrated and continued right up to them*

The simple past is normal. This is an exact parallel to the present tense usage described in paragraph 12a(iv). Similarly, German, like English, uses the pluperfect tense to refer to a series of separate actions or states [►12b(ix)].

Inzwischen *wohnte* ich aber schon seit zwanzig Jahren in der Stadt, und ich wußte ihre Namen nicht mehr.	Meanwhile, I *had been living* in the city for twenty years and I no longer knew their names.

(v) *Events, especially recent ones, whose effects can still be felt in the present*

Use the perfect.

Letzte Woche *hat* meine Frau mich an diesen Vorfall *erinnert*.	Last week my wife *reminded* me of this incident.

(vi) *A series of separate events leading up to the present (including events which did **not** happen)*

Use the perfect. Contrast this with the present tense in paragraph 12a(iv).

Seitdem *habe* ich mehrmals von den Schafen *geträumt* und *bin* immer voller Angst *aufgewacht*.	Since then I *have dreamed* about the sheep several times and *have* always *woken up* full of fear.

(vii) *The completion of a future activity*

Even in main clauses the perfect is often used instead of the future perfect [➤12c(iii)]. In subordinate clauses the perfect is always used.

Ich werde froh sein, wenn ich ihren Namen *entdeckt habe*. Bis dann *habe* ich aber bestimmt viel Schlaf *verloren*.	I will be glad when I *have discovered* their names. Until then, though, I *will* certainly *have lost* a lot of sleep.

(viii) *Events even further in the past than the main narrative*

Use the pluperfect. These may be single events or a whole series. The uses of the pluperfect correspond to the uses of the perfect listed in paragraphs 12b(i), (v) and (vi), shifted one stage further into the past.

Mag sein, aber bis letzte Woche *hatte* ich immer sehr gut *geschlafen*. Ich *hatte* nicht einmal Schafe *gezählt!*	Maybe, but up to last week I *had* always *slept* very well. I *had* not even *counted* sheep!

12c   The future tense

The normal way to refer to future action in German is to use the present tense [➤12a(iii)]. There are also two compound tenses: the *future*, **ich *werde* es *machen*** 'I *will do* it', and the *future perfect*, **ich *werde* es *gemacht haben*** 'I *will have done* it'. The compound future is used in the first three usages that follow; the future perfect is used in the fourth.

VERBS AND THEIR USES

(i) *To avoid ambiguity, where the present tense could mean either 'now' or 'soon'*

„Als Abgeordneter für diesen Wahlkreis *werde* ich immer in eurem Interesse *handeln!*", rief der Kandidat.	"As member for this electoral district I *will* always *act* in your interests!" shouted the candidate.

(ii) *To emphasize that you really are going to do the thing in question*

„Ich verspreche euch, ich *werde sicherstellen,* dass neue Arbeitsplätze hier geschaffen werden."	"I promise you, I *will ensure* that new jobs will be created here."

(iii) *To make a prediction or estimate the reason for something*

Wohl 'no doubt, probably' [➤29c(iii)] is often added (**dürfte** + infinitive has a similar meaning [➤9c(i)]).

Das *wird* wohl unser Herr Schwätzle *sein.* Später *wird* er sicherlich sein Versprechen *bereuen.*	That*'ll be* our Mr. Schwätzle. Later he *will* certainly *regret* his promise.

(iv) *To refer to events completed before the future time being talked about (the 'past in the future')*

Like English, German uses the future perfect for this in main clauses [but ➤12b(vii)] and the perfect tenses in subordinate clauses, for example after **bis** 'by the time that', **wenn** 'when' or **nachdem** 'after'.

Glaubst du? Bis er ins Parlament *gekommen ist, wird* er jedes Wort *vergessen haben.*	Do you think so? By the time he *has gotten* into parliament he *will have forgotten* every word.

13 Requests and commands: the imperative

13a   What does the imperative express?

The *imperative* is used for a variety of purposes including requests, commands, warnings, instructions, invitations and advice.

13b   What you are to do: second person imperatives

➤   Uses of second person forms: ➤25b(ii). Formation of the imperative: ➤17d. Reported commands: ➤5e, 9c(v).

(i)   The three second person imperatives (for **du, ihr** and **Sie**) come *first* in the sentence, apart of course from names or exclamations. The pronoun **Sie** is always included, after the verb; **du** and **ihr** are not usually included, but they may be added for emphasis or when different people are being asked to do different things.

Hans, *bring(e)* **(du)** das Geschirr in die Küche! Inge und Martin, *räumt* **(ihr)** eure Sachen *weg*! Frau Körner, *reichen Sie* mir bitte das Salz!	Hans, (you) *take* the dishes into the kitchen. Inge and Martin, (you) *clear away* your things. Mrs. Körner, please *pass* me the salt.

(ii)   Because straight imperatives are felt to be somewhat brusque, questions are often used instead. Auxiliaries like **würden Sie ...?** or **willst du/wollen Sie ...?** and **könnten Sie?** are also frequently used.

Hans, *bringst du* das Geschirr in die Küche? Inge und Martin, *wollt ihr* eure Sachen *wegräumen*? Frau Körner, *würden Sie* mir bitte das Salz *reichen*?	Hans, *(could you) take* the dishes into the kitchen? Inge and Martin, *will (would) you clear away* your things? Mrs. Körner, *would you* please *pass* me the salt?

13c   Instructions and firm commands

(i)   Imperative usage of the infinitive

The infinitive is often used in official warnings and directions and in instructions for games, recipes etc. It is also used in colloquial speech for urgent warnings.

Endstation! Alles aussteigen!	End of the line/Terminus! All *change!*
Bei Kurzschluss gleich *abschalten*!	In case of a short *switch off* immediately.
Äpfel *schälen*, **in Scheiben** *schneiden*, **mit Zucker** *bestreuen* **und mit etwas Rum** *übergießen.*	*Peel* the apples, *cut* in slices, *sprinkle* with sugar and *pour* a little rum *over.*
Aufpassen! Links *gucken*!	*Look out*! *Look* left!

(ii)   Imperative usage of the past participle

The past participle can be used as a very sharp command, for example in military language. In colloquial speech it is restricted to a few set phrases, including expletives, which are, after all, a sort of sharp command!

Verdammt **noch mal!**	*Damn!*
Abgemacht!	*Done!/Agreed!*
Stillgestanden!	*Attention!* (military)

13d   Wishes and suggestions

(i)   What we are to do

The German equivalents of 'let's go' include **gehen wir jetzt** (now felt to be rather stilted), **lass uns jetzt gehen** and (perhaps most commonly) **wollen wir jetzt gehen?**

Lass uns **heute Abend** *ausgehen.*	*Let's go out* tonight.
Wollen wir **ins Kino** *gehen*?	*Let's (shall we) go* to the cinema.

(ii)   If only ...

Free-standing **wenn** clauses with the verb in the conditional [►14b] express a heartfelt wish that something had or had not happened.

Wenn ich *doch nur* wüsste, welche Filme gezeigt werden! *Wenn* du *bloß* die Zeitung nicht weggeschmissen hättest!	*If only* I knew what movies were playing! *If only* you hadn't thrown away the newspaper!

(iii)   *Expressing a wish for the future*

The third person forms of **Konjunktiv I** [➤14b] can express a wish for the future, but nowadays only in some set phrases.

Gott *sei Dank!* Gott behüte!	*Thank* God! God *forbid*!

14 Areas of uncertainty: der Konjunktiv

14a Konjunktiv or subjunctive?

Konjunktiv is a term used in modern German grammar to refer to a series of tenses parallel to the indicative [➤ch. 12]. It is also called the *subjunctive*, but this is misleading as it has almost none of the usages which the subjunctive has in other languages. We shall therefore use the German term, with references to other terms where helpful.

14b The tenses of the Konjunktiv

➤ Formation of Konjunktiv: ➤17a.

(i) The **Konjunktiv** has two series of tenses, referred to in German simply as **Konjunktiv I** and **Konjunktiv II**. Each has one simple tense and two compound tenses. Older grammar calls the two simple tenses *present subjunctive* and *past subjunctive*, but in fact the first refers mainly to the past and the second often to the future.

(ii) With some additions, **Konjunktiv II** is used like the conditional in, for example, English and French, and it is sensible to think of it in this way in German and to call it the *conditional*.

(iii) In the following lists the tenses are given in the **es** form because this is a good marker for **Konjunktiv I**.

Konjunktiv I		*Konjunktiv II*	
Simple	**es warte/ komme**	Simple Conditional	**es wartete /käme**
Future	**es werde warten/ kommen**	Compound Conditional	**es würde warten/ kommen**
Perfect	**es habe gewartet/ sei gekommen**	Past Conditional	**es hätte gewartet/ wäre gekommen**

Konjunktiv tenses have two main uses.

(A) Indirect/Reported speech [➤14c.]

(B) Conditional clauses [➤14d.]

14c *What did they say? Indirect speech*

In *indirect* or *reported* speech, what was actually said is not repeated word for word but rephrased in a clause introduced by a suitable verb [➤5c for the syntax of the construction]. Usage on indirect speech has changed considerably over the years, and even educated Germans now find it hard to say what is 'correct' in every instance. The following guidelines take account of the differences between reporting in speech and in writing, but it is impossible in a book of this size to cover all possibilities.

(i) *Rules for indirect speech*

The traditional rule for indirect speech in written German has two stages. (See examples in the next paragraph.)

(A) As a first principle, the actual tense used is changed into the **Konjunktiv I** tense which best indicates the time zone spoken of. This is the only function of **Konjunktiv I**.

(B) If, however, the resulting **Konjunktiv I** form is the same as the corresponding indicative form, then the conditional **(Konjunktiv II)** is used.

The basis of this rule is that indirect speech should if possible be indicated by a distinct **Konjunktiv** form. As **sie seien** (from **sein** 'be') is the only **sie** (third person plural) form in **Konjunktiv I** which is different from the indicative, the effect is to put all other plural verbs into the conditional.

(ii) *Changes to the verb*

The resultant verb changes may be summarized as follows. The introductory verbs could be in any past tense. The reported speech clause may start:

• with **dass**, with the verb at the end, as in the last three examples shown below;
• simply with a comma, as in the first three examples, in which case normal main clause word order is used.

Words actually used	*Indirect speech*
Present	
„Ich *komme* aus Lübeck."	**Paul sagte, er *komme* aus Lübeck.**
"I *come* from Lübeck."	He said he *came* from Lübeck.

VERBS AND THEIR USES

Words actually used

Indirect speech

„Wir *sind* vier in der Familie."
"There *are* four of us in the family."

Er sagte, sie *seien* vier in der Familie.
He said there *were* four of them in the family.

„Wir *haben* dort eine Wohnung."
"We *have* an apartment there."

Er sagte, sie *hätten* dort eine Wohnung.
He said they *had* an apartment there.

Future

„Wir *ziehen* morgen nach Köln."
„Wir *werden* morgen nach Köln *ziehen*."
"We *are/will be moving* to Cologne tomorrow."

Er sagte, dass sie tags darauf nach Köln *ziehen würden*.
He said that they *were/would be moving* to Cologne the next day.

Past

„Ich *wohnte* als Junge dort."
„Ich *habe* als Junge dort *gewohnt*."
"I *lived/used to live* there as a boy."

Er erzählte uns, dass er als Junge dort *gewohnt habe/hätte*.
He told us that he *had lived* there as a boy.

„Meine Mutter *hatte* früher im Osten *gelebt*."
"My mother *had* earlier *lived* in the east."

Er behauptete, dass seine Mutter früher im Osten *gelebt habe/hätte*.
He claimed that his mother *had* earlier *lived* in the east.

(iii)   Variations to the rules

In any sort of non-personal writing these rules are generally adhered to, so that both **Konjunktiv I** and the conditional often appear in the same sentence. Newspapers use the construction frequently — reporting is, after all, their job. There are, however, important factors which often alter the indirect speech verb forms shown above.

(A) Apart from in a few set phrases, **Konjunktiv I** is virtually never used in everyday speech and seldom in personal writing.

• In speaking, indirect speech normally uses the same indicative tenses as were used by the speaker.

Paul sagt, er *kommt* **aus Lübeck.**	Paul says he *comes* from Lübeck.

• In writing, use of the same indicative tense is increasingly common when the subordinate clause begins with **dass** (which replaces the **Konjunktiv** as a marker of indirect speech).

Er hat uns erzählt, dass er als Junge in Köln *gewohnt hat.*	He told us that he *lived* in Cologne when he was a boy.

• Alternatively, and especially if what was said may not be true, the conditional may be used in both speech and writing.

Er behauptet, seine Mutter *hätte* **im Osten** *gelebt.*	He claims that his mother *had lived* in the east.

(B) In speech, and increasingly even in formal writing, there is now a strong tendency to use the compound conditional (e.g. **er würde kommen**) instead of the simple conditional (**er käme**) [➤14d(iv) Note]. The compound conditional is:

• *less* used with auxiliary verbs (**haben**, **sein** and the modals);
• *more* used when the simple conditional is either the same as the simple past (e.g. **machte**) or felt to be archaic (e.g. **stünde** from **stehen** 'stand').

Paul hat gesagt, er *würde* **gleich** *umziehen,* **wenn er das Geld** *hätte.* **Vor allem** *müsste* **er in Köln eine Stelle finden.**	Paul said he *would move* at once if he *had* the money. Above all he *had to/would have to* find a job in Cologne.

14d   *What if? Conditional statements (Konjunktiv II)*

A *conditional statement* deals not with what is so, but with what *would* be so *if* something else happened. Sentences therefore generally have the form:

Wenn ich zu viel denke, bekomme ich Kopfschmerzen.	If I think too much I get a headache.

Which tenses are used depends on how likely the event is and the time zone referred to. A very important difference between German and (for example) French and English is that the same type of tense is used both in the **wenn** 'if' clause and in the main clause.

Wenn ich den Grund dafür *wüsste, würde* **ich es dir sagen.**	If I *knew* (*would know*) the reason for it I *would* tell you.

(i)   Likely future events

Some future events are very likely to happen. The verb in the **wenn** clause is then in the normal present tense and the main verb is either also present, referring to the future [➤12a(iii)] or compound future (**werden** + infinitive) [➤12c].

Wenn es so *weitergeht, bitte* **ich den Arzt um Rat/***werde* **ich den Arzt um Rat** *bitten.*	If it *goes on* like this, I *will ask* the doctor for advice.

(ii)   Giving advice

As an extension of this, the conditional can be used in the main clause to give advice about something which is known to be happening. Here the **wenn** clause may well be replaced by a phrase such as **an Ihrer/deiner Stelle** 'if I were you', **in dem Fall** 'in that case' etc.

An Ihrer Stelle *würde* **ich mir keine Sorgen** *machen.*	If I were you I *would*n't *worry.*

(iii)   Possible events

Other future possibilities depend on events which may or may not happen. Here both the **wenn** clause verb and the main verb are in the conditional. The use of the compound conditional with **würde** in the **wenn** clause is more colloquial.

Wenn es ein gutes Mittel dagegen *gäbe* (*geben würde*), *würde* **ich es nehmen.**	If there *was/were* a good remedy for it, I *would* take it.

(iv) *Dependent events in the past*

Some past events only happened (or did not happen) because of something else. In such cases, the verbs in both clauses are in the past conditional. If we are talking about the effects now, then the main verb is in the normal conditional.

Wenn du meinem Rat nur *gefolgt wärst, hättest* **du diese Probleme nicht** *gehabt/würdest* **du dich jetzt viel wohler** *fühlen.*	If you *had* only *taken* my advice, you *would*n't *have had* these problems/you *would feel* much better now.

Note German use of the simple conditional (e.g. **käme**) as against the compound conditional (e.g. **würde kommen**) varies very greatly, making it difficult to make hard-and-fast rules for this usage [➤14c(iii)].

(A) In general, the simple conditional is more likely to be used:

• in the **wenn** clause;
• with auxiliaries (**haben, sein** and the modals) and other common verbs;
• in non-personal writing.

(B) Conversely, the compound conditional is more used:

• in all cases in colloquial speech;
• in the main clause;
• with weak verbs [➤16c] with no distinct simple conditional form (e.g. **wartete**);
• with strong verbs [➤16d] whose simple conditional is felt to be archaic or stilted (e.g. **begönne** 'begin', **hülfe** 'help').

(C) Almost all weak and a good many strong verbs are in the last two categories, which reinforces the tendency to use the compound conditional. It is considered clumsy to use **würde** + infinitive in both halves of the sentence, though this does not prevent its happening, even in writing.

Things done to you: the passive

15a What does the passive express?

In the *passive*, the subject does not perform the action of the verb but is the thing or person primarily affected by it. This is just what the direct object of a transitive verb describes, and only transitive verbs can be used in the passive [▶8d(i)]. All the same, the passive is not just another way of saying the same thing as the active form – it emphasizes different things, especially what happens to the subject. Who the doer of the action is usually matters less and may well not be stated.

Unser Haus *wird* **im Augenblick** *ausgebaut*. **Das Dach** *wird* **auch neu** *gedeckt*.	Our house *is being extended* at the moment. It *is* also *being re-roofed*.

15b The tenses of the passive

The passive has the same range of tenses as the active, but they are all compound, formed with the relevant tense of the auxiliary **werden** + past participle. (The English equivalent is 'be' + past participle.) The more complex tenses are rare in the passive – other tenses tend to be substituted for them.

In the following list, the terms *simple* and *compound* refer to the forms of **werden**, not to the whole tense; this helps to show how the passive and active tenses are parallel. Note that in the compound past tenses, the past participle of **werden** loses its **ge-** and becomes **worden**.

Present/		
Simple future:	**Es wird gemacht.**	It is being/will be done.
Simple past:	**Es wurde gemacht.**	It was being done.
Perfect:	**Es ist gemacht worden.**	It has been done.
Pluperfect:	**Es war gemacht worden.**	It had been done.
Compound future:	**Es wird gemacht werden.**	It will be done (*rare*).
Conditional:	**Es würde gemacht.**	It would be done.
Past conditional:	**Es wäre gemacht worden.**	It would have been done.

| *Konjunktiv I* *simple*: | **Es werde gemacht.** | (They said that) it was being done. |
| *Konjunktiv I* *perfect*: | **Es sei gemacht worden.** | (They said that) it had been done. |

15c By whom? How? With what? The agent, the means and the instrument

Three German prepositions translate the English 'by' with a passive.

(i) **von** + dative noun phrase describes the person who (or possibly thing which) did the action.

| **Zunächst wurde das alte Dach *von den Bauarbeitern* entfernt.** | First the old roof was removed *by the construction workers*. |

(ii) **durch** + accusative noun phrase describes the means by which the action was done.

| **Es war *durch die letzten Winterstürme* schwer beschädigt worden.** | It had been badly damaged *by the last winter storms*. |

(iii) **mit** + dative noun phrase describes the instrument with which the action was done. (**durch** + accusative can also be used).

| **Dann wurden die neuen Ziegel *mit langen Nägeln* an den Dachlatten befestigt.** | Then the new tiles were secured *by/with long nails* to the roof slats. |

15d The passive with intransitive verbs

(i) In German, unlike English, only the direct (accusative) object of an active verb can become the (nominative) subject of a passive verb. Dative objects [▶8d(ii), 8e] can be used with passive verbs but:

• they remain in the dative case;
• the main verb is in the third person singular;

VERBS AND THEIR USES

- main clauses must start with the dummy subject **es** if no other word or phrase occupies the first position.

Uns ist empfohlen worden, einen Architekte zu engagieren. *Es* ist *mir* geraten worden, es nicht alleine zu unternehmen.	*We* were recommended to hire an architect. *I* was advised not to undertake it alone.

(ii)   Prepositional objects [➤8g] can similarly be used with passives.

Für alle möglichen Fälle ist gesorgt worden.	*Every possible eventuality* was taken care *of*.

Note   In both cases alternative constructions are often preferable [➤15f].

15e   What is going on? Passive verbs with no subject

Unlike English, German can use a passive verb to refer generally to an activity. Such constructions have no subject, but main clauses must start with the dummy subject **es** if no other word or phrase is occupying the first position. Even intransitive verbs are sometimes used in this way.

Beim Richtfest *wird getrunken.* Am Abend *wird* wohl *gesungen* und *getanzt*.	At the roof completion ceremony *there is drinking.* In the evening *there is* probably *singing* and *dancing*.

15f   Alternatives to the passive

The passive is not uncommon in German, and it is certainly not to be avoided if it is the most suitable way of saying something. Indeed, it has uses like those in paragraph 15e which have no English equivalent. All the same, German does have a range of alternatives to the passive.

(i)   In English we may use the passive in order to stress something other than the doer of the action. In German this can easily be done by placing (say) the accusative or dative object at the start of the sentence.

Unseren Anbau **hat eine Fachzeitschrift ausführlich beschrieben.** *Dem Architekten* **hat der Verfasser insbesondere gratuliert.**	*Our extension* was extensively written up by a trade journal. *The architect* was especially congratulated by the writer.

(ii) Where in English we describe the process using the passive, German may well use an active verb describing the outcome. This is especially useful as a way of avoiding passive verbs with indirect objects [➤8e].

Ich *habe erfahren*, **dass der Architekt einen Preis** *erhalten hat*.	I *was told* that the architect *was given* a prize.

(iii) The indefinite pronoun: **man**

If the doer of an action is 'they' (people in general), the indefinite pronoun **man** 'one' is often used as the subject.

Solche Preise *verleiht man* **nicht ohne guten Grund.**	Such prizes *are* not *awarded* without good reason.

Note **man** cannot be used to narrate a chance event for which nobody is held responsible, so:

Ein Bauarbeiter wurde verletzt. A building worker was injured.

or **Ein Bauarbeiter hat sich verletzt.** A building worker injured himself.

(but not **Man hat einen Bauarbeiter verletzt.** They injured a building worker.)

(iv) Passive usage of reflexive verbs

A reflexive verb often replaces an English passive. Similarly, many German reflexive verbs translate the English construction 'be' + past participle, for example, **ich ärgere/ freue/schäme mich** 'I am annoyed/pleased/ashamed'.

VERBS AND THEIR USES

Ich *wundere mich* nur (darüber), dass der Artikel mich gar nicht erwähnt hat. Das *erklärt sich* wohl dadurch, dass ich kein Architekt bin!	I *am* only *surprised* that the article did not mention me at all. That *is* no doubt *explained* by the fact that I am not an architect!

(v)   *'Can be done' can be expressed using:*

(A) das lässt sich ... machen [➤8d(i)] and **das ist ... zu machen**. The latter can also mean 'must be done'. Notice that the normal infinitive is used (here **machen**), rather than the passive infinitive (**gemacht werden**).

(B) sein + an adjective formed from the verb stem + **-bar** or **-lich** (equivalent to the English ending '-able').

Solche Arbeit *lässt sich* leicht *machen*, wenn man Architekt ist. Sonst *ist* sie aber kaum *zu machen*/kaum *machbar*. Ein Fachmann *ist* immer *einzustellen*.	That sort of work *can* easily *be done* if you are an architect, but otherwise *is* hardly *to be done* (*is* hardly *doable*). An expert *must* always *be hired*.

(vi)   **bekommen** or the colloquial **kriegen** are sometimes used with a past participle.

Dadurch *bekommt/kriegt* man alle technischen Probleme *gelöst*.	That way you *get* all the technical problems *solved*.

15g   Action or description? The descriptive passive

The true passive always describes a process, but when it is over the same past participle, can describe the result. For this, German uses **sein** + past participle. This construction is often called the *descriptive passive,* but it must not be used instead of the true passive with **werden**.

The first example below describes a process which is still going on, the second a recently completed process and the third the result of a process which may have happened years before. In this last case, the participle could well be replaced by an adjective.

Die Mauern _werden_ gerade verputzt.	The walls _are_ just _being_ plastered.
Die Mauern _sind_ verputzt _worden_.	The walls _have been_ plastered.
Die Mauern _sind_ verputzt (weiß/sehr hoch).	The walls _are_ plastered (white/very high).

Types of German verbs

➤ Tense stems and endings: ➤ch.17. Verb tables: ➤ch.18.

16a Predictability: regular or irregular?

(i) Conjugation

The whole set of a verb's stems and endings is called its *conjugation*.

• *Regular* verbs are verbs in which you can predict any part of any tense from the spelling of the infinitive – plus of course a knowledge of the rules!
• Verbs in which some parts cannot be predicted in this way are known as *irregular* verbs. Some of the most common German verbs are irregular, but there are not very many of them, and the irregularities are often quite small.

(ii) Predicting the conjugation

The conjugation of German verbs is very systematic. In all but a handful of verbs you can predict any part just by knowing four basic forms:

• the *infinitive;*
• the **er/sie/es** (third person singular) form of the present tense and of the simple past;
• the past participle.
In fact, in the great majority the other forms can be predicted from the infinitive alone.

(iii) Compound verbs

Compound verbs [➤16e] always conjugate in the same way as their base verb. Apparent exceptions are in fact verbs made from nouns related to the base verb.

Sie trägt es/trug es/hat es ... getragen.	She carries/(has) carried it.
Sie erträgt es/ertrug es/hat es ... ertragen.	She endures/(has) endured it.
Sie trägt es ... ein/trug es ... ein/hat es ... eingetragen.	She enters/(has) entered it (on a list).

but:

Sie beantragt es/beantragte es/hat es ... beantragt.	She applies/(has) applied for it.

This last example is in fact formed from **der Antrag** 'application'.

16b   *Weak and strong verbs*

Like other Germanic languages (including English), German has two main categories of verbs, traditionally known as *weak* and *strong.* They have very different ways of forming their simple past tense and past participle.

Note   'Weak' and 'strong' are not the same as 'regular' and 'irregular'. In both categories most verbs are regular, that is, they follow the rules for their category.

16c   *Weak verbs*

If any new verb is coined (from another language, for example), it always follows the weak pattern.

(i)   *Regular weak verbs*

Weak verbs add endings to the stem of the infinitive (the infinitive minus **-(e)n**), as in the English 'walk, walked' or 'learn, learned(t)'. German weak verbs add:

• **-(e)te** to the stem to form the base of the simple past (that is, the basic form to which the endings are added [➤17a]);
• **-(e)t** to the stem to form the past participle.

For example, **lachen** 'laugh': **ich lache, ich lachte, ich habe, ... gelacht.**
The **-e-** is used if the stem ends in **d** or **t**, or in **m** or **n** preceded by any consonant other than **l** or **r**.

For example, **regnen** 'rain': **es regnet, es regnete, es hat ... geregnet.**

(ii)   *Irregular weak verbs*

There are only sixteen irregular weak verbs.

• They all add the normal weak endings in the simple past and past participle, but they have minor variations in the stem. The verbs can be grouped together according to these variations.

VERBS AND THEIR USES

• Only **haben** and the modals/**wissen** group are also irregular in the present tense.

The parts of the verb shown in the examples below are the infinitive, and the present (only if irregular), simple past and perfect tenses.

(A) **haben** loses its **-b-** in the **du** and **er/sie/es** forms of the present tense and in all of the simple past (where the **-t-** of the ending doubles). The past participle is regular.

haben, hast/hat, hatte, hat ... gehabt	have

(B) The six modal verbs [➤ch.9] and **wissen** form the largest group of irregular weak verbs.

• The present tense singular looks like the simple past of a strong verb, that is, the **ich** and **er/sie/es** forms (first and third persons) are the same, and neither has any ending. All but **sollen** change the stem vowel. The plural is regular.
• The four modals with **ö** or **ü** in the stem drop the Umlaut in the simple past and past participle; the **i** in **wissen** changes to **u**. [Infinitive-past participle: ➤9b(i).]

dürfen, darf, durfte, hat ... gedurft	allowed to (may)
können, kann, konnte, hat ... gekonnt	able to (can)
mögen, mag, mochte, hat ... gemocht	like (to)
müssen, muss, musste, hat ... gemusst	have to (must)
sollen, soll, sollte, hat ... gesollt	supposed to, ought to
wollen, will, wollte, hat ... gewollt	want to
wissen, weiß, wusste, hat ... gewusst	know (a fact)

(C) Four verbs change **-enn-** in the stem to **-ann-**. You will notice that they all rhyme.

brennen, brannte, hat ... gebrannt	burn
kennen, kannte, hat ... gekannt	know (a person, place, etc.)
nennen, nannte, hat ... genannt	name
rennen, rannte, ist ... gerannt	race, scamper

(D) Two verbs change **-end-** in the stem to **-and-**. **senden** 'broadcast' and **wenden** 'turn (a car) round, meat over' are regular (**sendete, wendete**), as are the compounds **entwenden** 'purloin' and **verwenden** 'use'.

senden, sandte, hat ... gesandt	send
wenden, wandte, hat ... gewandt	turn

(E) Two verbs change the last three letters of the stem to **-ach-**. Like their English counterparts, they therefore rhyme in the simple past and past participle but not in the infinitive or present tense.

bringen, brachte, hat ... gebracht   bring (brought)
denken, dachte, hat ... gedacht   think (thought)

16d   *Strong verbs*

(i)   *Formation of strong verbs*

Strong verbs change the stem vowel of the infinitive, as in the English 'bite, bit, bitten', 'give, gave, given' or 'sing, sang, sung'.

• In the **du** and **er/sie/es** forms of the present tense, the stem vowels **e**, **a** and **o** often change to **i(e)**, **ä** and **ö**.
• In all strong verbs the stem vowel changes in the simple past.
• In all strong verbs except **tun** (**getan**) the past participle ends in **-en**, and in four of the seven classes the stem vowel changes.

(ii)   *Vowel changes*

Strong verbs fall into seven major classes. Each class has a distinctive pattern of vowel changes, and the verbs within it often rhyme. You can predict the forms of most strong verbs by knowing which class they fall into. [For examples of verbs in each class ➤(v) below.] You will see that there is a clear progression both in the stem vowels of the infinitive (**ei ➜ ie ➜ i ➜ e/i ➜ e ➜ a ➜ a**) and in other ways, and this can be a great help when learning the parts of the verbs.

(iii)   *Irregular strong verbs*

Irregular strong verbs are of three kinds.

• Verbs with minor variations in the stem consonants. These are noted as they occur in each class.
• Verbs in which the simple past and past participle follow a regular pattern but the infinitive and present tense do not. The most common of these are listed below by class.
• Two verbs which do not fit into any class. These are:

stehen, steht, stand, hat ... gestanden   stand
tun, tut, tat, hat ... getan   do, put

(iv)   *Verbs with both weak and strong forms*

Some verbs have both weak and strong forms, sometimes with different meanings. The most common of these are noted below.

(v)   *The seven strong verb classes*

In the following listings these parts of the verb are given:

101

VERBS AND THEIR USES

• the infinitive
• the **er/sie/es** (third person singular) form of the present tense, the simple past and the perfect.

(The **du** form has the same stem vowel as the **er/sie/es** form.)

● *Class I*
-ei- in infinitive and present tense, changing to -ie- (before a single consonant) or -i- (before a double consonant) in both simple past and past participle.

• -f- and -t- are doubled, changing -eif- to -iff- and -eit- to -itt-.
• -eid- also usually becomes -itt- (but **meiden, mied**).

beißen, beißt, biss, hat ... gebissen	bite
bleiben, bleibt, blieb, ist ... geblieben	remain
greifen, greift, griff, hat ... gegriffen	grab at
schneiden, schneidet, schnitt, hat ... geschnitten	cut

● *Class II*
-ie- in infinitive and present tense, changing to -o- in both simple past and past participle.

• Note the -g- in **ziehen: zog**.

fliegen, fliegt, flog, ist ... geflogen	fly
gießen, gießt, goss, hat ... gegossen	pour

Irregular verbs. Class II has collected a number of verbs whose stem vowel is not -ie-.

bewegen, bewegt, bewog, hat ...bewogen	persuade
betrügen, betrügt, betrog, hat ... betrogen	deceive
erwägen, erwägt, erwog, hat ... erwogen	consider
gären, gärt, gor, hat/ist ... gegoren	ferment
glimmen, glimmt, glomm, hat ... geglommen	glow
heben, hebt, hob, hat ... gehoben	lift, raise
lügen, lügt, log, hat ... gelogen	(tell a) lie
melken, melkt, molk, hat ... gemolken	milk
scheren, schert, schor, hat ... geschoren	shear
schwören, schwört, schwor, hat ... geschworen	swear (an oath)

(**bewegen** 'move' and **gären** 'seethe (with rage, etc.)' are weak.)

• Some verbs change the vowel in the **du** and **er/sie/es** forms of the present tense, usually to -i-.

dreschen, drischt, drosch, hat ... gedroschen	thresh
erlöschen, erlischt, erlosch, ist ... erloschen	go out (of fire)
fechten, ficht, focht, hat ... gefochten	fence (fight)
flechten, flicht, flocht, hat ... geflochten	plait
quellen, quillt, quoll, ist ... gequollen	well up, stream

saufen, säuft, soff, hat ... gesoffen	drink (of animals), booze
schmelzen, schmilzt, schmolz, hat/ist ... geschmolzen	melt
schwellen, schwillt, schwoll, ist ... geschwollen	swell

(**löschen** 'extinguish' is weak.)

● ***Class III***
-ind-, -ing- or -ink- in infinitive and present tense, changing to -a- in the simple past and to -u- in the past participle.

finden, findet, fand, hat ... gefunden	find
singen, singt, sang, hat ... gesungen	sing
sinken, sinkt, sank, ist ... gesunken	sink

● ***Class IV***
-imm-, -inn-, or -e- + two consonants (except -ss-) in infinitive, changing -e- to -i- in the **du** and **er/sie/es** forms of the present tense, and -e-/-i- to -a- in the simple past and to -o- in the past participle.

erschrecken, erschrickt, erschrak, ist ... erschrocken	be frightened, startled
helfen, hilft, half, hat ... geholfen	help
sterben, stirbt, starb, ist ... gestorben	die
schwimmen, schwimmt, schwamm, ist/hat ... geschwommen	swim
beginnen, beginnt, begann, hat ... begonnen	begin

(**erschrecken** 'frighten' is weak.)

Irregular verbs. Note the single and double consonants.

kommen, kommt, kam, ist ... gekommen	come
nehmen, nimmt, nahm, hat ... genommen	take
treffen, trifft, traf, hat ... getroffen	meet, hit (target)
werden, wirst/wird, wurde, ist ... geworden	become

● ***Class V***
-e- + single consonant or -ss- in infinitive, changing to -i- in the **du** and **er/sie/es** forms of the present tense and to -a- in the simple past, but retaining the stem of the infinitive in the past participle.

• Note that only **essen** inserts a -g- into the past participle.

geben, gibt, gab, hat ... gegeben	give
essen, isst, aß, hat ... gegessen	eat

Irregular verbs.

liegen, liegt, lag, hat ... gelegen	lie (flat)
sitzen, sitzt, saß, hat ... gesessen	sit
sein, ist, war, ist ... gewesen	be

VERBS AND THEIR USES

(**sein** is very irregular, especially in the present [➤18b]. It is a mixture of two verbs, one of which fits the pattern of Class V.)

● *Class VI*

-a- in infinitive, changing to -ä- in the **du** and **er/sie/es** forms of the present tense and to -u- in the simple past, but retaining the stem of the infinitive in the past participle.

fahren, fährt, fuhr, ist ... gefahren	go (in a vehicle), drive
graben, gräbt, grub, hat ... gegraben	dig
laden, lädt, lud, hat ... geladen	load
schlagen, schlägt, schlug, hat ... geschlagen	hit, strike
wachsen, wächst, wuchs, ist ... gewachsen	grow
waschen, wäscht, wusch, hat ... gewaschen	wash

Irregular verbs. There are only two of these.

backen, backt, backte/(buk), hat ... gebacken	bake (**buk** is now archaic)
schaffen, schafft, schuf, hat ... geschaffen	create

(**schaffen** 'do, achieve' is weak)

● *Class VII*

-a- in infinitive, changing to -ä- in the **du** and **er/sie/es** forms of the present tense and to -ie- (after single consonant) or -i- (after a double) in the simple past, but retaining the stem of the infinitive in the past participle.

• Apart from the eight verbs in Class VI, all strong verbs with -a- in the infinitive stem belong to this class.

fangen, fängt, fing, hat ... gefangen	catch
schlafen, schläft, schlief, hat ... geschlafen	sleep

Irregular verbs. Class VII has collected some half dozen verbs whose stem vowel is not -a- but which follow this pattern in the past (participle) and sometimes in the present.

laufen, läuft, lief, ist ... gelaufen	run, walk
stoßen, stößt, stieß, hat ... gestoßen	push (sharply)
hängen, hängt, hing, hat ... gehangen	hang (*intransitive*)
gehen, geht, ging, ist ... gegangen	go (on foot or generally), walk
hauen, haut, hieb/haute, hat ... gehauen/gehaut	hew, bash (weak forms are more colloquial)
heißen, heißt, hieß, hat ... geheißen	be called, command
rufen, ruft, rief, hat ... gerufen	call, shout

(**hängen** [*transitive*] is weak)

16e *Compound verbs*

German has a wide range of compound verbs, which greatly extend the meanings of the simple verbs on which they are based. There are two forms of compound verbs:

(A) those formed with a *fixed prefix* [➤16e(i)] (often marked *insep. [inseparable]* in dictionaries).

(B) those combined with a *verbal particle* [➤16e(ii)] (marked *sep. [separable]* in dictionaries).

These are often called **(A)** *inseparable prefixes* and **(B)** *separable prefixes*. However, as all true prefixes are inseparable, making the second term confusing, we prefer to use the terms *(fixed) prefix* and *(verbal) particle* .

Note   The major distinctions between the two affect both speech and writing.

1) Fixed prefixes are never detached from the verb stem.

• They are never stressed, that is, they never receive the main emphasis within the word. The stress remains on the verb stem.
• Verbs with a fixed prefix do not add **ge-** for the past participle.
• **zu** and the infinitive (including the prefix) are two separate words.

Ich hatte ihnen *erlaubt*, meinen Wagen *zu verkaufen.*	I had *allowed* them *to sell* my car.

2) Verbal particles are always in the final block [➤4e[iii]].

• They are stressed, even when they are attached to their verb.
• When the verb is also in the final block, its particle is attached to it. Both **ge-** and **zu** (if present) are then 'sandwiched' between the two.

Sie hatten sich *angeboten,* mir den Wagen *abzukaufen.*	They had *offered to buy* the car *from* me.

(i)   *Fixed prefixes*

Fixed prefixes usually make verbs from other verbs, but they can also make verbs from adjectives and occasionally from nouns. They almost always add a sense of completion — they carry the action of the verb further or to a conclusion (for better or worse). The general sense of each prefix is given below, but you will find many verbs with different meanings. Only a few examples are listed.

105

VERBS AND THEIR USES

(A) be- makes transitive verbs from other verbs, nouns or adjectives (the latter usually ending in **-ig**), often applying the original meaning to something.

Ich begreife es.	I grasp, understand it.
Ich bespreche es.	I discuss it.
Ich betrete es.	I enter (a room etc.).
Ich bewässere es.	I water, irrigate it.
Ich berichtige es.	I correct it.
Ich beruhige mich.	I calm down.

(B) ent- with verbs of motion takes a dative object, meaning 'getting away from'.

Ich entkomme ihnen.	I escape from them.
Ich entlaufe ihm.	I run away from him.
Ich entwische ihr.	I slip away from her.
Ich entrinne ihm.	I escape him.

ent- with adjectives, nouns or other verbs often means 'removing'.

Ich entferne es/mich.	I remove it/move away.
Ich entziffere es.	I decipher it.
Ich entschuldige mich.	I say sorry.
Ich entwässere es.	I drain, dehydrate it.

(C) er- with verbs usually carries the action to a conclusion.

Ich ergreife es.	I seize, grasp, grip it.
Ich erhalte es.	I receive it.
Ich erlebe es.	I experience it.
Ich erreiche es.	I reach it (a place).
Ich erwarte es.	I await, wait for it.
Ich erzähle es.	I narrate, tell it.

er- with adjectives means 'making' or 'changing to'.

Es ermöglicht etwas.	It makes something possible.
Ich ermüde (ihn).	I tire (him).
Ich erröte.	I blush.

(D) ge- makes compounds which considerably alter the meaning of the base verb.

Ich gebrauche es.	I use it.
Das gefällt mir.	I like that.
Es gehört ihnen.	It is theirs, belongs to them.
Es gelingt mir.	I succeed.

(E) hinter- adds the meaning of 'behind' to verbs, usually in a metaphorical sense.

Ich hintergehe sie.	I do it behind their back.

Ich hinterlasse es ihr.	I leave it to her it (in my will).

(F) **miss-** has the same meaning as English 'mis-'.

• Note the double prefix in **er missversteht es** 'he misunderstands it' and the position of **-zu-** in **misszuverstehen** 'to misunderstand'.

Es misslingt.	It goes wrong.
Das missfällt mir.	I don't like that.
Ich misstraue ihnen.	I mistrust them.

(G) **ver-** is very common and has a range of meanings. With verbs it conveys the sense of 'finishing off' or 'wrongly, by mistake'. In a few cases it gives an opposite.

Ich verdiene es.	I earn, deserve it.
Ich verfahre mich.	I lose my way (driving).
Ich verlasse es.	I leave it (a place).
Ich verliere es.	I lose it.
Ich verlerne es.	I forget, 'unlearn' it.
Ich verschließe es.	I lock it (up).

ver- with adjectives means 'making' or 'becoming'. With nouns it conveys 'providing or applying'.

Sie vereinigen sich/es.	They unite (it).
Es verfärbt sich.	It discolors.
Sie verhaften ihn.	They arrest him.
Sie vergiften es.	They poison, pollute it.

(H) **zer-** with other verbs always adds the sense of 'in pieces'.

Ich zerlege es.	I dismantle it, take it apart.
Ich zerquetsche es.	I squash it.
Ich zerreiße es.	I tear it up.
Ich zerstöre es.	I destroy it.

(ii) *Verbal particles*

A *verbal particle* is a semi-independent word closely linked to a verb, whose meaning it modifies. Most are derived from prepositions, adverbs, other verbs, adjectives or nouns. There are far too many verbal particles to list. The following examples are grouped by their derivation or form.

VERBS AND THEIR USES

(A) Particles from prepositions (**ein** is the particle for **in**).

Dreh das Licht *aus*, sperr die Katze *ein*, und mach alle Fenster *zu*. Kommt Peter *mit*? Oder hat er *vor*, uns *nach*zufahren? Pünktlichkeit werden wir ihm nie *bei*bringen! Der Sechsuhrzug ist schon *ab*gefahren. Nun werden wir erst um Mitternacht in Berlin *an*kommen.	Turn the light out, shut the cat in and close all the windows. Is Peter coming with us? Or is he planning to follow us? We'll never teach him punctuality! The six o'clock train has already left. Now we will not arrive in Berlin before midnight.

(B) Compound particles.

Ich ging eine enge Gasse *hinunter*, da kam mir ein Mann *entgegen*. Als er an mir *vorbei*ging, schob er mich *beiseite*. Ich ließ meine Papiere fallen, die ganz *durcheinander* kamen. „Passen Sie doch auf!", stieß ich *hervor* und fügte *hinzu*: „Sind Sie betrunken?" Ohne zu antworten lief er *davon*, ich ihm *hinterher*.	As I was walking down a narrow alley, a man came towards me. As he passed me, he pushed me aside. I dropped my papers, which got into a complete mess. "Look out!" I gasped, adding, "Are you drunk?" Without answering he ran off, with me behind him.

(C) Particles from other verbs (infinitives or past participles). These are usually linked to just one or two verbs.

Meinen Wagen hatte ich auf der Hauptstraße *stehen* (lassen). Kurz davor blieb er *stehen*. Ich wollte ihn wieder anreden, da erkannte ich ihn – ich hatte ihn vor ein paar Wochen *kennen* gelernt. Ich wusste, an ihm würden meine Worte *verloren* gehen, also ließ ich mein Vorhaben *fallen* und ging weiter *spazieren*.	I had parked my car on the main street. Just before it he stopped. I was going to speak to him again, then I recognized him – I had met him a few weeks earlier. I knew that my words would be wasted on him, so I abandoned my plan and continued with my walk.

(D) Particles from adverbs, adjectives or nouns. These also are usually linked to just one or two verbs.

Ich nahm an Verhandlungen *teil*, die in einem großen Hotel *statt*fanden. Sie waren im Allgemeinen *glatt* gegangen. Am Abend ging ich in die Bar, wo verschiedene Leute *fern*sahen. Plötzlich hielt mich jemand am Ärmel *fest*, und eine Stimme sagte: „Ich höre, Sie arbeiten die meiste Zeit *schwarz*!"	I was taking part in negotiations which were taking place in a big hotel. In general they had gone smoothly. In the evening I went into the bar, where various people were watching television. Suddenly someone caught me by the sleeve, and a voice said, "I hear you spend most of your time moonlighting!"

(iii) *Dual use as prefix and particle*

A few words can be both fixed prefixes and particles. The particles (in italics in the following examples) usually have more literal meanings than the prefixes.

(A) durch-

Ich habe eben Ihren Bericht *durch*gelesen. Jetzt durchschaue ich die Lage besser.	I have just read through your report. Now I understand the situation better.

(B) über-

Wir gehen ja bald zu einem neuen Computersystem *über*. Ich bitte Sie, die Verantwortung dafür zu übernehmen.	Of course we are soon going over to a new computer system. I am asking you to take over responsibility for it.

(C) um-

Das Computernetz umspannt unser ganzes Unternehmen. Viele Angestellte müssen *um*geschult werden.	The computer network covers our whole operation. Many employees will have to be retrained.

(D) unter-

Wir müssen alles unternehmen, um konkurrenzfähig zu bleiben, sonst gehen wir *unter*.	We must do everything to remain competitive, otherwise we will go under.

(E) wider- : used as a particle with only two verbs, **widerhallen** 'echo' and **widerspiegeln** 'reflect'.

Das spiegelt unseren festen Entschluss *wider*, in diesem Bereich aller Konkurrenz zu widerstehen.	This reflects our strong resolve to stand firm against all the competition in this field.

(F) wieder- : used as a prefix with only one verb **wiederholen** 'repeat'.

Ich wiederhole es, wir sind entschlossen, unseren ehemaligen Marktanteil *wieder*zugewinnen.	I repeat, we are determined to regain our former market share.

17 The formation of tenses: how are verbs conjugated?

Any part of any simple tense is made up of the basic stem ('base') for that tense plus the ending which goes with the verb's subject.

➤ Compound tenses: ➤17c. Imperative: ➤17d. Passive: ➤Chapter 15.

17a The basic form (base) of simple tenses

(i) Tense bases are more complex than endings. For this reason, they have been discussed fully in paragraphs 16c (weak verbs, especially irregular) and 16d (strong verbs). Once the base is known, the endings are added to it as shown in paragraph 17b.

(ii) The bases of the four simple tenses are summarized below.

Present: = stem of infinitive (i.e. infinitive minus **-(e)n**)
  e.g. **setz-, wart-, lächel-, wander-, hab-, bleib-, geb-, trag-, tu-**

Simple past
– *weak*: = infinitive stem + **-(e)te**
  e.g. **setzte-, wartete-, lächelte-, wanderte-**
– *strong*: = infinitive stem with change of vowel
  e.g. **blieb-, gab-, sang-, trug-**

Konjunktiv I:
  = infinitive minus **-n**
  e.g. **setze-, warte-, lächle-, wandere-, habe-, bleibe-, gebe-, trage-, sei-**. Note **tue-**.

Simple conditional:
  (*a*) if the simple past is regular weak: = simple past
  e.g. **setzte-, wartete-, lächelte-, wanderte-, sollte-**
  (*b*) if strong or irregular weak: = simple past + Umlaut if stem vowel is **a**, **o** or **u**, + final **-e** if not already there
  e.g. **bliebe-, gäbe-, trüge-, wäre-, würde-, hätte-, wüsste-, möchte-**

Note The rules for the simple conditional are very consistently applied, except that:

1) there are some strong verbs which change their stem vowel again, for example, **half → hülfe, schwamm → schwömme, schwor → schwüre, stand → stünde**;
2) irregular weak verbs which change **-enn-/-end-** to **-ann-/-and-** in the simple past and past participle [➤16c(i)] return here to the infinitive

VERBS AND THEIR USES

stem, for example, **brannte → brennte, kannte → kennte, sandte → sendete, wandte → wendete**. (**ä** would of course be pronounced like **e** in any case.)

In both instances, the compound conditional (**würde** + infinitive) would usually be preferred [➤14d(iv)Note].

17b   Tense endings

(i)   German tense endings are very straightforward. Apart from the **ich** and **er/sie/es** forms of the present tense, all tenses add the same set of endings to the base of the tense [➤17a]. With the fairly minor variations listed in (iii) below, this goes for almost all weak and strong verbs. The only major exceptions are in the present tenses of **sein** [➤18b], **wissen** and the modals [➤16c(ii)].

(ii)   In each tense there are three *persons* in both *singular* (one person) and *plural* (more than one):

First person:	the speaker(s)	**ich** 'I', **wir** 'we'
Second person:	the person(s) spoken to	**du, ihr** 'you' (familiar singular, plural)
		Sie 'you' (polite singular/plural)
Third person:	the person(s) or thing(s) spoken about	**er/sie/es** 'he/she/it', **sie** 'they' or any noun phrase

Singular endings   *Examples*

First person **ich**:
     present tense = base + **-e**   **mache, warte, bleibe**
     other tenses = base (no   **machte, wartete, blieb, würde,**
     ending)   **käme**

Second person **du**:
     all tenses = base + **-(e)st**   **machst, wartest, bleibst, machtest, würdest**

Third person **er/sie/es**:
     present = base + **-(e)t**   **macht, wartet, bleibt**
     other tenses = base (no   **machte, wartete, blieb, würde,**
     ending)   **käme**

Plural endings

First person **wir**:
     all tenses = base + **-(e)n**   **machen, bleiben, warteten, blieben, würden**

Second person **ihr**:
     all tenses = base + **-(e)t**   **macht, wartet, bleibt, machtet, würdet**

Third person **sie/(Sie)**:
     all tenses = base + **-(e)n**   **machen, bleiben, warteten, blieben, würden**

(iii)   *Variations in the pattern of endings*

Most of these variations simply make the word easier to pronounce.

(A) The linking **-e-** is included before **-st** and **-t** after bases ending in **t** or **d**, or in **m** or **n** preceded by any consonant except **l** or **r**, e.g. **wartest, findet, atmest, regnet** but **qualmt, wärmst, warnt.**

Note   1) In strong verbs, there is no **-e-** after a vowel change in the present tense or in the (little used) **du** form of the simple past, e.g. **trittst, tritt, lädst, lädt**; **fandst, tratst**.

2) In **werden**, note the dropping of the **d** in **du wirst** and of the **t** in **er/sie/es wird**.

(B) The linking **-e-** is always included before **-n** *unless* the base ends in **e**, **el** or **er**, e.g. **warten, finden, atmen** but **möchten, lächeln, wandern**. Note also **tun**.

(C) After present tense bases ending in **s**, **ß**, **x** or **z** the **du** ending **-st** reduces to **-t** e.g. **niest, heißt, boxt, sitzt** (replacing the older form **niesest,** etc.).

(D) Bases ending in **-el** lose the **e** of the base before the **ich** ending **-e**; particularly in speech, this also sometimes happens to bases ending in **-er**, e.g. **ich klingle, lächle, (wandre).**

(E) The **b** in **haben** is dropped in present tense **du hast** and **er/sie/es hat** (as also in the base of the simple past **hatte**).

17c   *Compound tenses*

(i)   *Compound past tenses*

These are formed with the auxiliaries **haben** or **sein** + past participle. (Paragraphs 18a/b list **haben** and **sein** in full.).

Note   In German, it is the meaning of the verb that determines which auxiliary it takes. This is why some verbs can take either **sein** or **haben** [➤(C) below]. For example:

• To say that people have just gone into town you would always start „Sie *sind* in die Stadt ...“ whether you then finished with „ ... **gegangen**", „ ... **gefahren**" or whatever.
• However, if the verb had a direct object, you would always use **haben**, as in **er hat das Auto in die Garage gefahren**.

(A) The following groups of verbs take **sein**. Note that some take an object in the dative but none takes an object in the accusative.

VERBS AND THEIR USES

- Intransitive verbs of motion:

Das Kind ist in den Garten *gegangen/gerannt/gekommen/gekrochen.*	The child *went/ran/came/crawled* into the yard.
Es ist *hingefallen,* **ist aber gleich** *aufgestanden.*	He (It) *fell down* but *got up* again at once.
Es war vorher auf die Bank *gestiegen* **und dann in den Sandkasten** *gesprungen.*	He had earlier *climbed* onto the bench, and then had *jumped* into the sandbox.
Es ist im Sandkasten der Katze *begegnet* **und ist ihr ins Haus** *gefolgt.*	He *met* the cat in the sandbox and *followed* it into the house.

- Intransitive verbs describing a change of state. This often includes the start or end of a process:

Es war wärmer *geworden.* **Die Eisblumen waren schon** *geschmolzen/getaut/verschwunden.*	It had *become* warmer. The frost patterns had already *melted/thawed/disappeared.*
Bis das Feuer *erloschen* **war, war das Kind schon** *eingeschlafen.* **Erst zehn Stunden später ist es wieder** *aufgewacht.*	By the time the fire had *gone out*, the child had *gone to sleep*. He only *woke up* ten hours later.
Das Kind ist im Mai 1990 *geboren.* **Einen Monat später ist sein Großvater** *gestorben.*	The child was *born* in May 1990. One month later his grandfather *died.*

- Most verbs meaning 'happen', 'succeed' or 'fail':

Es ist mir nicht *gelungen,* **ins Parlament zu kommen. Das ist mir schon dreimal** *passiert/geschehen/zugestoßen.*	I have not *succeeded* in getting into Parliament. That has *happened* to me three times already.

- The verbs **sein** and **bleiben**:

Wo bist du gestern *gewesen?* **Ich bin den ganzen Tag allein** *geblieben.*	Where *were* you yesterday? I *remained* alone the whole day.

(B) All other verbs take **haben**. This includes:

• All transitive verbs except **ich *bin* es losgeworden** 'I got rid of it':

Der Feuerwehrmann hat das Haus *betreten*, eine Leiter *bestiegen* und das Feuer *gelöscht*. Dafür hat er viel Lob *bekommen*.	The fireman *entered* the house, *mounted* a ladder and *put out* the fire. For that he *received* a lot of praise.

• All reflexive verbs except for a few verbs with **sein** where **sich** means 'each other':

Ich habe *mich gewaschen*, *rasiert* und *angezogen*, dann habe ich *mich* zu Tisch *gesetzt*. but	I *washed, shaved* and *dressed (myself)*, then I *sat down* at the table.
Wir *sind uns* zufällig in Rom *begegnet*.	We *met (each other)* by chance in Rome.

• Intransitive verbs not included in (A) above:

Ich habe drei Stunden lang in einem Meeting *gesessen*, dann noch zwei Stunden bei einer Abschiedsparty *gestanden*. Kein Wunder, dass ich gut *geschlafen* habe.	I *sat* for three hours in a meeting, then *stood* for two more hours at a farewell party. No wonder I *slept* well.

• The modal auxiliaries, even used with verbs taking **sein** [Perfect of modals: ➤9b(i) and (iii)]:

Wir haben nicht länger bleiben *können*, weil wir nach Hause haben zurückkehren *müssen*.	We *could* not stay longer, because we *had to* return home.

(C) Two groups of verbs may take either **sein** or **haben**.

• Some verbs of motion or change of state may also be transitive, possibly with a different meaning.

Sie *sind* sehr langsam *gefahren.* but	They *drove* very slowly.
Sie *haben* mich zum Bahnhof *gefahren.*	They *drove* me to the station.
Ich *bin* auf meinen Freund Hans *gestoßen.* but	I *bumped* into my friend Hans.
Ich *habe* ihn in die Rippen *gestoßen.*	I *nudged* him in the ribs.

• A few verbs of motion also describe physical activities, with no sense of moving in a given direction. They then take **haben**.

Wir *haben* vier Stunden lang *geschwommen/gesegelt/ gerudert/geritten/getanzt.*	We *swam/sailed/rowed/rode/ danced* for four hours.

(ii) The compound future
This is formed from the present tense of **werden** + infinitive. [➤12c(i)-(iii)]. (Paragraph 18c lists **werden** in full.)

Keine Angst! Wir *werden* am Sonntag bestimmt da *sein.* Elisabeth *wird* wohl auch *mitkommen.*	Don't worry! We *will* certainly *be* there on Sunday. Elisabeth *will* probably *come* too.

The future perfect uses the present tense of **werden** + the perfect infinitive (past participle + **haben** or **sein**) [➤12c(iii)].

Bis dann *wird* sie ihren Bericht *fertig geschrieben haben.* By then she *will have finished*	*writing* her report.

(iii) The compound conditional
This is formed with **würde** + infinitive [➤14d(ii)].

Sie hat gesagt, sie *würde* ihn spätestens Samstag *abschicken.*	She said she *would send* it *off* on Saturday at the latest.

The past conditional (conditional perfect) is formed with **hätte** or **wäre** + past participle [➤14d(iv)].

Wenn sie fleißiger *gewesen wäre, hätte* sie ihn schon längst beendet.	If she *had (would have) been* more industrious, she *would have finished* it long ago.

17d Formation of the imperative

➤ Uses of imperative: ➤ch.13. First and third persons: ➤13d.

Each of the three second persons [➤25b(ii)] has its own imperative.

(i) *du* form (singular)

Infinitive stem + **-e**, but note:

(A) The **-e** is often dropped in speech (though not with verbs that use the linking **-e-** in the **du** form of the present tense [➤17b(iii)]).

Komm her! Mach schnell! Sag mal! Sei ruhig! Lächle nicht! but **Antworte doch! Lade sie ein! Atme langsam!**	Come here! Hurry up! Tell me! Be quiet! Don't smile! (Do) Answer! Invite them! Breathe slowly!

(B) Strong verbs which change **-e-** to **-i(e)-** in the present tense also change in the **du** imperative. These have no final **-e**.

Gib her! Nimm es! Lies das vor!	Give it to me! Take it! Read that out loud!

(ii) *ihr* form (plural)

This is the same as **ihr** form present tense:

Macht schnell! Seid ruhig! Lächelt nicht! Antwortet doch! Ladet sie ein! Atmet langsam! Gebt her! Nehmt es! Lest das vor!	Hurry up! Be quiet! Don't smile! (Do) Answer! Invite them! Breathe slowly! Give it to me! Take it! Read that out loud!

(iii)   *Sie* form *(*singular and plural)

This is the same as the **Sie** form present tense inverted, except for **sein → seien Sie!** The pronoun **Sie** is always included.

Kommen Sie herein!	Come in!
Seien Sie bitte ruhig!	Please be quiet!
Laden Sie sie ein!	Invite them!
Atmen Sie langsam!	Breathe slowly!
Nehmen Sie es!	Take it!
Lesen Sie das bitte vor!	Please read that out loud!

Verb tables

This chapter contains:

(A) The full conjugation of the three auxiliary verbs **haben, sein** and **werden** [➤18a/b/c]. These also show the use of **haben** and **sein** to form the compound past tenses and serve as general models for weak and strong verbs.

(B) The conjugation of the verb **warnen** 'warn' in the passive [➤18d].

(C) A list of about 150 strong verbs in current use, giving the infinitive and the present (if the vowel changes), simple past and perfect tenses [➤18e]. These are the verbs' *principal parts*, so called because all other parts can be formed from them.

➤ The following sections give further information which you should use in conjunction with these tables.

- conjugation of modal auxiliaries: ➤9b(v).
- formation of the present participle: ➤10b(i).
- formation of the past participle: ➤10b(iii).
- summary of active tenses: ➤11d.
- summary of **Konjunktiv I** and conditional (**Konjunktiv II**) tenses: ➤14b.
- choice of simple or compound conditional: ➤14d Note.
- summary of passive tenses: ➤15b.
- principal parts of irregular weak verbs: ➤16c(ii).
- summary of seven strong verb classes: ➤16d(v).
- tense bases and endings: ➤17a and b.
- choice of **haben** or **sein** for compound past tenses: ➤17c(i).
- formation of the compound future: ➤17c(ii).

18a *haben* *to have*

[Weak irregular. Auxiliary verb. Example of verb making perfect tenses with **haben**.]

Present participle
habend

Past participle
gehabt

VERBS AND THEIR USES

Imperative

(du) hab(e)!   (ihr) habt!   haben Sie!

Present		**Simple past**	
ich	habe	ich	hatte
du	hast	du	hattest
er/sie/es	hat	er/sie/es	hatte
wir	haben	wir	hatten
ihr	habt	ihr	hattet
sie/Sie	haben	sie/Sie	hatten

Konjunktiv I		**Simple conditional (Konjunktiv II)**	
ich	habe	ich	hätte
du	habest	du	hättest
er/sie/es	habe	er/sie/es	hätte
wir	haben	wir	hätten
ihr	habet	ihr	hättet
sie/Sie	haben	sie/Sie	hätten

Perfect		**Past perfect (Pluperfect)**	
ich habe	... gehabt	ich hatte	... gehabt
du hast	... gehabt	du hattest	... gehabt
er/sie/es hat	... gehabt	er/sie/es hatte	... gehabt
wir haben	... gehabt	wir hatten	... gehabt
ihr habt	... gehabt	ihr hattet	... gehabt
sie/Sie haben	... gehabt	sie/Sie hatten	... gehabt

Future		**Future perfect**	
ich werde	... haben	ich werde	... gehabt haben
du wirst	... haben	du wirst	... gehabt haben
er/sie/es wird	... haben	er/sie/es wird	... gehabt haben
wir werden	... haben	wir werden	... gehabt haben
ihr werdet	... haben	ihr werdet	... gehabt haben
sie/Sie werden	... haben	sie/Sie werden	... gehabt haben

Compound conditional		**Past conditional**	
ich würde	... haben	ich hätte	... gehabt
du würdest	... haben	du hättest	... gehabt
er/sie/es würde	... haben	er/sie/es hätte	... gehabt
wir würden	... haben	wir hätten	... gehabt
ihr würdet	... haben	ihr hättet	... gehabt
sie/Sie würden	... haben	sie/Sie hätten	... gehabt

Konjunktiv I perfect		**Konjunktiv I future**	
ich habe	... gehabt	ich werde	... haben
du habest	... gehabt	du werdest	... haben
er/sie/es habe	... gehabt	er/sie/es werde	... haben
wir haben	... gehabt	wir werden	... haben
ihr habet	... gehabt	ihr werdet	... haben
sie/Sie haben	... gehabt	sie/Sie werden	... haben

18b *sein* *to be*

[Strong irregular. Auxiliary verb. Example of verb making perfect tenses with **sein**.]

Present participle	**Past participle**
seiend	gewesen

Imperative

(du) sei!   (ihr) seid!   seien Sie!

Present		**Simple past**	
ich	bin	ich	war
du	bist	du	warst
er/sie/es	ist	er/sie/es	war
wir	sind	wir	waren
ihr	seid	ihr	wart
sie/Sie	sind	sie/Sie	waren

Konjunktiv I		**Simple conditional (Konjunktiv II)**	
ich	sei	ich	wäre
du	sei(e)st	du	wärest
er/sie/es	sei	er/sie/es	wäre
wir	seien	wir	wären
ihr	seiet	ihr	wäret
sie/Sie	seien	sie/Sie	wären

Perfect		**Past perfect (Pluperfect)**	
ich bin	... gewesen	ich war	... gewesen
du bist	... gewesen	du warst	... gewesen
er/sie/es ist	... gewesen	er/sie/es war	... gewesen
wir sind	... gewesen	wir waren	... gewesen
ihr seid	... gewesen	ihr wart	... gewesen
sie/Sie sind	... gewesen	sie/Sie waren	... gewesen

VERBS AND THEIR USES

Future
ich werde	... sein
du wirst	... sein
er/sie/es wird	... sein
wir werden	... sein
ihr werdet	... sein
sie/Sie werden	... sein

Future perfect
ich werde	... gewesen sein
du wirst	... gewesen sein
er/sie/es wird	... gewesen sein
wir werden	... gewesen sein
ihr werdet	... gewesen sein
sie/Sie werden	... gewesen sein

Compound conditional
ich würde	... sein
du würdest	... sein
er/sie/es würde	... sein
wir würden	... sein
ihr würdet	... sein
sie/Sie würden	... sein

Past conditional
ich wäre	... gewesen
du wärst	... gewesen
er/sie/es wäre	... gewesen
wir wären	... gewesen
ihr wäret	... gewesen
sie/Sie wären	... gewesen

Konjunktiv I perfect
ich sei	... gewesen
du seiest	... gewesen
er/sie/es sei	... gewesen
wir seien	... gewesen
ihr seiet	... gewesen
sie/Sie seien	... gewesen

Konjunktiv I future
ich werde	... sein
du werdest	... sein
er/sie/es werde	... sein
wir werden	... sein
ihr werdet	... sein
sie/Sie werden	... sein

18c   *werden*   *to become/will*

[Strong irregular. Auxiliary verb. Example of verb making perfect tenses with **sein**.]

Present participle
werdend

Past participle
geworden

Imperative
(du)   werde!   (ihr)   werdet!   werden Sie!

Present
ich	werde
du	wirst
er/sie/es	wird
wir	werden
ihr	werdet
sie/Sie	werden

Simple past
ich	wurde
du	wurdest
er/sie/es	wurde
wir	wurden
ihr	wurdet
sie/Sie	wurden

Konjunktiv I

ich	werde
du	werdest
er/sie/es	werde
wir	werden
ihr	werdet
sie/Sie	werden

Simple conditional (Konjunktiv II)

ich	würde
du	würdest
er/sie/es	würde
wir	würden
ihr	würdet
sie/Sie	würden

Perfect

ich bin	... geworden
du bist	... geworden
er/sie/es ist	... geworden
wir sind	... geworden
ihr seid	... geworden
sie/Sie sind	... geworden

Past perfect (Pluperfect)

ich war	... geworden
du warst	... geworden
er/sie/es war	... geworden
wir waren	... geworden
ihr wart	... geworden
sie/Sie waren	... geworden

Future

ich werde	... werden
du wirst	... werden
er/sie/es wird	... werden
wir werden	... werden
ihr werdet	... werden
sie/Sie werden	... werden

Future perfect

ich werde	... geworden sein
du wirst	... geworden sein
er/sie/es wird	... geworden sein
wir werden	... geworden sein
ihr werdet	... geworden sein
sie/Sie werden	... geworden sein

Compound conditional

ich würde	... werden
du würdest	... werden
er/sie/es würde	... werden
wir würden	... werden
ihr würdet	... werden
sie/Sie würden	... werden

Past conditional

ich wäre	... geworden
du wärst	... geworden
er/sie/es wäre	... geworden
wir wären	... geworden
ihr wäret	... geworden
sie/Sie wären	... geworden

Konjunktiv I perfect

ich sei	... geworden
du seiest	... geworden
er/sie/es sei	... geworden
wir seien	... geworden
ihr seiet	... geworden
sie/Sie seien	... geworden

Konjunktiv I future

ich werde	... werden
du werdest	... werden
er/sie/es werde	... werden
wir werden	... werden
ihr werdet	... werden
sie/Sie werden	... werden

123

18d   *gewarnt werden*   *to be warned*

[Example of the passive.]

Present participle	Past participle
–	gewarnt worden

Imperative

(du) sei ... gewarnt!   (ihr) seid ... gewarnt!   seien Sie .. gewarnt!

Present		Simple past	
ich werde	... gewarnt	ich wurde	... gewarnt
du wirst	... gewarnt	du wurdest	... gewarnt
er/sie/es wird	... gewarnt	er/sie/es wurde	... gewarnt
wir werden	... gewarnt	wir wurden	... gewarnt
ihr werdet	... gewarnt	ihr wurdet	... gewarnt
sie/Sie werden	... gewarnt	sie/Sie wurden	... gewarnt

Konjunktiv I		Simple conditional (Konjunktiv II)	
ich werde	... gewarnt	ich würde	... gewarnt
du werdest	... gewarnt	du würdest	... gewarnt
er/sie/es werde	... gewarnt	er/sie/es würde	... gewarnt
wir werden	... gewarnt	wir würden	... gewarnt
ihr werdet	... gewarnt	ihr würdet	... gewarnt
sie/Sie werden	... gewarnt	sie/Sie würden	... gewarnt

Perfect		Past perfect (Pluperfect)	
ich bin	... gewarnt worden	ich war	... gewarnt worden
du bist	... gewarnt worden	du warst	... gewarnt worden
er/sie/es ist	... gewarnt worden	er/sie/es war	... gewarnt worden
wir sind	... gewarnt worden	wir waren	... gewarnt worden
ihr seid	... gewarnt worden	ihr wart	... gewarnt worden
sie/Sie sind	... gewarnt worden	sie/Sie waren	... gewarnt worden

Future		Future perfect	
ich werde	... gewarnt werden	ich werde	... gewarnt worden sein
du wirst	... gewarnt werden	du wirst	... gewarnt worden sein
er/sie/es wird	... gewarnt werden	er/sie/es wird	... gewarnt worden sein
wir werden	... gewarnt werden	wir werden	... gewarnt worden sein
ihr werdet	... gewarnt werden	ihr werdet	... gewarnt worden sein
sie/Sie werden	... gewarnt werden	sie/Sie werden	
			... gewarnt worden sein

Compound conditional (rare)		Past conditional	
ich würde	... gewarnt (werden)	ich wäre	... gewarnt worden
du würdest	... gewarnt (werden)	du wärst	... gewarnt worden
er/sie/es würde	... gewarnt (werden)	er/sie/es wäre	... gewarnt worden
wir würden	... gewarnt (werden)	wir wären	... gewarnt worden
ihr würdet	... gewarnt (werden)	ihr wäret	... gewarnt worden
sie/Sie würden	... gewarnt (werden)	sie/Sie wären	... gewarnt worden

Konjunktiv I perfect		Konjunktiv I future (rare)	
ich sei	... gewarnt worden	ich werde	... gewarnt (werden)
du seiest	... gewarnt worden	du werdest	... gewarnt (werden)
er/sie/es sei	... gewarnt worden	er/sie/es werde	... gewarnt (werden)
wir seien	... gewarnt worden	wir werden	... gewarnt (werden)
ihr seiet	... gewarnt worden	ihr werdet	... gewarnt (werden)
sie/Sie seien	... gewarnt worden	sie/Sie werden	... gewarnt (werden)

18e *List of strong verbs*

The following alphabetical list gives the principal parts of about 150 strong verbs, using the **er/sie/es** form. Weak or alternative strong/weak forms are given where they are in current usage. [I/II/III etc. after the infinitive refers to the strong verb class: ➤16d(v).]

Infinitive	English	Present (if vowel changes)	Simple past	Perfect
backen (VI)	*bake*		backte	hat ... gebacken
befehlen (IV)	*command*	befiehlt	befahl	hat ... befohlen
beginnen (IV)	*begin*		begann	hat ... begonnen
beißen (I)	*bite*		biss	hat ... gebissen
betrügen (II)	*deceive*		betrog	hat ... betrogen
bewegen (II)	*persuade*		bewog	hat ... bewogen
biegen (II)	*bend*		bog	hat/ist ... gebogen
bieten (II)	*offer*		bot	hat ... geboten
binden (III)	*tie*		band	hat ... gebunden
bitten (V)	*ask, request*		bat	hat ... gebeten
blasen (VII)	*blow*	bläst	blies	hat ... geblasen
bleiben (I)	*remain*		blieb	ist ... geblieben
braten (VII)	*roast, grill*	brät	briet	hat ... gebraten
brechen (IV)	*break*	bricht	brach	hat/ist ... gebrochen
dreschen (II)	*thresh*	drischt	drosch	hat ... gedroschen

125

VERBS AND THEIR USES

dringen (III)	*penetrate*		drang	ist ... gedrungen
empfehlen (IV)	*recommend*	empfiehlt	empfahl	hat ... empfohlen
erlöschen (II)	*go out (fire)*	erlischt	erlosch	ist ... erloschen
[**löschen** *put out, extinguish* is weak]				
erschrecken (IV)	*start (fright)*	erschrickt	erschrak	ist ... erschrocken
[**schrecken** *frighten, scare* is weak]				
essen (V)	*eat*	isst	aß	hat ... gegessen
fahren (VI)	*go, drive*	fährt	fuhr	ist/hat ... gefahren
fallen (VII)	*fall*	fällt	fiel	ist ... gefallen
fangen (VII)	*catch*	fängt	fing	hat ... gefangen
fechten (II)	*fight, fence*	ficht	focht	hat ... gefochten
finden (III)	*find*		fand	hat ... gefunden
fliegen (II)	*fly*		flog	ist/hat ... geflogen
fliehen (II)	*flee*		floh	ist ... geflohen
fließen (II)	*flow*		floss	ist ... geflossen
fressen (V)	*eat, gobble*	frisst	fraß	hat ... gefressen
gären (II)	*ferment*		gor/gärte	hat/ist ... gegoren/gegärt
gebären (IV)	*bear (child)*		gebar	hat ... geboren
geben (V)	*give*	gibt	gab	hat ... gegeben
gedeihen (I)	*prosper*		gedieh	ist ... gediehen
gehen (VII)	*go, walk*		ging	ist ... gegangen
gelingen (III)	*succeed*		gelang	ist ... gelungen
gelten (IV)	*be valid, true*	gilt	galt	hat ... gegolten
genesen (V)	*recover (health)*		genas	ist ... genesen
genießen (II)	*enjoy*		genoss	hat ... genossen
geschehen (V)	*happen*	geschieht	geschah	ist ... geschehen
gewinnen (IV)	*win*		gewann	hat ... gewonnen
gießen (II)	*pour*		goss	hat ... gegossen
gleichen (I)	*resemble*		glich	hat ... geglichen
gleiten (I)	*slide, glide*		glitt	ist ... geglitten
glimmen (II)	*glow, glimmer*		glomm	hat ... geglommen
graben (VI)	*dig*	gräbt	grub	hat ... gegraben
greifen (I)	*grab, grasp*		griff	hat ... gegriffen
halten (VII)	*hold, keep*	hält	hielt	hat ... gehalten
hängen (VII)	*hang (intr)*		hing	hat ... gehangen
hauen (VII)	*hew, bash*		haute/hieb	hat ... gehauen
heben (II)	*lift, raise*		hob	hat ... gehoben
heißen (VII)	*be called, command*		hieß	hat ... geheißen
helfen (IV)	*help*	hilft	half	hat ... geholfen

klimmen (II)	*clamber*		klomm/klimmte	
			ist ... geklimmt/geklommen	
klingen (IV)	*sound*		klang	hat ... geklungen
kneifen (I)	*pinch*		kniff	hat ... gekniffen
kommen (IV)	*come, get (somewhere)*		kam	ist ... gekommen
kriechen (II)	*crawl*		kroch	ist ... gekrochen
laden (VI)	*load*	lädt	lud	hat ... geladen
lassen (VII)	*let*	lässt	ließ	hat ... gelassen
laufen (VII)	*run, walk*	läuft	lief	ist ... gelaufen
leiden (I)	*suffer*		litt	hat ... gelitten
leihen (I)	*lend*		lieh	hat ... geliehen
lesen (V)	*read*	liest	las	hat ... gelesen
liegen (V)	*lie (flat)*		lag	hat ... gelegen
lügen (II)	*(tell a) lie*		log	hat ... gelogen
mahlen (–)	*grind (grain)*		mahlte	hat ... gemahlen
melken (II)	*milk*		melkte/(molk)	
			hat ... gemolken/(gemelkt)	
messen (V)	*measure*	misst	maß	hat ... gemessen
nehmen (IV)	*take*	nimmt	nahm	hat ... genommen
pfeifen (I)	*whistle*		pfiff	hat ... gepfiffen
quellen (II)	*well, gush*	quillt	quoll	ist ... gequollen
raten (VII)	*advise*	rät	riet	hat ... geraten
reiben (I)	*rub*		rieb	hat ... gerieben
reißen (I)	*tear*		riss	hat ... gerissen
reiten (I)	*ride*		ritt	ist/hat ... geritten
riechen (II)	*smell*		roch	hat ... gerochen
ringen (III)	*wrestle*		rang	hat ... gerungen
rinnen (IV)	*trickle*		rann	ist ... geronnen
rufen (VII)	*call*		rief	hat ... gerufen
saufen (II)	*drink, booze*	säuft	soff	hat ... gesoffen
saugen (II)	*suck*		sog/saugte	hat ... gesogen/gesaugt
schaffen (VI)	*create*		schuf	hat ... geschaffen
[**schaffen** *do, achieve* is weak]				
scheiden (I)	*divorce; (depart)*		schied	hat/(ist) ... geschieden
scheinen (I)	*seem; shine*		schien	hat ... geschienen
scheißen (I)	*shit*		schiss	hat ... geschissen
schelten (II)	*scold*	schilt	scholt	hat ... gescholten
scheren (II)	*shear, clip*		schor	hat ... geschoren
schieben (II)	*push, shove*		schob	hat ... geschoben
schießen (II)	*shoot*		schoss	hat ... geschossen
schinden (III)	*maltreat, overwork*		schindete	hat ... geschunden

VERBS AND THEIR USES

schlafen (VII)	*sleep*	schläft	schlief	hat ... geschlafen
schlagen (VI)	*strike, hit*	schlägt	schlug	hat ... geschlagen
schleichen (I)	*creep, slink*		schlich	ist ... geschlichen
schleifen (I)	*sharpen, whet*		schliff	hat ... geschliffen
[**schleifen** *drag* is weak]				
schließen (II)	*close, shut*		schloss	hat ... geschlossen
schmeißen (I)	*hurl, chuck*		schmiss	hat ... geschmissen
schmelzen (II)	*melt, smelt*	schmilzt	schmolz	hat/ist ... geschmolzen
schneiden (I)	*cut*		schnitt	hat ... geschnitten
schreiben (I)	*write*		schrieb	hat ... geschrieben
schreien (I)	*shout, cry out*		schrie	hat ... geschrie(e)n
schreiten (I)	*stride; proceed*		schritt	ist ... geschritten
schweigen (I)	*be(come) silent*		schwieg	hat ... geschwiegen
schwellen (II)	*swell*	schwillt	schwoll	ist ... geschwollen
schwimmen (IV)	*swim, float*		schwamm	ist/hat ... geschwommen
schwingen (III)	*swing*		schwang	hat ... geschwungen
schwören (II)	*swear (oath)*		schwor	hat ... geschworen
sehen (V)	*see, look*	sieht	sah	hat ... gesehen
sein (V)	*be*	ist	war	ist ... gewesen
singen (III)	*sing*		sang	hat ... gesungen
sinken (III)	*sink*		sank	ist ... gesunken
sinnen (IV)	*ponder*		sann	hat ... gesonnen
sitzen (V)	*sit*		saß	hat ... gesessen
speien (I)	*spew*		spie	hat ... gespie(e)n
spinnen (IV)	*spin*		spann	hat ... gesponnen
sprechen (IV)	*speak*	spricht	sprach	hat ... gesprochen
springen (III)	*jump, spring*		sprang	ist ... gesprungen
stechen (IV)	*sting, prick*	sticht	stach	hat ... gestochen
stehen (IV)	*stand*		stand	hat ... gestanden
stehlen (IV)	*steal*	stiehlt	stahl	hat ... gestohlen
steigen (I)	*rise, climb*		stieg	ist ... gestiegen
sterben (IV)	*die*	stirbt	starb	ist ... gestorben

stinken (III)	*stink*		stank	hat ... gestunken
stoßen (VII)	*push*	stößt	stieß	hat ... gestoßen
streichen (I)	*spread; stroke*		strich	hat/ist ... gestrichen
streiten (I)	*quarrel, argue*		stritt	hat ... gestritten
tragen (VI)	*carry*	trägt	trug	hat ... getragen
treffen (IV)	*meet, hit*	trifft	traf	hat ... getroffen
trinken (III)	*drink*		trank	hat ... getrunken
tun (–)	*do, put*		tat	hat ... getan
verderben (IV)	*spoil*	verdirbt	verdarb	hat ... verdorben
verdrießen (II)	*annoy*		verdross	hat ... verdrossen
vergessen (V)	*forget*	vergisst	vergaß	hat ... vergessen
verlieren (II)	*lose*		verlor	hat ... verloren
verschlingen (III)	*engulf, swallow*		verschlang	hat ... verschlungen
verschwinden (III)	*disappear*		verschwand	ist ... verschwunden
verzeihen (I)	*forgive*		verzieh	hat ... verziehen
wachsen (VI)	*grow*	wächst	wuchs	ist ... gewachsen
waschen (VI)	*wash*	wäscht	wusch	hat ... gewaschen
weichen (I)	*yield, give way*		wich	ist ... gewichen
[**weichen** *soak* is weak]				
weisen (I)	*point*		wies	hat ... gewiesen
werben (IV)	*advertise*	wirbt	warb	hat ... geworben
werden (IV)	*become*	wird	wurde	ist ... geworden
werfen (IV)	*throw*	wirft	warf	hat ... geworfen
wiegen (II)	*weigh*		wog	hat ... gewogen
winden (III)	*wind*		wand	hat ... gewunden
wringen (III)	*wring*		wrang	hat ... gewrungen
ziehen (II)	*pull; move*		zog	hat/ist ... gezogen
zwingen (III)	*force, compel*		zwang	hat ... gezwungen

129

D

PEOPLE, THINGS AND IDEAS: NOUNS AND NOUN PHRASES

19   *Labeling the world: nouns*

20   *Classes of German noun: the three genders*

21   *One or more? Singular and plural*

22   *The role of the noun phrase in the sentence: the four cases*

23   *Specifying nouns: determiners*

24   *Describing nouns: adjectives*

25   *Representing nouns: pronouns*

26   *Giving vent to your feelings: exclamations and interjections*

Labeling the world: nouns

19a What does a noun do?

Nouns answer the questions **Wer ist das?** 'Who is that?' and **Was ist das?** 'What is that?'. They are the labels we attach to everything in the world around us or in our own minds: people, animals, things, events, processes, ideas.

Meine jüngste *Tochter* studiert *Physik* an der *Universität*.	My youngest *daughter* is studying *physics* at the *university*.

19b Adding details: the noun phrase

The noun phrase often consists of more than just a noun – it can be extended so as to provide more information, as in the phrase **meine jüngste Tochter** in the previous example. The additional words and phrases which supply this information are:

- determiners [➤ch.23];
- adjectives and adjectival phrases [➤ch.24];
- relative clauses [➤5b, 25j];
- following prepositional phrases [➤19h, ch.27].

To avoid repetition, noun phrases are often represented by pronouns [➤ch.25].

19c Individual names and general labels: proper and common nouns

A *proper noun* (or 'proper name') is the name of a particular individual person like **Willi Brandt, Steffi Graf**, of a place like **Innsbruck, Österreich, Europa** or of a thing (such as a commercial product). All other nouns are *common nouns*. In German all nouns are written with a capital (not just proper names, as in many other languages).

der Sohn, Löffel, Hass	son, spoon, hate
die Tochter, Gabel, Liebe	daughter, fork, love
das Kind, Messer, Mitleid	child, knife, pity

Note In recent years there has been a movement to abolish capital letters for nouns, but this is still far from being regarded as correct. It can in fact be a real help to be able to pick out the nouns in a sentence.

19d *Names of people*

Personal names are treated in German very much as in English. The main points to note are:

(i) For the possessive, **-s** is added to both first names and surnames. There is no apostrophe.

Käthe*s* Fahrrad ist kaputt, und Frau Kerner*s* Rad ist zu groß für sie.	Käthe*'s* bicycle is broken, and Mrs. Kerner*'s* bike is too big for her.

• If the name ends in **-s**, **-ß**, **-x** or **-z**, the possessive **-s** is usually replaced in writing by an apostrophe; with short names, the ending **-ens** is sometimes used. In speech, a following phrase with **von** is usual; **von** is in fact much used colloquially with all names. For example **Max'/Maxens Familie – die Familie *von* Max** 'Max's family', **Moritz' Freund – der Freund *von* Moritz** 'Moritz's friend'.

• Titles and forms of address like **Frau** 'Mrs.' or **Dr.** 'Dr.' are generally treated as a whole with the following name. **Herr** always adds **-n**. For example, **Frau Dr. Stauffens Job** 'Dr. Stauffen*'s* job', **Herrn Kerners Anschrift** 'Mr. Kerner's address', **Onkel Konrads Hörgerät** 'Uncle Konrad's hearing aid'.

• When not used with a name, any words used to address members of the family add **-s**. For example, **Omas Wagen** 'Grandma's car', **Vatis Regenschirm** 'Dad's umbrella', **Tantes Haus** 'Aunt's house'.

(ii) A plural **-s** is added to surnames to refer to the whole family. Surnames ending in **-s**, **-ß**, **-x** or **-z** add **-ens**. The definite article **die** is often omitted, especially after prepositions or when the family name is the possessive.

(*Die*) Gauß*ens* sind nette Leute. Wir haben sie bei *Brandts* kennen gelernt. Frau Gauß ist *Brandts* Tochter.	*The Gauss's* are nice people. We met them at *the Brandts*. Mrs. Gauss is *the Brandts'* daughter.

NOUNS AND NOUN PHRASES

(iii) The definite article **der, die** etc. is used when a name is preceded by an adjective, except at the start of a letter. This is also done:

• as a sign of familiarity (which may be either affectionate or disparaging);
• when referring to well-known people, especially performing artists, and to characters in plays.

Lieber Heiner/*Sehr geehrte* Frau Beck, ...	*Dear* Harry/*Dear* Mrs. Beck
Der alte Konrad – das ist der Großonkel *der kleinen* Angelika – wollte gestern mit Jenny ins Kino gehen. *Der* Konrad ist doch ein dummer Kerl! In unserem letzten Laienspiel wollte er *den* Romeo spielen! Bloß weil er *die* Garbo gekannt hat!	*Old* Konrad – that's *little* Angelika's great-uncle – wanted to go to the movies yesterday with Jenny. *(That)* Konrad really is a silly fellow! In our last amateur dramatics he wanted to play (*the part of*) Romeo! Just because he used to know Garbo!

19e   Geographical names

(i)   Names of places

• All continents and towns, and almost all countries and provinces, are neuter. The article **das** is used only when the name is defined or described in some way.
• The '-ia' ending on the English name of some countries and continents becomes **-ien** in German, but plain '-a' endings do not change, for example, **Asien** 'Asia' but **Afrika** 'Africa'.
• The prepositions of position and motion are **aus** 'originally from', **in** 'at, in', **nach** 'to' and **von** 'from (also of)'.

(nach) Österreich/Wien;	(to) Austria/Vienna;
(in) Amerika/Pittsburgh;	(in) America/Pittsburgh;
(von) Hessen/Frankfurt;	(from/of) Hessen/Frankfurt;
das mittelalterliche Venedig;	medieval Venice;
vom industriellen Wolfsburg;	from industrial Wolfsburg;
im ländlichen Skandinavien	in rural Scandinavia

However, some countries and provinces are masculine, feminine or plural. These are always used with the article **der** or **die**. **in** + dative is normally used for 'in', **in** + accusative for 'to', though **nach** + dative may also be used.

Masculine **der Irak, in den Iran, im Jemen, vom Libanon**	Iraq, to Iran, in the Yemen, from Lebanon
Feminine **(in) die Schweiz, in der Türkei, von der Pfalz**	(to) Switzerland, in Turkey, from the Palatinate
Plural **(in) die Niederlande, in den Vereinigten Staaten (in den USA)**	(to) the Netherlands, in the United States (in the USA)

(ii)   *Names of oceans, seas, lakes, rivers and mountains*

These tend to follow the gender of the word which describes them: **der Ozean** 'ocean', **das Meer** 'sea (often warmer)' or **die See** 'sea (usually colder)', **der See** 'lake', **der Fluss** 'river', **der Berg** 'mountain'. The main exceptions are:

• all but half a dozen native German names of rivers, and almost all others which end in **-a** or **-e**, are feminine;

• mountains which end in an ordinary word have the same gender as that word. A few mountain ranges are feminine, while many are plural.

der Atlantik, der Stille Ozean (der Pazifik);	the Atlantic, the Pacific;
das Mittelmeer, das Sargassomeer, die Ostsee, die Tasmansee;	the Mediterranean, the Sargasso Sea, the Baltic, the Tasman Sea;
der Bodensee, der Genfer See, der Ontario-See;	Lake Constance, Lake Geneva, Lake Ontario;
der Inn, der Lech, der Neckar, der Main, der Regen, der Rhein, der Nil, der Shannon, der Hudson but **die Donau, die Oder, die Ruhr, die Weichsel, die Wolga, die Themse;**	the Inn, the Lech, the Neckar, the Main, the Regen, the Rhine, the Nile, the Shannon, the Hudson but the Danube, the Oder, the Ruhr, the Vistula, the Volga, the Thames;
der Brocken, der Montblanc, der Vesuv but **das Matterhorn, die Zugspitze;**	the Brocken, Mont Blanc, Vesuvius but the Matterhorn, the Zugspitze;
der Harz, der Himalaja, der Jura but **die Eifel** (*feminine*)**, die Pyrenäen, die Ardennen, die Dolomiten** (*plural*)	the Harz, the Himalayas, the Jura but the Eifel, the Pyrenees, the Ardennes, the Dolomites

19f   Nationalities and languages

(i)   The precise forms of nouns of nationality and inhabitants of towns and regions are hard to predict and best looked up. Note that:

(A) the great majority end in **-er**, sometimes **-ier** or **-aner**, and form their feminine by adding **-in**, without Umlaut;

Europa → die Europäer	Europe → the Europeans
Amerika → die Amerikaner	America → the Americans
Australien → die Australier	Australia → the Australians

(B) about a dozen nationalities and some regional and ethnic names end in **-e**. These are weak masculine nouns [➤22g(i)], which drop the **-e** before adding **-in** for the feminine; only **der Franzose – die Französin** 'French' has an Umlaut on the feminine;

die Chinesen, die Dänen,	the Chinese, the Danes,
die Franzosen, die Iren, die Polen,	the French, the Irish, the Poles,
die Portugiesen, die Russen,	the Portuguese, the Russians,
die Schotten, die Schweden,	the Scots, the Swedes,
die Tschechen, die Sachsen,	the Czechs, the Saxons,
die Schwaben	the Swabians

(C) only one nationality is an adjective-noun [➤24d];

der Deutsche	the German (man)
ein Deutscher	a German (man)
die/eine Deutsche	the/a German (woman)
die Deutschen	the Germans
Deutsche	Germans

(ii)   The names of all languages are the same as the national adjectives. Apart from **Deutsch** most of the more widely spoken languages end in **-isch** and are normally spelled with a capital. They have two forms, both neuter.

(A) The stem without any ending is the general name for the language.

Meine Muttersprache ist Französisch.	My mother tongue is French.

Ich kann/spreche auch Englisch, Ungarisch und Jiddisch, und ich lese ziemlich gut Deutsch. Ich träume immer auf Ungarisch!	I also speak English, Hungarian and Yiddish, and I can read German quite well. I always dream in Hungarian!

(B) The stem with **-e/-en** adjective endings [➤24b(ii)] has a sense of 'the ~ version', 'the ~ way of putting it'.

Dieses Handbuch ist aus dem Englischen ins Französische übersetzt worden.	This handbook has been translated from English into French.

19g *Nouns formed from other parts of speech*

German nouns are formed from other words in a number of ways. The most common examples are listed below. The English equivalents given are only approximate.

➤ The great and the good: adjectives used as nouns ➤24d.
Singing and dancing: infinitive-nouns ➤10a(iii).

(i) Other parts of speech used as nouns are neuter, except for numerals, which are feminine (**die Eins, eine Sechs, eine Million**).

das Wenn und Aber	ifs and buts
ein großes A	a big A
das Schwarz-Rot-Gold	black, red and gold (German national colors)
das ewige Hin und Her	the continual back and forth
ein völliges Durcheinander	a complete mess

(ii) A series of masculine nouns are made from the stem of strong verbs [➤16d(v)].

Plurals add **-e**, often with Umlaut. No firm rules can be given for the choice of vowel, but it is useful to be aware of the series.

(A) with the vowel of the infinitive:

der Fall, Gewinn, Hang, Lauf, Rat, Ruf, Schlaf, Schlag, Schrei, Stoß, Streit	fall/case, profit, slope, run, advice, call/reputation, sleep, blow, shout, push, quarrel

NOUNS AND NOUN PHRASES

(B) with the vowel of the simple past:

der Griff, Klang, Pfiff, Riss, Ritt,	grip, sound, whistle, tear, ride,
Schnitt, Schritt, Trieb, Zwang	cut, step/stride, drive/urge, compulsion

(C) with a third vowel, often **u**:

der Bruch, Flug, Fluss, Gang,	break, flight, river, corridor/gait/walk,
Guss, Schluss, Schub,	gush/casting, conclusion, shove,
Spruch, Sprung, Tritt,	saying, leap/jump, (foot)step,
Wurf, Zug	throw, pull/train/draft (draught)

(iii)   Forming nouns with suffixes

Some nouns are formed from other words by adding the following suffixes. Most of these nouns are feminine.

• **~chen, ~lein** '~kin, ~let, ~ling'. A small or young ~. Forms neuter nouns from other nouns, usually with Umlaut if possible (**-chen** is more common; **-lein** is mainly southern German).

das Häuschen, Hühnchen,	little house, pullet,
Kätzchen, Mädchen	kitten, girl,
das Büchlein, Entlein	booklet, duckling

• **~e** Usually the result of ~ing, or a related object. Forms feminine nouns from verbs (by dropping the **-n** from the infinitive). Note **helfen – die Hilfe** 'help'.

die Anleihe, Binde, Bitte, Falle,	loan, bandage, request, trap,
Fliege, Fresse, Klinge, Lüge,	fly, gob/trap (*slang*), blade, lie/untruth,
Pfeife, Quelle, Wende	pipe, source, turning point

~e The quality of being ~. Forms feminine nouns from adjectives, with Umlaut if possible. Only possible with some adjectives, often describing physical qualities. Note **heiß – die Hitze** 'hot – heat'

die Breite, Ferne, Höhe,	breadth, distance (in general), height,
Kälte, Kürze, Länge,	cold, brevity, length,
Schwäche, Stärke	weakness, strength

• **~ei**. The workplace or activity of a ~. Forms feminine nouns from other nouns, without Umlaut.

die Brauerei, Metzgerei,	brewery/brewing, butcher's shop,
Schlosserei, Wäscherei	metalworking (shop), laundry

• **~er, ~ler** '~er'. A person or thing that ~s. Forms masculine nouns from verbs, verb phrases and a few nouns, sometimes with Umlaut. [Nouns of nationality: ➤19f(i).]

der Arbeiter, Bäcker, Bohrer,	worker, baker, drill,

Briefträger, Sportler, Staubsauger   mailman, sportsman, vacuum cleaner

- **~heit, ~(ig)keit** '~ness'. The quality of being ~. Forms feminine nouns from adjectives. **-keit** is used with adjectives which themselves end in a suffix [➤24f(i)] and a few others. **-igkeit** is used with adjectives in **-haft** and **-los** and a few others.

die Dummheit, Gleichheit,	stupidity, equality,
Schönheit, Weisheit,	beauty, wisdom,
Freundlichkeit,	friendliness,
Haltbarkeit, die Geschwindigkeit,	durability/lastingness, speed,
Hilflosigkeit, Lebhaftigkeit	helplessness, liveliness

- **~in** '~ess'. The female of most persons and many animals. Plural **-innen.** Persons usually with Umlaut, and some animals.

die Arbeiterin, Ärztin, Bäckerin,	female worker, doctor, baker,
Freundin, Heldin, Köchin, Müllerin,	friend, heroine, female cook, miller,
Professorin, Sportlerin,	professor, sportswoman,
die Füchsin, Löwin, Tigerin	vixen, lioness, tigress

- **~nis** '~ness, ~ion'. The effect of ~. Forms feminine and neuter nouns from verbs and adjectives. Plural **-nisse.**

die Erkenntis, Finsternis;	realization, darkness;
das Erlebnis, Gedächtnis,	experience, memory,
Geheimnis, Verhältnis	secret, relationship

- **~schaft** '~ship, ~hood'. A quality or organization associated with ~s. Forms feminine nouns from other nouns, usually referring to people, without Umlaut.

die Brüderschaft, Freundschaft,	brotherhood/'du' friendship, friendship,
Landschaft, Schwesternschaft,	landscape, sisterhood/nursing staff,
Studentenschaft	student body

- **~tum** '~dom'. An institution or feature associated with ~s. Forms neuter nouns from other nouns, usually referring to people. (Note however *der* **Irrtum** 'error' and *der* **Reichtum** 'wealth'.)

das Beamtentum,	civil servants,
Bistum (from **Bischof**)**, Fürstentum**	diocese, principality

- **~ung** '~ing, ~ion'. The action or fact of ~ing. Forms feminine nouns from verbs, without Umlaut.

die Ahnung, Empfindung,	inkling/idea, feeling,
Erfahrung, Erwartung, Hoffnung,	experience, expectation, hope,
Kreuzung, Öffnung, Verbindung,	crossroads, opening, connection,
Verwirrung	confusion

NOUNS AND NOUN PHRASES

(iv) Forming nouns with prefixes

Nouns can also be formed from other words by adding prefixes. Apart from **Haupt-, Mit-** and **Fehl-**, the only prefixes listed here are those which are not words in their own right. Only **Ge-** changes the gender of the original noun.

• **Erz~** 'arch~, complete ~'. Can be added to both nouns and adjectives, magnifying their position or qualities, whether good or bad. (Do not confuse these words with compounds of **das Erz** meaning 'ore'!)

der Erzengel, Erzbischof,	archangel, archbishop,
Erzfeind, Erzreaktionär	arch-enemy, ultra-reactionary

• **Fehl~** 'mis~, wrong ~'. Compared to **Miss-**, a fairly neutral negative.

der Fehldruck, Fehlschlag,	misprint, failure,
Fehlschluss, Fehlstoß;	false conclusion, miskick/miscue;
die Fehldiagnose,	wrong diagnosis,
Fehlgeburt	miscarriage

• **Ge~** 1) A collection of ~. Forms neuter nouns from other nouns, with Umlaut if possible. (**-e-** in the stem changes to **-i-**.)

das Gebirge, Gebiss,	mountain range, set of teeth/dentures,
Geflügel, Getriebe, Gewitter	poultry, gears, thunderstorm

• **Ge~** 2) Repeated, probably irritating ~ing. Forms usually neuter nouns from verbs.

das Gekreisch(e), Gelächter,	screeching, laughter,
Geschwätz, Getue	gossip/chatter, fuss

but

der Gebrauch, Gedanke, Gehalt,	custom, thought, content(s),
Geruch, Geschmack, Gewinn;	smell, taste, profit;
die Gebärde, Geduld, Gemeinde,	gesture, patience, community,
Gewalt	force

• **Haupt~** 'main ~'.

der Hauptbahnhof, Hauptmann;	main station, (army) captain;
die Hauptstadt, Hauptpost,	capital (city), main post office,
Hauptsache;	main thing;
das Hauptbüro, Hauptfach	headquarters, main subject

• **Miss~** 'mis~, wrong ~'. Usually gives a stronger emphasis than **Fehl-**.

der Missbrauch, Misserfolg, Missmut;	abuse, failure/flop, sullenness/discontent;
die Missgeburt, Misshandlung;	deformed creature, maltreatment;
das Misstrauen, Missverständnis	mistrust, misunderstanding

- **Mit~** 'co-~, fellow ~'.

der (die) Mitarbeiter(in), Mitwisser(in);	colleague, accomplice/accessory;
die Mitarbeit, Mithilfe;	collaboration, assistance;
das Mitgefühl, Mitglied, Mitleid	sympathy, member, pity

- **Un~** 'un~, abnormal ~'.

der Unfall, Unfug, Unmensch, Unsinn;	accident, mischief, (human) monster, nonsense;
die Ungeduld, Unmenge, Unruhe, Unschuld;	impatience, vast number, disquiet, innocense;
das Ungeziefer, Unglück, Unkraut, Unrecht	vermin, misfortune, weeds, injustice

- **Ur~** 'original ~, ancient ~, typical ~'.

der Urbayer, Urgroßvater, Urwald;	typical Bavarian, great-grandfather, jungle;
die Uraufführung, Urenkelin, Ursache	première, great-granddaughter, cause/reason

19h   Nouns governing phrases and clauses

As a rule, nouns govern the same type of clause or prepositional phrase as their corresponding verbs or adjectives, as shown below.

Verbs + prepositions: ➤8g

Ich arbeite/Meine Arbeit *an diesem Projekt* ...	I am working/My work *on this project* ...

Verbs + zu + infinitive: ➤8h(ii)

Er versprach, /Sein Versprechen, mir *zu helfen*, ...	He promised/His promise *to help* me ...

NOUNS AND NOUN PHRASES

Verbs + ***dass*** *clauses:* ➤*8i*

Sie erwarten,/Ihre Erwartung, **dass du mitkommst, ...**	They expect/Their expectation *that* *you will come too* ...

Adjectives + prepositions: ➤*24g(ii)*

Sie war wütend/hatte eine Wut **auf mich.**	She was furious *at me*.

Adjectives + ***zu*** *+ infinitive/+* ***dass*** *clauses:* ➤*24g(ii)*

Sie sind bereit,/Ihre **Bereitschaft, mit***zuhelfen***, ...**	They are willing/Their willingness *to help* ...
Ich bin stolz darauf,/Mein Stolz **darauf,** ***dass es gelungen ist***, ...	I am proud of the fact/My pride in the fact *that it was a success* ...

Note Nouns related to verbs or adjectives followed by the accusative or dative generally use the genitive or whatever preposition best conveys the meaning.

Das Schiff **wurde versenkt.**	*The ship* was sunk.
Nach Versenkung *des Schiffs* **...**	After the sinking *of the ship* ...
Wir haben *sie* **gebeten, hier zu** **warten. Unsere Bitte** *an sie* **...**	We asked *them* to wait here. Our request *to them* ...
Alle gehorchen *ihm.* **Ihr** **Gehorsam** *ihm gegenüber* **...**	They all obey *him*. Their obedience *to him* ...
Er ist *seiner Oma* **sehr ähnlich.** **Seine Ähnlichkeit** *mit ihr* **...**	He is very like *his grandmother*. His resemblance *to her* ...

20 Classes of German nouns: the three genders

20a What is meant by gender?

The word *gender* means 'kind' or 'type'. All German nouns belong to one of three genders: *masculine*, *feminine* or *neuter*. Each gender has its own set of case endings [►ch.22]. The gender of a noun is not the same thing as the sex of the person or animal it may refer to.

• Nouns which refer to people and animals are normally masculine for males and feminine for females, but there are important exceptions [►20b(iii) and (iv)].
• Other nouns can be of any of the three genders.
• There are some groupings of meanings which will help you [►20b], but the best thing is to learn a noun with its definite article **der, die** or **das**, which always shows the gender.

Note   There are some endings which indicate the gender of a noun but, apart from the suffixes listed in paragraph 19g, most of them either are too uncommon or have too many exceptions to be of much use.

20b What does it mean? Gender groupings by meaning

► Geographical names: ►19e.

(i) These groups of nouns are normally masculine.

(A) Male persons and animals:

der Bock, Kater, Mann, Onkel, Neffe, Richter, Sohn, Stier, Vater	buck (deer), tom-cat, man, uncle, nephew, male judge, son, bull, father

(B) Rocks and minerals:

der Diamant, Felsen, Lehm, Kalk, Kies, Kiesel, Kristall, Schlamm, Stein, Ton	diamond, rock, loam, lime, gravel, pebble, crystal, mud, stone, clay
but	but
die Erde, Kohle, Kreide; **das Erz, Mineral**	earth, coal, chalk; ore, mineral

(C) Compass directions, kinds of weather:

der Norden, Süden, Osten, Westen,	North, South, East, West,

NOUNS AND NOUN PHRASES

der Frost, Hagel, Nebel,	frost, hail, mist/fog,
Schnee, Sturm, Wind	snow, storm, wind
but	but
das Eis, Gewitter, Wetter	ice, thunderstorm, weather

(D) Days of the week, months, seasons [➤31b(i) on].

(E) Makes of car [compare (ii)(C) below]:

der BMW, Cadillac, Mercedes,	BMW, Cadillac, Mercedes,
Peugeot, Trabant	Peugeot, Trabant

(ii) These groups of nouns are normally feminine.

(A) Female persons and animals:

die Frau, Hündin, Kuh, Mutter,	woman, bitch, cow, mother,
Nichte, Richterin, Tante, Tochter	niece, female judge, aunt, daughter

(B) Names of numerals [➤30a(ii)].

(C) Names of ships, makes of airplanes and motorbikes:

die Bremen, Graf Spee,	the Bremen, Graf Spee,
Mayflower, Titanic	Mayflower, Titanic
die Boeing, Concorde, Dakota	Boeing, Concorde, Dakota
die BMW, Harley-Davidson,	BMW, Harley-Davidson,
Honda	Honda [compare (i)(E) above]

(iii) These groups of nouns are normally neuter.

(A) The young of persons and animals, and all nouns with the endings **-chen** and **-lein** [➤19g(iii)]. Note that **das Junge – ein Junges** 'young (of animals)' takes adjective endings [➤24d].

das Baby, Ferkel, Kalb, Kind,	baby, piglet, calf, child,
Küken, Lamm	chick, lamb

(B) Metals and chemical elements, except compounds (for example, of **der Stoff**); scientific units.

das Aluminium, Blei, Eisen, Gold,	aluminum, lead, iron, gold,
Kupfer, Messing, Silber, Uran,	copper, brass, silver, uranium,
but	but
der Stahl, Schwefel	steel, sulphur
das Atom, Gramm	atom, gram(me)
Neutron, Pfund, Volt	neutron, pound, volt
der Liter, der Meter	liter, meter

(C) Letters of the alphabet

das ABC	the ABC/alphabet
z.B. – mit kleinem z und	z.B. 'e.g.' – with a small z and
großem B (zum Beispiel)	a capital B (for example)
Er läßt sich kein X für ein	He's not easily fooled.
U vormachen.	

(D) Names of theaters (theatres), movie houses, hotels, cafés and restaurants.

(iv) *Unexpected genders*

The gender of some nouns is different from the sex of the person or animal they refer to. Sometimes, as in the neuter examples in (A) below, this is because they are compounds taking the gender of the final part.

(A) Many names of animals have no separate masculine and feminine forms. If necessary, **das ~männchen** 'male ~' and **das ~weibchen** 'female ~' can be used.

der Adler, Elefant, Frosch, Kuckuck;	eagle, elephant, frog, cuckoo;
die Eule, Giraffe, Kröte, Maus, Ratte;	owl, giraffe, toad, mouse, rat;
das Eichhörnchen, Nilpferd, Nashorn, Rotkehlchen	squirrel, hippopotamus, rhinoceros, robin

(B) Some nouns refer to both women and men.

der Mensch, Vormund;	human being/person, legal guardian;
die Geisel, Person, Wache, Waise;	hostage, person, sentry, orphan;
das Mitglied, Mündel	member, legal ward

20c *Gender benders: nouns with double gender*

Several dozen words have different genders for different meanings. These are some of the most common, with their plurals.

der Band – Bände	volume, book	**das Band – Bänder**	ribbon
		die Band – Bands	(music) band
(**die Bande – Banden**	gang, band)	**das Band – Bande**	fetter, bond
der Bund – Bünde	union, federation	**das Bund – Bunde**	bunch, bundle
der Erbe – Erben	heir	**das Erbe – Erbschaften**	inheritance
der Gefallen – Gefallen	favo(u)r	**das Gefallen –** *no plural*	pleasure
der Gehalt – Gehalte	content(s)	**das Gehalt – Gehälter**	salary

NOUNS AND NOUN PHRASES

der Heide – Heiden	heathen	**die Heide – Heiden**	heath
der Junge – Jungen	boy	**das Junge –** *adj.-noun*	young (animal)
der Kiefer – Kiefer	jaw	**die Kiefer – Kiefern**	pine
der Laster – Laster	truck	**das Laster – Laster**	vice
der Leiter – Leiter	leader, chief	**die Leiter – Leitern**	ladder
der Mangel – Mängel	lack	**die Mangel – Mangeln**	mangle
der Messer – Messer	surveyor; gauge	**das Messer – Messer**	knife
der Moment – Momente	moment (time)	**das Moment – Momente**	factor
der Schild – Schilde	shield	**das Schild – Schilder**	sign, metal plate
der See – Seen	lake	**die See –** *no plural*	sea
die Steuer – Steuern	tax	**das Steuer – Steuer**	steering wheel

21 One or more? Singular and plural

21a Predicting the plural

(i) In German the *plural* of a noun is not as easy to predict as in English. This is because German has kept the older Germanic endings and vowel changes which are still to be seen in the English 'one ox, two oxen' **ein Ochse, zwei Ochsen** and 'one mouse, two mice' **eine Maus, zwei Mäuse**. As with genders, there are some guidelines to help you, but you should always learn the plural of a noun together with its meaning and gender.

(ii) German nouns fall into five groups according to the ending (if any) which they add to make their plural. In three of these groups the stem vowel may also take Umlaut when possible (that is, **a(u)** → **ä(u)**, **o** → **ö**, **u** → **ü**). You will see from the following paragraphs that feminine nouns have the fewest ways of making their plurals and are therefore easiest to predict. Neuters are fairly predictable, but masculines have a wide range of possibilities.

➤ Four *bottles* of wine and two *dozen* sausages, please!: plural measures ➤3d(ii).

21b Plural groupings

(i) *-(e)n* group

This group is never combined with Umlaut. The **-e-** is included when the noun ends in a consonant. All nouns ending in **-e** add **-n**, except **der Käse** and neuters starting with **Ge-**, which do not change. The group includes:

• a good number of masculine nouns, including the weak masculines [➤22g(i)] and the eight nouns like **der Name** [➤22g(ii)], but also foreign borrowings ending in unstressed **-or** (which shift their stress to the **-or** in the plural) and some two dozen others:

der Dorn – Dornen	thorn
der Muskel – Muskeln	muscle
der Schmerz – Schmerzen	pain

NOUNS AND NOUN PHRASES

der See – Seen	lake
der Professor – Professoren	professor
der Staat – Staaten	state
der Stachel – Stacheln	barb, prickle
der Strahl – Strahlen	ray, beam
der Vetter – Vettern	male cousin

• the great majority (many thousands) of feminine nouns:

die Ecke – Ecken	corner
die Frau – Frauen	woman, wife
die Schulter – Schultern	shoulder
die Schüssel – Schüsseln	bowl
die Schwester – Schwestern	sister
die Station – Stationen	(small) station

• about a dozen neuter nouns, the most common being:

das Auge – Augen	eye
das Bett – Betten	bed
das Ende – Enden	end
das Hemd – Hemden	shirt
das Herz – Herzen	heart
das Insekt – Insekten	insect
das Interesse – Interessen	interest
das Juwel – Juwelen	jewel
das Ohr – Ohren	ear
das Elektron – Elektronen	electron

(and other scientific terms ending in **-on**).

(ii)   *No ending group*

This group is sometimes combined with Umlaut. The group includes:

• all masculine nouns ending in **-el**, **-en** or **-er** except **der Bauer – Bauern** 'farmer' and **der Vetter – Vettern** 'cousin'. Most do not add Umlaut, but about 20 do:

der Löffel – Löffel	spoon
der Schlüssel – Schlüssel	key
der Reifen – Reifen	tire
der Wagen – Wagen	car, railroad carriage
der Fehler – Fehler	mistake
der Koffer – Koffer	suitcase
der Apfel – Äpfel	apple

der Nagel – Nägel	nail
der Garten – Gärten	yard, garden
der Laden – Läden	store, shop
der Acker – Äcker	(plowed/ploughed) field
der Bruder – Brüder	brother

• two feminine nouns, both with Umlaut:

die (Groß)mutter – (Groß)mütter	(grand)mother
die Tochter – Töchter	daughter

• all neuter nouns ending in **-el**, **-en** or **-er**, or in the diminutive endings **-chen** and **-lein** [➤19g(iii)]. The only ones with Umlaut are **das Kloster – Klöster** 'convent, monastery', and **das Abwasser – Abwässer** 'effluent' and other compounds of -**wasser**:

das Mittel – Mittel	means; medicine
das Kissen – Kissen	cushion, pillow
das Fenster – Fenster	window
das Mädchen – Mädchen	girl
das Möbel – Möbel	furniture
das Zeichen – Zeichen	sign (indication)
das Muster – Muster	pattern, model
das Büchlein – Büchlein	booklet

• neuter nouns with the prefix **Ge-**, often collective nouns [➤19g(iv)]:

das Gebäude – Gebäude	building
das Gebirge	mountain range
das Gebüsch	bushes, undergrowth
das Gehäuse – Gehäuse	casing; snail shell

(iii)   -e *group*

This group is sometimes combined with Umlaut. The group includes:

• a great many masculine nouns, especially one-syllable words. Of those which could add Umlaut, about half do, including all those in paragraph 19g(ii). For example:

der Arm – Arme	arm
der Hund – Hunde	dog, hound
der Ort – Orte	place
der Punkt – Punkte	point, full stop/period
der Tag – Tage	day

der Schuh – Schuhe	shoe
der Arzt – Ärzte	doctor
der Rock – Röcke	skirt
der Stuhl – Stühle	chair
der Anlass – Anlässe	immediate cause
der Einwand – Einwände	objection
der Vertrag – Verträge	contract

• about a quarter of one-syllable feminine nouns. All have Umlaut:

die Hand – Hände	hand
die Stadt – Städte	town/city
die Wand – Wände	internal wall
die Wurst – Würste	sausage

• about three-quarters of those neuter nouns which are not in the no ending group. The only one with Umlaut is **das Floß – Flöße** 'raft':

das Bein – Beine	leg
das Brot – Brote	bread, loaf
das Ding – Dinge	thing, object
das Haar – Haare	hair
das Jahr – Jahre	year
das Ziel – Ziele	aim, objective

(iv)   -er *group*

This group is always combined with Umlaut where possible. The group includes:

• about a dozen masculine nouns, for example:

der Geist – Geister	spirit/ghost
der Irrtum – Irrtümer	error
der Mann – Männer	man
der Rand – Ränder	edge
der Ski – Skier	ski
der Strauch – Sträucher	shrub
der Wald – Wälder	woods, forest
der Wurm – Würmer	worm

• no feminine nouns.
• about a quarter of those neuter nouns which are not in the no ending group, mostly one-syllable, but also all those ending in **-tum** [➤19g(iii)] and eight others:

das Ei – Eier	egg
das Haus – Häuser	house
das Kind – Kinder	child
das Schild – Schilder	sign (notice)
das Gehalt – Gehälter	salary
das Geschlecht – Geschlechter	sex
das Gespenst – Gespenster	ghost
das Mitglied – Mitglieder	member

(v)   -s *group*

These are never combined with Umlaut. Not a native Germanic plural ending, but increasingly common. The group includes nouns from all three genders:

• large numbers of recent borrowings from English or French:

das Atelier – Ateliers	studio
der Bankier – Bankiers	banker
das Motel – Motels	motel
der Streik – Streiks	strike

• words ending in a consonant + a vowel other than **-e**:

das Auto – Autos	car
das Baby – Babys	baby
das Büro – Büros	office
die Party – Partys	(celebration) party
das Taxi – Taxis	taxi

• abbreviations (initials or shortened words). The **-s** is sometimes left off in speech:

der LKW – LKW(s)	truck
die Uni – Unis	university

• family names [➤19d(ii)].

Noun plural endings have no effect whatsoever on the other parts of the noun phrase (determiners, adjectives, etc.). These are governed by very different rules, which are discussed in Chapters 23 and 24.

21c   *Double plurals*

A few nouns have different plurals with different meanings. For example:

das Band – Bande	fetters, bonds, chains	**das Band – Bänder**	ribbons

die Bank – Banken	banks (financial)	**die Bank – Bänke**	benches
der Block – Blöcke	blocks (large chunks)	**der Block – Blocks**	blocks (apartments, pad of paper)
die Mutter – die Mütter	mothers	**die Mutter – die Muttern**	nuts (for bolts)
der Stock – Stöcke	sticks	**der Stock – Stockwerke**	storeys
der Strauß – Sträuße	bunches	**der Strauß – Strauße**	ostriches
das Wort – Wörter	(separate) words	**das Wort – Worte**	words (speech)

21d   Plurals with no singular

Some of these have exact English equivalents, but others are singular in English. For example:

die Eltern	parents
die Ferien	vacation, holidays
die Leute	people (in general)
die Flitterwochen	honeymoon
die Lebensmittel	food
die Zinsen	interest (on capital)

21e   Singulars for plurals

(i)   In some English words the final '-s' is a false plural, that is, the thing itself is singular and there is often no singular form with the same meaning. The German for these words is often singular. For example:

die Brille	glasses, spectacles
das Fernglas	binoculars
die Hose	pants, trousers
der Inhalt	contents
die Kaserne	barracks
der Lohn	wages
die Mathe(matik)	math(ematics)
die Physik	physics
die Politik	politics
der Pyjama	pyjamas
die Schere	scissors
die Treppe	stairs
die Umgebung	surroundings
die Waage	scales

| die Zange | pincers, tongs |

(ii) Conversely, some English singular nouns are plural in German. The German singular then often means 'piece or item of ...'.

die Auskünfte	information
die Fortschritte	progress
die Hausaufgaben	homework
die Kenntnisse	knowledge
die Möbel	furniture
die Nachrichten	news

22 The role of the noun phrase in the sentence: the four cases

22a What are cases?

(i) What do cases tell us?

All languages have ways of showing what role each noun phrase is playing in the sentence, for example, as subject [➤4b], as object [➤8d/e] or as part of an adverbial expression [➤28c]. In some languages, such as English and French, this is shown mainly by the position of the noun phrase. Position can be important in German too [➤4e], but the role of a noun phrase or pronoun is shown most clearly by its *case*. Each case has its own set of endings. English has similar forms in the possessive 's, as in 'a child's toy', and in the pronoun forms 'I - me, she - her, he - him, we - us, they - them', but German cases are much more significant.

(ii) German cases

German noun phrases and pronouns have four cases: *nominative*, *accusative*, *genitive* and *dative*. These are traditional names which are useful labels. Each case has a number of uses. Most of these are dealt with in other sections of this *Handbook*, but they are summarized for ease of reference in paragraphs 22c to f below.

22b Case endings on nouns

The case of a noun phrase is most commonly shown by a determiner [➤ch.23] or possibly by an adjective [➤ch.24], not by the noun itself. The only case endings added to nouns are detailed below.

(i)

Weak masculine nouns add **-(e)n** to all cases except the nominative singular [➤22g(i)]. Eight other irregular masculine nouns add both **-en** to all cases and **-s** to the genitive singular [➤22g(ii)]. One neuter, **das Herz**, also follows this pattern, except that it does not change in the accusative singular.

| Mit meinem *Kollegen* ist bestimmt etwas los. Er ist nicht mehr mit ganzem *Herzen* bei der Arbeit. Am Telefon sagt er statt seines *Namens* bloß „Huh?". Mich behandelt er wie einen *Dummen*. Ich würde lieber mit unserem *Vorgesetzten* arbeiten. | There is certainly something the matter with my *colleague*. His *heart* is no longer in his work. On the telephone, instead of his *name*, he just says "Huh?". He treats me like a dumb person. I would rather work with our supervisor. |

(ii) Other masculine nouns, and all neuter nouns, add **-(e)s** to the genitive singular. The **-e-** is used mainly to aid pronunciation. It must be used after **-s, -ß, -sch, -x** and **-z**.

| Während des *Mittagessens* bin ich trotz des schrecklichen *Wetters* rausgegangen. Mein Wagen stand am anderen Ende des *Parkplatzes*. | During *lunch* I went out, despite the terrible *weather*. My car was at the other end of the *parking lot*. |

(iii) Short masculine and neuter nouns may add **-e** for the dative singular, though nowadays this is mainly confined to set phrases.

| Im *Laufe* der Zeit bin ich mit dem ganzen Konkurrenzkampf unzufrieden geworden. Nur zu *Hause* fühle ich mich wohl. | In the *course* of time I have become discontented with the whole rat-race. Only at *home* do I feel at ease. |

(iv) All nouns except those which add **-s** for their plural [➤21b(v)] must end in **-n** in the dative plural. This means that any noun plural which does not already end in an **-n** must add one for the dative.

| Mit Büro*s* und Hotel*s* hätte ich lieber nichts mehr zu tun. Ich möchte gern mehr Zeit mit meinen *Kindern* und meinen *Freunden* verbringen. | I would rather have nothing more to do with offices and hotels. I would like to spend more time with my *children* and my *friends*. |

22c   Uses of the nominative case

This is the basic form of the noun, the form listed in dictionaries. It is used:

NOUNS AND NOUN PHRASES

(i)   for the subject of the sentence [➤4b]:

Mein ältester Bruder Martin hat Grafik - Design studiert.	*My eldest brother* Martin studied graphic design.

(ii)   for the complement of joining verbs such as **sein, werden, bleiben** [➤8c]:

Er ist *ein sehr kompetenter Zeichner.*	He is *a very competent draftsman/draughtsman.*

(iii)   for certain noun phrases used in isolation, as when addressing people or in exclamations:

Aber *Herr Ganz*! Was für *ein interessanter Entwurf*!	Well, *Mr. Ganz*! What *an interesting design*!

22d   Uses of the accusative case

This has the same forms as the nominative except in the masculine singular. It is used:

(i)   for the direct object of transitive verbs [➤8d]:

Mein Bruder leitet *ein ziemlich großes Team.*	My brother leads *a fairly large team.*

(ii)   for free-standing adverbial expressions of time, value or measurement, that is, those not governed by a preposition:

Jeden Morgen fährt er *mehrere Kilometer* zur Arbeit.	*Every morning* he drives *several kilometers* to work.

(iii)   after some prepositions always [➤27b(i)]:

Ohne den Wagen wäre der Weg *für ihn* viel länger.	*Without the car* the journey would be much longer *for him.*

(iv)   after some prepositions to indicate motion towards a place [➤27b(iii)]:

Am Wochenende fährt die Familie *in die Berge* **oder** *ans Meer.*	On the weekend the family drives *into the mountains* or *to the seaside.*

(v)   for many common greetings and wishes:

Guten Tag! Alles Gute! Vielen Dank! Einen Augenblick! Guten Appetit!	Good morning/day! All the best! Many thanks! One moment! Enjoy your meal!

22e   Uses of the genitive case

The genitive has a range of uses, but it is now less used in speech, where it is more normal to use a prepositional phrase (especially with **von**). It is, however, widely used in written German, and it is not hard to find everyday texts in which it is the most common case.

• Except with proper names and certain set expressions, the genitive almost always follows the noun it depends on. To put it first sounds old-fashioned or mock-solemn.
• The main uses of the genitive are:

(i)   to express possession:

Martins **Haus/Das Haus** *meines Bruders* **ist sehr schön gelegen.**	*Martin's/My brother's* house is very beautifully situated.

(ii)   to define the scope of the preceding noun:

Es liegt auf der anderen Seite *der Stadt* **am Rande** *eines Wald(e)s.*	It lies on the other side *of town* on the edge *of a wood (woods).*

(iii)   after nouns of quantity [➤3d]:

In seinem Garten steht eine Gruppe *uralter Eichen.*	In his yard there is a clump *of ancient oaks.*

(iv) after certain prepositions. A few of these are common, but a large number are only used in official or commercial writing [➤27b(iv)]:

Dank *seiner Ausbildung* hat Martin ein gutes Gefühl für Design. Während *des vergangenen Jahres* hat er den Garten neu angelegt.	Thanks to *his training*, Martin has a good sense of design. During *the last year* he redesigned the garden.

(v) after a few verbs and adjectives, including some set expressions after the verb **sein** [➤8d(iii), 24g(i)]. Most of these are hardly used in colloquial German:

Er bedurfte *der Hilfe* eines Fachmanns nicht – *dessen* war er sicher. Danach war er *sehr guter Laune/guter Dinge.*	He did not need *the help* of a specialist – *of that* he was certain. Afterwards he was *in a very good mood/in high spirits.*

(vi) in some set adverbial expressions:

***Eines Tages* hat er mir gesagt: „*Letzten Endes* braucht man diese Fachleute nicht." *Meines Wissens* hat er nicht sich selber gemeint!**	*One day* he said to me, "*When it really comes to it* you don't need these experts." *To the best of my knowledge* he didn't mean himself!

22f   Uses of the dative case

The dative case is common in both speech and writing. It is used:

(i) for indirect objects [➤8e]:

Er hat *mir* das Bäumchen gezeigt, das meine Nichte *ihm* geschenkt hatte.	He showed *me* the sapling which my niece had given *him*.

(ii) as the only object of certain verbs [➤8d]:

Sie wollte *ihm* dafür danken, dass er *ihr* bei ihren Prüfungsvorbereitungen geholfen hatte.	She wanted to thank *him* for helping *her* with her examination preparations.

(iii) after some prepositions always [➤27b(ii)]:

Bei *der Prüfung* ist sie mit *sehr guten Noten* durchgekommen.	She passed *the examination* with *very good grades*.
Seit *letzter Woche* arbeitet sie als Forschungsassistentin.	Since *last week* she has been working as a research assistant.

(iv) after some prepositions to indicate position [➤27b(iii)]:

Das Labor(atorium) befindet sich in *der Stadtmitte*, hinter *der Hauptpost*.	The lab(oratory) is in *the town center*, behind *the main post office*.

22g *Masculine nouns with irregular case endings*

(i) *Weak masculine nouns*

The so-called 'weak masculine' nouns add the ending **-(e)n** to all cases (singular and plural) except the nominative singular. Almost all these nouns refer to humans or animals. The nouns which belong to this group are:

(A) all masculine nouns ending in **-e** except **der Käse**, **der Charme** and the eight nouns listed in paragraph 22g(ii). For example:

der Biologe – Biologen	biologist
der Junge – Jungen	boy
der Matrose – Matrosen	sailor
der Neffe – Neffen	nephew

(B) some native German nouns which do not end in **-e**. Note that **Herr** adds **-n** in the singular and **-en** in the plural. Especially in colloquial speech, there is a tendency for many of these nouns to have the normal endings in all or part of the singular. For example:

NOUNS AND NOUN PHRASES

der Bär – Bären	bear
der Bauer – Bauern	peasant, farmer
der Bayer – Bayern	Bavarian
der Herr – Herrn – Herren	gentleman
der Mensch – Menschen	person, human
der Nachbar – Nachbarn	neighbor
der Narr – Narren	fool
der Oberst – Obersten	colonel
der Ochs – Ochsen	ox
der Papagei – Papageien	parrot
der Spatz – Spatzen	sparrow
der Untertan – Untertanen	subject (politics)

(**C**) a large number of nouns brought in from other languages, especially those ending in **-and, -ant, -arch, -at, -ent, -ist, -krat** and **-nom**. For example:

der Elefant – Elefanten	elephant
der Automat – Automaten	slot machine
der Student – Studenten	student
der Telefonist – Telefonisten	telephone operator
der Demokrat – Demokraten	democrat
der Astronom – Astronomen	astronomer

Note   Weak masculine nouns do not have the **-n** ending in the singular if they are used without a determiner [➤ch.23]. This avoids confusion between singular and plural.

Das Verhältnis zwischen Professor und *Assistent* ist immer sehr wichtig.	The relationship between professor and *assistant* is always very important.

Do not confuse weak masculine nouns with adjective-nouns like **der Deutsche – ein Deutscher** or **der Beamte – ein Beamter**, which have the variable endings of adjectives [➤24d].

(ii)   Eight masculine nouns ending in **-e** add **-n** in the accusative and dative singular and the whole of the plural, and **-ns** in the genitive singular. One neuter, **das Herz**, also follows this pattern, except that it does not change in the accusative singular.

der Buchstabe – Buchstaben(s)	letter (ABC...)
der Friede –Frieden(s)	peace
der Funke – Funken(s)	spark
der Gedanke – Gedanken(s)	thought
der Glaube – Glauben(s)	belief

das Herz – Herzen(s)	heart
der Name – Namen(s)	name
der Same – Samen(s)	seed
der Wille – Willen(s)	will, intention

Note Three of these nouns have alternative nominative singulars ending in
-n which are now more usual: **der Frieden, der Funken** and **der
Samen**. Indeed, it is helpful to think of them all as following the same
pattern as **der Wagen** 'car', but without the **-n** in the nominative
singular.

23 Specifying nouns: determiners

23a   What are determiners?

You will not find the word *determiner* in older grammar, but it is a very useful term, which takes in some of the most common words in any language.

• Unlike ordinary adjectives, determiners do not describe nouns but are used to place them in a context. They say whether they are assumed to be known or not, to whom they belong, how many there are and so on.
• Determiners come first in the noun phrase. In German they are the main indicators of the noun's gender, number and case.
• Most determiners have corresponding pronouns, which replace the whole noun phrase [➤ch.25].
• Numerals are also determiners, but it is convenient to discuss them separately [➤ch.30].

23b   Case endings on determiners

In most noun phrases, it is the determiner which best shows the case. With the exception of the three forms **die** and **das** 'the' [➤23d] and **ein** 'a(n)' [➤23e], all determiners have the same set of standard case endings (also known as 'strong' case endings). These are shown in paragraph 23c(i), taking **welcher?** 'which?' as a model. Note that:

• in the singular, the feminine has only two forms, the neuter three and the masculine four. Only the masculine has a separate accusative;
• the masculine and neuter are the same in the singular genitive and dative;
• for all determiners, adjectives, and pronouns, the plural case endings are the same for all three genders.

23c   Which ...? What sort of ...? Interrogative determiners
(i)   *Welcher ...?* Which ...? [➤6d(iii)]

This determiner is used very much as in English, to ask someone to choose from a known collection.

> **Entschuldigen Sie!** *Welches* **Hundefutter kaufen Sie am meisten? – Immer das billigste.**
>
> Excuse me. *Which* dog food do you buy most? – Always the cheapest.

Case endings

In the following table the standard case endings are shown in italics.

	Masculine	*Feminine*
Nominative	**welch**er **Mann?**	**welch**e **Frau?**
Accusative	**welch**en **Mann?**	**welch**e **Frau?**
Genitive	**welch**es **Mann(e)s?**	**welch**er **Frau?**
Dative	**welch**em **Mann(e)?**	**welch**er **Frau?**

	Neuter	*Plural*
Nominative	**welch**es **Kind?**	**welch**e **Leute?**
Accusative	**welch**es **Kind?**	**welch**e **Leute?**
Genitive	**welch**es **Kind(e)s?**	**welch**er **Leute?**
Dative	**welch**em **Kind(e)?**	**welch**en **Leuten?**

Note 1) In the masculine and neuter genitive singular, **welchen** is often used instead of **welches** when the noun has the ending **-(e)s**.

2) Before an adjective, **welcher** ...? may be used without any ending. The adjective then has the standard (strong) ending. This only occurs in formal written German.

(ii) **Was für (ein) ...?** *What kind of ...? [➤6d(iv)]*

This asks someone to describe something more closely. The **ein** is used with singular countable nouns (that is, anything you can count) and has its normal case endings [➤23e]. The case of the whole phrase is decided by its function in the sentence, not by **für**.

> *Was für* **Haustiere haben Sie? – Einen Schäferhund, einen Dackel und einen Gecko.**
>
> *What sort of* pets do you have? – An alsatian, a dachshund and a gecko.

Especially (but not only) in speech, the phrase is often split and the **für (ein) ...** put later in the sentence.

Einen Gecko? *Was* **ist das denn** *für ein* **Hund? – Kein Hund, eine Eidechse.**	A gecko? *What kind of a* dog is that? – Not a dog, a lizard.

(iii) *Wie viel ...? Wie viele ...? How much/many ...? [➤6d(viii)]*

This determiner is used to ask about quantity. **Wie viel** is used almost always in the singular and increasingly in the plural; it has no case endings. [Compare **viel(e)** in paragraph 23g(ix).]

Wie viel **Futter/***Wie viele* **Dosen Futter kaufen Sie pro Woche? – Eine ganze Menge.**	*How much* pet food/*How many* cans of pet food do you buy per week? – A great deal.

➤ *What* a beautiful lizard! Interrogatives used as exclamations: ➤26a.

23d Already known: the definite article 'the'

(i) When the definite article is used we know precisely what the noun phrase refers to, because it has already been mentioned, because it is closely defined or because it is obvious. It often answers the question **Welcher ...?** 'Which ...?' [➤23c(i)].

I*m* **(In** *dem***) 17. Jahrhundert war** *das* **Schloss** *das* **Landhaus** *der* **Familie Borkewitz.**	In *the* 17th century *the* castle was *the* country house of *the* Borkewitz family.

(ii) *Case endings*

Note the irregular **die** in the feminine and plural and **das** in the neuter. All other cases have the standard endings.

	Masculine	*Feminine*
Nominative	**der Mann**	**die Frau**
Accusative	**den Mann**	**die Frau**
Genitive	**des Mann(e)s**	**der Frau**
Dative	**dem Mann(e)**	**der Frau**

	Neuter	*Plural*
Nominative	**das Kind**	**die Leute**
Accusative	**das Kind**	**die Leute**
Genitive	**des Kind(e)s**	**der Leute**

Dative	**dem Kind(e)**	**den Leuten**

(iii) Uses of the definite article

Especially with nouns referring to concrete objects and people, German uses the definite article much as English does. At other times, though, German uses the definite article where English would not, and in ways which are impossible to tie down exactly. If in doubt, it is safer to use the article.

Set phrases with verb (+ preposition) + noun are particularly variable and must be learned as you meet them [➤8g]. Otherwise, as a rule of thumb:

(A) the article is more likely to be used to refer to something in general. It is almost always used before infinitive-nouns [➤10a(iii)];

(B) the article is less likely when talking about something in a particular situation. It is often left out in idioms with **sein** 'be' and after prepositions which are not linked to a verb.

In the following passage German usage is sometimes the same as English, sometimes not.

Zu der Zeit *war* **im ganzen jetzigen Deutschland** *Krieg. Das Volk* **wollte** *in Frieden* **leben, aber** *der Frieden* **kam nicht.** *Die Treue* **und** *die Ehrlichkeit* **schienen verloren gegangen zu sein.** *Die Pest* **tötete Tausende, in allen Dörfern litten** *(die) Leute* **an** *Unterernährung,* **sogar** *der Kannibalismus* **war nicht unbekannt.** *Im Winter* **fehlte** *Brennstoff. Die Geschichte* **kennt keine schlimmere Zeit – wer** *Geschichte* **studiert, wird das schon wissen.**	At that time *there was war* in the whole of what is now Germany. *The people* wanted to live *in peace*, but *peace* did not come. *Loyalty* and *honesty* seemed to have been lost. *(The) plague* killed thousands; in every village *(the) people* were suffering from *malnutrition*; even *cannibalism* was not unknown. *In winter* there was no *fuel. History* knows no worse period – anyone who studies *history* will already know that.

➤   Personal names ➤19d. Geographical names ➤19e. Weights and measures ➤23e(iii). Languages ➤19f(ii).

(iv) Shortened forms of the definite article

The definite article can be shortened, both distinguish **der** 'the' from **der** 'this, that' [➤23f(i).]

In speech and writing shortened forms are commonly used after certain

NOUNS AND NOUN PHRASES

prepositions.

an + das → ans	an + dem → am	in + das → ins	in + dem → im
auf + das → aufs		von + dem → vom	
bei + dem → beim		zu + dem → zum	zu + der → zur

Note   In speech, other compounds with **das** are common, for example: **durchs**, **übers**, **ums**, **unters**. Except in certain set phrases like **ums Leben kommen** 'die', these are less used in writing.

23e   Unknown individuals: the indefinite article 'a(n)'

(i)   A noun phrase with the indefinite article emphasizes the type of person or thing being referred to, rather than the individual. The phrase often answers the question **was für (ein) ...?** 'what sort of ...?' [➤23c(ii)].

| **Hier sehen wir das Porträt** *eines* **Herrn aus dem 18. Jahrhundert. Er war** *ein* **leidenschaftlicher Jäger.** | Here we see the portrait of *a* gentleman from the 18th century. He was *an* avid hunter. |

(ii)   Case endings

ein has no ending in the masculine nominative and neuter nominative/accusative. All other cases have the standard endings. Because **ein** has no plural, its opposite **keine** 'no ...' is given in the table.

	Masculine	*Feminine*
Nominative	ein Mann	eine Frau
Accusative	einen Mann	eine Frau
Genitive	eines Manns	einer Frau
Dative	einem Mann(e)	einer Frau

	Neuter	*Plural*
Nominative	ein Kind	keine Leute
Accusative	ein Kind	keine Leute
Genitive	eines Kinds	keiner Leute
Dative	einem Kind(e)	keinen Leuten

Note   All possessives (for example, **mein** 'my', **unser** 'our', **ihr** 'her, their') have the same endings as **ein** [➤23h].

(iii)   Uses of the indefinite article

German usage is similar to English except that:

(A) no article is used after a linking verb [➤8c] to refer to someone's job, profession, nationality or religion. **ein(e)** is used if there is an adjective before the noun – being a doctor is a profession, being a *bad* doctor is not!

Seine Frau war *Österreicherin.* **Sie war** *Katholikin*, **während ihr Mann** *Lutheraner* **war.** but **Sie war** *eine begabte Malerin.* **Er war aber** *ein ziemlich schlechter Jäger*!	His wife was *Austrian.* She was *(a) Catholic*, whereas her husband was *(a) Lutheran.* but She was *a gifted painter*, but he was *a fairly bad hunter*!

(B) the definite article is used in phrases of measurement (weights, frequency, etc.). **pro** 'per' is another way of saying this.

Der Honig kostet vier Euro *das* **Glas, die Pralinen kosten acht Euro** *das* **Pfund und die Ansichtskarten 60 Cent** *das* **Stück.** **Wir bekommen hier Tausende von Besuchern** *pro* **Woche.**	The honey costs four euros *a* jar, the chocolates cost 8 euros *a* pound and the postcards 60 cents *a* piece. We get thousands of visitors *a/per* week here.

23f *Pointing and showing: demonstrative determiners 'that, this' etc.*

Demonstratives are like a strong definite article. They point to something near to or far from the speaker in time or place, or to something of a certain kind.

• Except after the **allerlei** group [➤(vi) below] and some usages with **solch-** [➤(v) below], adjectives following demonstratives have the **-e/-en** endings [➤24b(ii)A].

(i) *der, die, das* 'this, that'

These are the most common demonstratives in German. Colloquially they are often reinforced with **da** after the noun. They have exactly the same forms as the definite article [➤23d(ii)], but in speech they are always stressed and never shortened as

der 'the' usually is [➤23d(iv)]. This makes the difference between **zu der Zeit** 'then' and **in dem Augenblick** 'at that moment', and **zurzeit** 'now' and **im Augenlick** 'at the moment'.

In *dem* Zimmer (da) sehen Sie ein prachtvolles Himmelbett.	In *that* room (there) you can see a magnificent four-poster bed.

(ii)   *dieser* 'this'

dieser has the standard case endings [➤23c(i)]. It is used very much like the English 'this', except that in speech **der ... (hier/da)** is often used instead.

In *diesem* Bett soll Albrecht der Bär geschlafen haben.	Albrecht the Bear is said to have slept in *this* bed.

(iii)   *jener, derjenige* 'that'

jener is used mainly in formal written German, but **derjenige** is used in both speech and writing. It is mainly followed by a relative clause [➤5b] defining who or what is being spoken of, as in English 'those people who ... '.

derjenige etc. is always written as one word, but the two halves are treated separately: **der-** has its normal case endings and is never shortened; **-jenige** has the **-e/-en** adjective endings, for example **diejenige, dasjenige, denjenigen, demjenigen**; (plural) **diejenigen**.

Aber *diejenigen* Historiker, die *jene* Zeit studiert haben, glauben diese Geschichte nicht.	But *those* historians who have studied *that* period do not believe this story.

(iv)   *derselbe* 'the same'

This classes people and things together. The two parts are treated separately, as with **derjenige**, except that the **der** part does combine with prepositions [➤23d(iv)]. It is then written as two words. 'The same *as*' is **derselbe *wie*** [➤comparatives 24e(ii)].

Dieselbe Geschichte wird von so vielen Schlössern erzählt!	*The same* story is told of so many castles!

Im *selben* Zimmer steht ein so genannter Bibliothekarsstuhl.	In *the same* room stands a so-called librarian's chair.

(v) solch-, so ein *'such (a)'*

These determiners place people and things in a certain class. They are used in various ways. Note that adjective endings vary according to the construction chosen:

• adjectives take the **-e/-en** endings after **solcher** and after any part of **ein** which has standard case endings [➤24b(ii)A];
• adjectives have the standard case endings after **so** and after endingless **ein** and **solch** [➤24b(ii)B].

(A) In the singular the possibilities are:

• 'such (a) ...' (without an adjective): **(ein) solcher** ... or, more colloquially, **so ein** .... In formal usage **solch ein** ... is an emphatic alternative; here **solch** never takes an ending.

Ein solcher Stuhl dient zugleich als Stuhl und als Trittleiter.	*Such a* chair serves both as chair and as stepladder.

• 'such (a) ... ' (with an adjective): **(ein) so** ... or, much more formally, **(ein) solcher**....

Ein so schönes Beispiel wie dieses ist selten zu finden.	*Such a* fine example as this is seldom to be found.

(B) In the plural the possibilities are:

• 'such ...' (without an adjective): **solche** ... is normal in both speech and writing.

Solche Möbel wurden nur auf Bestellung hergestellt.	*Such* furniture was only made to order.

• 'such ...' (with an adjective): **solche** ... or **so** ... The latter is more colloquial, but there may also be a difference between the two, as shown in the example. In literary writing endingless **solch** + adjective is also used.

Solche geschickten Schreiner ...	Skilled cabinet makers *like these* ...
So geschickte Schreiner ...	Cabinet makers *who were so* skilled ...
... wurden hoch bezahlt.	... were highly paid.

(vi) **allerlei, allerhand, vielerlei** 'all sorts of', **einerlei** '(all) the same', **keinerlei** 'no ... at all', **zweierlei** 'two kinds of'

None of these add endings. Any adjectives have the standard case endings [➤24b(ii)B].

Sie sehen, wir haben hier *allerlei/allerhand* faszinierende Sachen. Wir haben sogar *zweierlei* patentierte Wasserklosetts aus dem 19. Jahrhundert!	As you see, we have *all sorts of* fascinating things here. We even have *two kinds of* patented water-closets/flush toilets from the 19th century!

23g How much? How many?: the indefinite quantifiers 'some, all' etc.

Like the indefinite article, these quantifiers do not identify specific individuals. Some refer to the whole or none of some thing or group, others to some part or some members of it.

(i) For singular and plural materials (money, food, work materials etc.), phrases without an article are used much as in English. They are also used where English might have 'some, any'; here **etwas** can add emphasis.

Hast du *Geld*? Ich habe schon *Bier* für die Party gekauft, aber wir brauchen noch *Gurken* und (*etwas*) *Wein*.	Have you *any money*? I've already bought (*some*) *beer* for the party, but we still need *gherkins* and (*some*) *wine*.

(ii) **kein ...** 'no ..., not a(ny) ...'

This has exactly the same endings as **ein**, except that it has plural forms [➤23e(ii)].

(A) In general, **kein** is used instead of **nicht (ein)** as the negative of **ein**/no article (+ adjective) + noun. If in doubt always use **kein**.

Wir haben auch *kein* **frisches Brot,** *keinen* **Käse und** *keine* **Würstchen! Hoffentlich haben unsere Gäste** *keinen* **Hunger.**	We do not have *any* fresh bread, (*any*) cheese or (*any*) sausages either! I hope our guests are *not* hungry.

(B) Note the use of **noch kein** to mean 'not yet' or 'not even'.

Von Carl haben wir *noch keine* **Antwort bekommen.**	We haven*'t* received a reply from Carl *yet*.

(C) nicht (ein) is used in several contexts:

• in verb + noun constructions where the meaning is 'not' rather than 'no' or 'not a(ny)':

Weißt du, er fährt *nicht* **Auto, nur Moped, und das ist kaputt.**	You know, he doesn*'t* drive a car, only a moped, and that's broken.

• to stress the idea of 'not a single one', though **kein einziger** can also be used:

Stimmt. Das letzte Mal wollte *nicht ein* **(kein einziger) Freund ihn mitbringen.**	You're right. Last time *not one* friend would give him a lift.

• starting a sentence with an **ein** or article-less phrase and placing **nicht** later emphasizes the negative:

Eine **andere Möglichkeit, zu uns zu kommen, hat er ja** *nicht*.	After all he doesn*'t* have *any* other way of getting to us.

(iii) *aller, all der* '*all (the)*'

These are used in various ways. Note that adjectives take the **-e/-en** endings [▶24b(ii)A] after all constructions with **all-**.

(A) In the singular, endingless **all** is normally used before other determiners. Before an adjective, **aller** with standard case endings is used, but this is rare outside set phrases (**mit allem modernen Komfort** 'with all modern conveniences'). Singular **all/aller** is far less common than the English 'all', which is usually expressed by **der ganze ...**, **mein ganzer ...** 'the whole ..., my whole ...' etc.

Fast (*all* der Wein) der *ganze* Wein ist schon weg, und wir haben (*all* unser Geld) unser *ganzes* Geld ausgegeben.	Almost *all* the wine is gone, and we've spent *all* our money.

(B) In the plural, **alle** (+ other determiner) + noun is the commonest usage, though **all die** and occasionally **alle die** are also used. Note that **alle** is *never* followed by a genitive, so **alle Kinder** means both 'all children' and 'all (of) the children'.

Wo kommen *alle* diese Leute nur her? Haben wir *alle* Einwohner des Viertels eingeladen?	Just where do *all* these people come from? Did we invite *all (of) the* local residents?

(iv) **jeder** *'each, every'*, **jeglicher** *'any at all'*

These both have standard case endings [➤23c(i)]. **jeder** can only be used in the singular. **jeglicher**, an emphatic alternative used mainly in formal written style, also has plural forms.

Das nächste Mal kann *jeder* Gast eine Flasche mitbringen. So vermeiden wir *jegliche* Probleme.	The next time *every* guest can bring a bottle. In that way we'll avoid *any* problems.

(v) **beide** *'both, the two'*

beide has the standard case endings [➤23c(i)]. Any following adjectives end in **-en**. **beiden** can also be used after another determiner, as in **seine beiden ...** 'both his .../his two ...'.

Ich bin froh, dass wir deine *beiden* Brüder eingeladen haben. *Beide/Die beiden* jungen Leute mag ich gern.	I'm glad that we invited your *two* brothers. I like *both (the)* young people.

(vi) **einig-** *'some'*

This refers to a fairly small amount or number. It has the standard case endings throughout, but following adjectives have different types of ending in the singular and the plural.

(A) The singular **einiger** is used mainly with abstract nouns ['some' with materials: ➤23g(i)]. Following adjectives have the **-e/-en** endings [➤24b(ii)A].

Es tut mir leid, dass wir sie seit *einiger* **Zeit nicht gesehen haben.**	I'm sorry that we haven't seen them for *some* time.

(B) The plural **einige** is common, though it is often left out where English might have 'some'. Following adjectives have the same endings as **einige**.

Einige **ältere Verwandte haben ihnen gegenüber** (*einige*) **Bedenken, aber ich finde sie sympathisch.**	*Some* older relatives have *some* misgivings about them, but I find them likeable.

(vii) *manch- 'many (a)'*

This has the sense of 'a fair amount but some way short of all'. It is more common in writing than in speech.

(A) In both singular and plural, **mancher** is most often used with standard case endings. Following adjectives then take the **-e/-en** endings [➤24b(ii)A].

Mancher **junge Mann ist ...** *Manche* **jungen Leute sind ...** **... viel ausgelassener als sie.**	*Many* a young man is ... *Many* young people are ... ... much more boisterous than them.

(B) Endingless **manch** is common in the singular:

• before adjectives, which then have the standard case endings [➤24b(ii)B].
• in formal writing, before **ein**. Following adjectives then have the **-e/-en** endings except after endingless **ein**.

Manch (ein) **alter Mensch hat eine wilde Jugend gehabt.**	*Many an* old person had a wild youth.

NOUNS AND NOUN PHRASES

(viii) *etlicher* 'quite a lot of', *etliche* 'quite a few', *mehrere* 'several'

These have the standard case endings, as do any following adjectives [➤24b(ii)B].

Etliche gutbürgerliche Leute haben ein untadeliges Leben geführt – und bereuen es später! Ich kenne *mehrere* Rentner, die das nun nachholen wollen.	*Quite a lot of* solid middle-class people have led a irreproachable life – and regret it later! I know *several* pensioners who are now trying to make up for it.

(ix) *viel* 'much/a lot', *viele* 'many', *wenig* 'little, *wenige* 'few'; *ein wenig*, *ein bisschen* 'a little' (singular); *ein paar* 'a few', *ein oder zwei* 'one or two' (plural).

With one exception [➤(A) below], following adjectives have the standard case endings [➤24b(ii)B].

(A) In the singular, endingless **viel** and **wenig** are normally used. **viel-** and **wenig-** with singular case endings occur in some set phrases and in formal writing; any following adjectives then have the **-e/-en** endings.

Recht *vielen* Dank für die Party! Wir haben *viel* Spaß gehabt. Ich bin nur erstaunt, dass ihr so *viel* Arbeit in so *wenig* Zeit gemacht habt.	Very *many* thanks for the party! We enjoyed ourselves *a lot*. I am just amazed that you did so *much* work in so *little* time.

(B) In the plural, **viele** and **wenige** with standard case endings are the rule.

Es bleiben nur noch *wenige* unersättliche Gäste. *Viele* Leute sind nach Hause gegangen.	Only *a few* insatiable guests remain. *Many* people have gone home.

(C) Both **viel-** and **wenig-** can be used after **der** or another determiner, when they take the usual adjective endings.

Das viele Essen und *die vielen* Getränke sind alle – *unser weniges* Geld auch!	*The quantities of* food and *the many* drinks are all gone– so is *what little* money *we had!*

174

(D) ein wenig, ein bisschen, ein paar and **ein oder zwei**
remain unchanged in all cases.

Übers Wochenende müssen wir mit *ein paar* kleinen Würstchen, *ein wenig/ein bisschen* altem Käse und *ein oder zwei* Gurken auskommen!	Over the weekend we will have to get by on *a few* small sausages, *a little* stale cheese and *one or two* gherkins (pickles)!

(x)   *irgendein ..., irgendwelcher* ... *'just any ..., any ... at all, some ... or other.'*

These are used in the same way as **ein** (singular only) and **welcher** (singular and plural).

Ich glaube, in *irgendeinem* Schrank findest du *irgendwelche* Büchsen. In der Gefriertruhe ist noch *irgendwelches* Fleisch.	I think you'll find *some (sort of)* cans in *some* cabinet *or other*. There is still *some kind of* meat in the freezer (chest).

23h   *Belonging together: possessive determiners 'my, our' etc.*

Possessives are used to show that the noun belongs to somebody or something. Which possessive is used depends on the possessor, but they add the endings belonging to the same gender and case of the thing possessed.

(i)   *Forms of the possessives*

The following table shows the two nominative forms of the possessives, with their subject pronouns. Note that the **-er** in **unser** and **euer** is part of the word, not an ending; especially in speech, the **-e-** is often dropped before case endings. [Use of second persons **du/ihr** as against **Sie**: ➤25b.]

	Singular			*Plural*		
First person	ich	*mein, meine*	my	wir	*unser, uns(e)re*	our
Second person	du	*dein, deine*	your	ihr	*euer, eu(e)re*	your
	Sie	*Ihr, Ihre*	your	Sie	*Ihr, Ihre*	your
Third person	er	*sein, seine*	his, its	sie	*ihr, ihre*	their
	sie	*ihr, ihre*	her, its			
	es	*sein, seine*	its			

NOUNS AND NOUN PHRASES

Note   All these possessives have the same case endings as **ein** [➤23e(ii)]. Following adjectives have the **-e/-en** endings except when the possessive has no ending, that is, when it is **mein**, **dein**, **sein**, **ihr**, **unser**, **euer**.

(ii)   *Use of possessives*

Possessives are used in German very much as in English, except that the definite article is normally used instead of a possessive:

(A) when referring to clothes or parts of the body. A dative pronoun is often added for clarity [➤8e(iii)].

Hans, steck *die* **Finger bitte nicht in** *den* **Mund! Zieh** *das* **Hemd an, und kämme** *dir die* **Haare! Hast du** *die* **Zähne geputzt?**	Hans, please don't stick *your* fingers in *your* mouth! Put *your* shirt on and comb *your* hair! Have you brushed *your* teeth?

(B) with the adjective **eigen** 'own'.

Hoffentlich hast du diesmal *die eigene* **Zahnbürste gebraucht.**	I hope you used *your own* toothbrush this time.

However, possessives are used to avoid ambiguity, especially with the subject of the sentence.

Seine Mutter sah ihn an. *Sein* **Gesicht war nicht sehr sauber,** *sein* **Hemd war zerrissen, und er hatte** *ihren* **Pullover an!**	His mother looked at him. *His* face was not very clean, *his* shirt was torn, and he had *her* sweater on!

(C) dessen can be used for 'his' and **deren** for 'her' when **sein** and **ihr** would be ambiguous [➤25g(i)].

Sie dachte an ihre Schwester und *deren* **Sohn. Ob der ordentlicher war als ihr Sohn?**	She thought of her sister and *her* (sister's) son. Was he neater than her son?

24 Describing nouns: adjectives

24a What do adjectives do?

Adjectives describe nouns. They can do this either as part of a noun phrase [➤24b] or as a separate element in the sentence [➤24c]. The former are known as attributive adjectives, the latter as predicative adjectives. Only attributive adjectives have added endings.

➤ A bad writer writes *badly*: adverbs formed from adjectives ➤28b(i).

24b Accompanying the noun: adjectives within a noun phrase

(i) Noun phrases can consist of any combination of determiners, adjectives and nouns. The adjectives in the phrase add endings according to the following rule:

• If either the determiner or the noun has a case ending, then the adjective has the so-called weak endings:
-e in the nominative singular of all three genders and in the feminine and neuter accusative singular,
-en in all other cases, singular and plural.
• Otherwise, the adjective has the same standard (strong) case endings as determiners [➤23c(i)]. **-e** and **-en** are of course also two of the standard endings, so in some cases it makes no difference.

(ii) The following tables show how this works. You can see that in practice adjectives end in **-e** or **-en** unless they come first in the phrase or the determiner has no ending.

(A) Adjectives ending in **-e/-en** (shown here in small capitals). In the table **der** etc. stands for all determiners with standard case endings. Parts of **ein, kein** or the possessives have been given where they too have these endings.

	Masculine	*Feminine*
Nominative	der rote Wein	die/meine frische Milch
Accusative	den/einen roten Wein	die/meine frische Milch
Genitive	des/keines roten Weins	der/meiner frischen Milch
Dative	dem/seinem rotenWein	der/meiner frischen Milch

	Neuter	Plural
Nominative	das helle Bier	die/deine kalten Getränke
Accusative	das helle Bier	die/eure kalten Getränke
Genitive	des/unseres hellen Biers	der/Ihrer kalten Getränke
Dative	dem/eurem hellen Bier	den/ihren kalten Getränken

(B) Adjectives with standard case endings.

Note the three cases where **ein, kein** and the possessives have no ending and so make no difference to the adjective ending. In the masculine and neuter genitive singular, the noun almost always has the case ending **-s**, so the adjective ends in **-en**.

	Masculine	Feminine
Nominative	(sein) roter Wein	frische Milch
Accusative	roten Wein	frische Milch
Genitive	[roten Weins]	frischer Milch
Dative	rotem Wein	frischer Milch

	Neuter	Plural
Nominative	(unser) helles Bier	kalte Getränke
Accusative	(Ihr) helles Bier	kalte Getränke
Genitive	[hellen Biers]	kalter Getränke
Dative	hellem Bier	kalten Getränken

In einem modernen Zoo sind viele gefährdete Tierarten zu sehen. Das heutige Leben ist oft langweilig, und bei schönem Wetter zieht ein seltenes Tier oder ein exotischer Vogel Tausende von neugierigen Besuchern an. Wir sehen eine Gruppe afrikanischer Schimpansen und fragen uns, was für interessante Gedanken sie wohl haben. Unsere nächsten Verwandten schauen zurück und stellen sich dieselbe Frage!

In a modern zoo there are many endangered species to be seen. Life nowadays is often boring, and in good weather a rare animal or an exotic bird attracts thousands of inquisitive visitors. We look at a group of African chimpanzees and wonder what sorts of interesting thoughts they have. Our closest relatives return the gaze and ask themselves the same question!

(iii) Some further points on the endings of adjectives within the noun phrase.

(A) If there is more than one adjective they all have the same ending. [Use of commas: ➤2d(ii).]

Im nächst*en*, enger*en* Käfig sind ein Dutzend groß*e* und klein*e* südamerikanisch*e* Vögel.	In the next, narrower cage are a dozen large and small South American birds.

(B) Sometimes the noun is 'understood' (omitted because obvious), but this does not affect the rest of the phrase. Adjectives still have the same endings and (unlike adjective nouns, ➤24d) are not spelled with a capital.

Die groß*en* (Vögel) sind meistens Kraniche, die klein*en* sind Finken. Der größt*e* ist ein Storch.	The big *ones* are mostly cranes; the small *ones* are finches. The biggest (*one*) is a stork.

(C) Some adjectives brought in from other languages (mainly colo(u)rs) do not take endings.

Die Finken sind *prima* kleine Vögel, mit *orange* und gelben Schnäbeln und roten, *rosa* und sogar *lila* Federn.	The finches are *great* little birds, with *orange* and yellow beaks and red, *pink* and even *purple* feathers.

(D) Adjectives made by adding **-er** to town names or numerals: ➤24f, 30a(iv).

➤ You *lucky* people: adjectives after personal pronouns ➤25b(iii). Something/nothing *special*: adjectives after indefinites ➤25h(ii) and (iv), 24d(iii).

(iv) *The spellings of some adjectives*

(A) hoch 'high' changes to **hoh-** before case endings and in the comparative (**höher**).

Auf einem *hohen* Felsen hockt eine Gruppe Paviane.	On a *high* rock a group of baboons is squatting.

(B) Adjectives in **-el, -auer** and **-euer** drop the **-e-** before case endings and in the comparative, and so do foreign adjectives in **-er**.

| Das alte Männchen hat ein *dunkles* Fell und einen etwas *sauren* Gesichtsausdruck. | The old male has *dark* fur and a rather *sour* expression. |

(C) Some adjectives end in an **-e**, which is often dropped in speech though not usually in writing. Case endings are added to the stem without the **-e**. For example:

| Irgendwie macht er einen *müden*, *trägen* Eindruck. Er schaut *trübe* vor sich hin und grunzt *leise*. *Blöd(e)* ist er aber nicht, nur *böse*! | Somehow he gives the impression of being *tired* and *lethargic*. He gazes *dully* into space and grunts *quietly*. He is not *stupid* though, just *cross*! |

24c   At a distance: adjectives as separate elements

Adjectives which are not part of a noun phrase never have case endings in German. They usually describe the subject and are linked to it by a verb like **sein** 'be', **bleiben** 'remain' or **werden** 'become' [►8c]. They can also describe the object, as in the next to last sentence in the example given below, or form a free-standing phrase, as in the last sentence.

| Viele Tiersorten sind *gefährdet*. In Zoos sind sie wenigstens *gesund* und *sicher*. Ihre Käfige sind aber oft *klein* und *kahl*, und ihr Bewegungsraum ist sehr *begrenzt*. Die aktiveren Tiere finden dieses Dasein *frustrierend*. *Verwirrt* und *verzweifelt* rennen sie unaufhörlich hin und her. | Many animal species are *endangered*. In zoos they are at least *healthy* and *safe*. However, their cages are often *small* and *bare*, and their room for movement is very *limited*. The more active animals find this existence *frustrating*. *Confused* and *desperate* they run ceaselessly to and fro. |

24d   Adjectives used as nouns

(i)   All German adjectives can be used as nouns. These *adjective-nouns* are spelled with a capital and almost always take the normal adjective endings [►24b(ii)]. Some typical adjective-nouns are:

der/die Abgeordnete	elected representative
der/die Angestellte	employee
der Beamte/die Beamtin	official (male/female)
der/die Deutsche	German
der/die Fremde	stranger
der/die Reisende	traveler

(ii) Masculine adjective-nouns are often confused with weak masculine nouns [➤22g(i)]. The following table shows where they differ. [Nouns of nationality: ➤19f.]

Singular

	Adjective-noun: 'German'	Weak masculine: 'Frenchman'
Nominative	**der Deutsche –** **ein Deutscher**	**der/ein Franzose**

Plural

Nominative/ *Accusative*	**die Deutschen –** **zehn Deutsche**	**die/zehn Franzosen**
Genitive	**der Deutschen –** **zehn Deutscher**	**der/zehn Franzosen**

In both adjective-nouns and weak masculine nouns, all other cases end in **-en**.

A further difference is that many weak masculine nouns have a feminine form ending in **-in** [➤19g(ii)], thus: **der Franzose – die Französin, der Löwe – die Löwin** 'lion/lioness'. The only feminine adjective-noun in **-in** is **die Beamtin** 'official'.

(iii) In speech, adjective-nouns sound just like a noun phrase with the noun understood [➤24b(iii)], but they have much more general meanings.

(A) Masculines and feminines usually refer to representatives of a whole class of people.

Die *Grünen* sind meist gegen Zoos. Trotzdem besuchen sowohl *Erwachsene* als auch *Jugendliche* sie gern. Zu Hagenbecks Tierpark in Hamburg kommen *Fremde* aus aller Welt, *Reisende* auf der Durchfahrt und viele andere.	The *Greens* are mostly against zoos. All the same, both *adults* and *young people* like visiting them. *Strangers* from far and wide, *travelers* passing through and many others come to Hagenbecks Zoo in Hamburg.

(B) Neuters refer to general ideas or qualities. They are often used after indefinites like **alles, nichts, viel, wenig** [➤25h(ii) and (iv)].

Wenn man *nichts Besonderes* zu tun hat, wird man dort immer *etwas Neues* finden, mit sehr *viel Interessantem* aus allen Ländern.	If you have *nothing special* to do, you will always find *something new* there, with *much of great interest* from every country.

Note A number of neuter adjective-nouns are almost always spelled with a capital letter, for example:

Akten, Berichte und *Ähnliches.*	Files, reports and *the like.*
Wir wollen es im *Einzelnen* besprechen.	Let's discuss it in *detail.*
Ich hätte das *Gleiche* getan.	I would have done the *same.*
Wir tun alles Mögliche.	We are doing everything *imaginable/* everything we can.
Das Übrige wissen Sie schon.	The *rest* you know already.
im *Allgemeinen*	in *general*
im *Großen und Ganzen*	on *the whole*
vor kurzem	*a short while* ago
Ich halte Sie auf dem *Laufenden.*	I'll keep you *informed.*
aufs neue	*anew/again*

There are some exceptions though:

Er ist alles *andere* als gescheit.	He is *anything* but bright.

➤ The best thing *that* ever happened: relative clauses after neuter adjective-nouns ➤25j(vi).

24e   *More and most: comparative and superlative*

Note For ease of reference, this section deals with both adjectives and the adverbs formed from them [➤28b(i)]. Unless otherwise stated, all references to adjectives apply also to their adverbs.

Most adjectives can be used to make comparisons: for this we use the *comparative* form. If we are comparing more than two people or things, then we use the *superlative*.

(i)   *Formation of comparatives and superlatives*

(A) Almost all German adjectives add **-er** for their comparative and **-(e)st** for their superlative.These forms then add the normal adjective endings when they are part of a noun phrase [➤24b].

Unsere elektrischen Handwerkzeuge sind die *erfolgreichsten* auf dem Markt. Wir haben einen *höheren* Umsatz als viele *bekanntere* Marken.	Our electrical hand-tools are the *most successful* on the market. We have a *higher* turnover than many *better known* makes.

Note   In a very few instances **mehr** and **am meisten** can be used for comparatives and superlatives (for example, with participles which are not normally used as adjectives). Normally, ***mehr* faul *als* dumm** means 'lazy *rather than* stupid', and ***meist* faul** means '*mostly/usually* lazy'.

Unser *meist gekauftes* Werkzeug ist ein elektrischer Schraubenzieher.	Our *most purchased* tool is an electric screwdriver.

(B) About 20 common one-syllable adjectives (and **gesund**) have Umlaut in the comparative and superlative. Note the irregular forms in **groß**, **hoch** and **nah**.

alt 'old'	älter	ältest-
arm 'poor'	ärmer	ärmst-
dumm 'stupid'	dümmer	dümmst-
gesund 'healthy'	gesünder	gesündest-
groß 'big, great'	größer	*größt-*
hoch 'high'	*höher*	höchst-
jung 'young'	jünger	jüngst-
klug 'clever'	klüger	klügst-
kurz 'short'	kürzer	kürzest-
lang 'long'	länger	längst-
nah(e) 'near'	näher	*nächst-*
scharf 'sharp'	schärfer	schärfst-
schwach 'weak'	schwächer	schwächst-
stark 'strong'	stärker	stärkst-
warm 'warm'	wärmer	wärmst-

(C) Three adjectives have completely different comparatives and superlatives. **minder** 'less' is used only as an adverb and **mindest-** usually means 'slightest'; otherwise, **weniger** and **wenigst-** are used.

gut 'good'	besser	best-
viele 'much/many'	mehr	meist-
wenige 'little/few'	minder	mindest-

NOUNS AND NOUN PHRASES

(D) Two non-adjectival adverbs have a comparative and superlative. **Das mache ich *gern*** is the usual way to say 'I *like* doing that' [➤29a]. **eher/am ehesten** often refers to preferences rather than time.

gern 'willingly', 'readily'	**lieber**	**am liebsten**
bald 'soon'	**eher**	**am ehesten**

Die Werkzeuge sind *eher* für den Amateur gedacht als für den Profi. Sie werden *am liebsten* von Bastlern gekauft.	The tools are intended for the amateur *rather* than the professional. They are bought *most (readily)* by do-it-yourself enthusiasts.

(E) -est- is used in the superlative for ease of pronunciation, especially with adjectives stressed on the last syllable, or ending in **-s, -x, -z, -sk** and often **-d, -t** and **-sch**.

leisest-, laxest-, wildest-, amüsantest-, raschest-	quietest, laxest, wildest, most amusing, swiftest

(F) Half a dozen adjectives of position have only comparative and superlative forms. They are only used before nouns.

der äußere/innere	outer/inner
der äußerste/innerste	outermost, utmost/innermost
(also **äußerlich/innerlich**)	(external/internal)
der obere/untere	upper/lower
der oberste/unterste	uppermost, top/lowest, bottom
der vordere/hintere	front/back
der vorderste/hinterste	foremost, furthest front/back

(ii)   Using comparatives

(A) The comparatives of some adjectives (and one adverb) can mean **ziemlich ...** 'fairly ...'. Thus **eine ältere Dame** is not as old as **eine alte Dame**. For example:

alt	old	**älter**
dick	thick, fat	**dicker**
dunkel	dark	**dunkler**
dünn	thin	**dünner**
groß	big, great	**größer**
hell	light	**heller**
jung	young	**jünger**
klein	little, small	**kleiner**
neu	new	**neuer**
oft	often	**öfters**

(B) Superiors and inferiors are compared using **(noch) ~er als ...**
'(even) more ~ than ...' and **weniger ~ als ...** 'less ~ than ...'.

Unsere Produkte sind *billiger* *als* **die Konkurrenz, aber nicht** *weniger verlässlich*.	Our products are *cheaper than* the competition but no(t) *less reliable*.

(C) Equals are compared using **(genau)so ~ wie ...** or **(eben)so ~ wie ...** '(just) as ~ as ...'.

Auf der letzten Industriemesse hatten wir *genauso viele* **Interessenten** *wie* **im vorigen Jahr.**	At the last industrial fair we had *just as many* inquiries *as* the year before.

(D) 'More and more ~ ' is **immer ~er**.

Die Nachfrage wird *immer größer*, **also haben wir** *immer mehr* **Arbeiter anstellen müssen.**	The demand gets *greater and greater*, so we have had to employ *more and more* workers.

(E) 'The more ~ ..., the more ~ ...' is **je ~er ..., umso ~er/desto ~er ....** (**desto** is more used in written German.) The first half of the sentence is a subordinate clause; the second part is the main clause. Note the positions of the verbs in each half of the sentence.

Je länger **die Rezession andauert,** *umso (desto) häufiger* **machen die Leute selber ihre Hausreparaturen,** *umso mehr* **brauchen sie unsere Werkzeuge.**	*The longer* the recession continues, *the more frequently* people do their own house repairs and *the more* they need our tools.

(iii)   *Using superlatives*

Superlatives have several forms.

(A) der ~ste etc. and **mein ~ster** etc. are used when an adjective describes a particular noun.

Unsere beste Zeit ist im November, wo *die meisten* Leute ihre Weihnachtsgeschenke kaufen.	*Our best* time is in November, when *most* people buy their Christmas presents.

(B) am ~sten is used:

• after **sein** 'be' in the sense of 'at its most ~'. It is also often used instead of **der ~ste** etc. [➤(A) above]:

Dann ist die Nachfrage *am größten* und unser Umsatz *am höchsten*.	That is when demand is *(at its) greatest* and our sales volume *(at its) highest*.

• for the normal superlative of adverbs:

Unsere Leute arbeiten *am schnellsten*, weil sie *am besten* bezahlt werden.	Our people work *(the) fastest*, because they are paid *(the) best*.

(C) Any superlative adjective can mean 'extremely ~'. It must be followed by a noun, often with no article.

Auch während des *schlechtesten* Wetters kommen sie zur Arbeit, manchmal nur mit *größter* Mühe.	Even during the *worst* weather they come in to work, sometimes only with *the greatest* difficulty.

(D) There are various emphatic superlative adverb forms:

• A few consist simply of the stem, ending in **~st:**

äußerst	extremely	**längst**	long since
herzlichst	most cordially	**meist**	mostly, usually
höchst	highly, extremely	**möglichst ~**	as ~ as possible

• **aufs ~ste** 'most ~ly' is used in formal written German:

Wir möchten ihnen allen *aufs herzlichste* danken.	We would like to thank them all *most warmly*.

• There are several common adverbs in **~stens**, usually meaning 'at (the) ~st':

höchstens	at (the) most	**schnellstens**	with utmost speed
meistens	mostly, for the most part	**strengstens**	very strictly
mindestens	at (the) least	**wenigstens**	at least, at any rate

24f Adjectives formed from other parts of speech

(i) Adjectives formed by using a suffix

As in English, adjectives are often made from nouns and verbs by adding a *suffix*. Unless otherwise stated, the suffixes listed below are all added to nouns. An Umlaut is frequently added if the suffix has an **-i-** in it, but not normally otherwise.

• **~bar** '~able, ~ible' can be used with any suitable verb, sometimes with change of stem.

hörbar, machbar, sichtbar, trinkbar   audible, feasible, visible, drinkable

• **~(e)n, ~ern** 'made of ~'. **~ern** does usually add an Umlaut.

bleiern, eisern, golden, hölzern, kupfern, silbern   leaden, iron, golden, wooden, copper, silver

• **~er** makes adjectives from names of towns and villages where English would normally just use the name. These adjectives are spelled with a capital and do not add case endings.

Bostoner, Edinburger, Hamburger, Pariser, Wiener   Boston(ian), Edinburgh, Hamburg, Parisian, Viennese

~er also makes adjectives from numerals [▶30a(iv)].

• **~haft** 'like a ~'.

heldenhaft, mädchenhaft, pöbelhaft   heroic, girlish, uncouth (rabble-like)

• **~ig** '~y' is a very common suffix which often means 'having the look or qualities of ~'.

freudig, grünäugig, rothaarig, staubig, traurig   joyful, green-eyed, red-haired, dusty, sad

~ig also makes useful adjectives from some phrases and adverbs of place and time.

damalig, dortig, ehemalig, einmalig, gestrig, heutig, hiesig, zweitägig   (the) then, of that place, former, unique, yesterday's, today's, local, lasting two days

• **~(i)sch** '~ish' makes adjectives from foreign words, from names of people and from countries and provinces, including

NOUNS AND NOUN PHRASES

their languages [➤19f]. Some towns have adjectives in **-isch**, usually in set phrases or meaning 'the dialect of ~'.

algebräisch, arithmetisch,	algebraic, arithmetic,
geometrisch, taktisch,	geometric, tactical,
beethovensch, kopernikanisch,	Beethoven's, Copernican,
shakespearisch,	Shakespearian,
bayerisch, bremisch,	Bavarian, Bremen,
sächsisch, Kölnisch Wasser	Saxon, eau de Cologne

~**isch** also makes often uncomplimentary adjectives from some nouns referring to people.

heidnisch, kindisch, wählerisch	heathen, childish, choosy

• ~**lich** '~ly' is a very common suffix meaning 'relating to ~'.

beruflich, glücklich, wöchentlich,	professional, happy, weekly,
zweitäglich	every two days

~**lich** '~able, ~ible' is used with some verbs.

möglich, verlässlich, verständlich,	possible, reliable, understandable,
wahrscheinlich	probable

~**lich** '~ish' can be added to colo(u)r adjectives.

blässlich, bläulich, gelblich,	palish, blueish, yellowish,
rötlich, schwärzlich	reddish, blackish

• ~**los** '~less, lacking ~'.

hilflos, ratlos, sinnlos,	helpless, at a loss, senseless,
ziellos	aimless/random

• ~**mäßig** is much used in official writing to mean 'related to ~' or 'in accordance with ~'.

planmäßig, verhältnismäßig,	according to plan, relative,
verkehrsmäßig	relating to traffic

• ~**sam** 'having the quality of ~'. Makes adjectives from nouns and verbs.

biegsam, grausam, gewaltsam,	flexible, cruel, violent,
ratsam	advisable

(ii) *Adjectives formed by using a prefix*

Two *prefixes* in common use are added to adjectives to modify their meaning:
• **un~** 'un~, in~, dis~' etc., meaning 'not ~' or sometimes 'not very ~'.

unehrlich, unerhört, unglaublich,	dishonest, scandalous, incredible,
unschön, untypisch, unweit	not very nice, untypical, not far

• **ur~** 'very' or sometimes 'typically'.

uralt, urdeutsch,	ancient, typically German,
urgemütlich, urverwandt	extremely cosy, cognate (words)

24g Adjectives governing phrases and clauses

A large number of adjectives can govern noun phrases or clauses in the same way as the verbs discussed in paragraphs 8d on. Usually:

• the adjective follows the noun phrase;
• the verb is **sein** or another linking verb [➤8c]. In fact, the adjective often acts as a verbal particle [➤16e(ii)], except that it is never written as one word with the verb.

The main constructions are given below with a few common examples and cross-references to the corresponding verb usages.

(i) Adjectives + noun phrases

(A) A few adjectives are used with the accusative [verbs: ➤8d(i)].

Ich bin es *gewohnt/satt*.	I am *used to* it/*fed up with* it.
Ich möchte es *los* sein/werden.	I would like to be/get *rid of* it.
Es ist nicht viel *wert*.	It isn't *worth* much.

(B) Many adjectives are used with the dative [verbs: ➤8d(ii)].

Das Baby ist der Mutter sehr *ähnlich*.	The baby is very *like (similar to)* its mother.
Er/Das ist mir *bekannt*.	I *know* him/about it.
Sie war mir sehr *behilflich/dankbar*.	She was very *helpful/grateful* to me.
Sie waren dem Kind sehr *böse*.	They were very *cross* with the child.
Was bin ich Ihnen *schuldig*?	What do I *owe* you?
In Mathe ist sie ihm *überlegen*.	In math(s) she is *better* than (*superior* to) him.

This group includes common idioms referring to feelings and sensations [➤8k] and a number of adjectives meaning 'all the same to ~', at varying levels of politeness:

NOUNS AND NOUN PHRASES

Das ist mir *gleich/einerlei/egal/wurs(ch)t*!	That's all the same to me! I couldn't care less!

(C) Some adjectives are used with the genitive. Very few are used outside very formal written German [verbs: ➤8d(iii)].

Ich bin der ganzen Hetze *müde.*	I am *tired* of the whole mad rush.
Der Verbrecher war des Verbrechens *schuldig.*	The criminal was *guilty* of the crime.
Ich bin dessen *sicher.*	I am *sure* of that.
Er ist dieser Ehre nicht *würdig.*	He is not *worthy* of this honor.

(ii) *Adjectives + prepositions + noun phrases*

(A) Adjectives can be used with any of the prepositions used with verbs [➤8g]. The following examples show how the construction works.

Wir Bauern sind vom Wetter *abhängig.*	We farmers are *dependent* on the weather.
Das Land ist *arm/reich* **an Mineralien.**	The country is *poor/rich* in minerals.
Er ist zu allem *bereit/fähig.*	He is *ready* for/*capable* of anything.
Sie war *blass* **vor Zorn/** *bleich* **vor Furcht.**	She was *pale* with anger/*pale* with fear.
Wir waren *böse/zornig/wütend* **auf sie.**	We were *cross/angry/furious* with them.
Sind Sie mit unserem Plan *einverstanden*?	Are you *in agreement* with our plan?
Wann werden Sie damit *fertig* **sein?**	When will you be *finished* (with) it?
Ich bin auf Ihre Antwort *gespannt/neugierig.*	I am *eager/curious* to hear your answer.
Er ist *schuld* **an der ganzen Sache.**	The whole thing is his *fault*.
Wir sind *stolz* **auf unsere Kinder.**	We are *proud* of our children.
Das ist *typisch* **für diese Gegend.**	That is *typical* of this area.

(B) With many adjectives of this type the noun phrase can be replaced by a **zu** + infinitive clause [verbs: ➤8h(ii)] or, if the subject changes, by a **dass** clause [➤8i]. As with the verbs, this clause is then normally introduced by an adverb formed from **da(r)-** + the preposition, though especially in speech the adverb is often left out.

Ich bin (*dazu*) bereit, Ihnen *zu helfen.*	I am ready *to help* you.
Wir sind stolz *darauf*, an diesem Projekt teilgenommen *zu haben.*	We are proud *of having* taken part in this project.
Sie sind nicht *damit* einverstanden, *dass* wir den Bericht *veröffentlichen.*	They do not agree *to our publishing* the report.
Wer ist schuld *daran, dass* du müde *bist*?	Whose fault is it *that* you're tired?

25 Representing nouns: pronouns

25a What pronouns do

(i) The word *pronoun* means 'in place of a noun.' Pronouns are used instead of nouns as a way of avoiding clumsy repetitions. Remember that:

• all pronouns take their gender (masculine/feminine/neuter) and number (singular/plural) from the noun they refer to;
• things can have any of the three genders, so **er/sie** can mean 'it' as well as 'he/she';
• all pronouns take their case from their function in the sentence they are in;
• unless they do not change at all, all third person pronouns have some form of the standard case endings [➤23c(i)].

(ii) The types of pronoun discussed in paragraphs 25f to 25(i) below have corresponding determiners in chapter 23, to which cross-references are given.

➤ 'We gave *it* to *her/it* to *the woman/her the money*': order of objects ➤4e(ii).

25b Personal pronouns

(i) These are the most neutral pronouns – they simply replace nouns without adding further information. They may refer to the person(s) speaking (first person 'I, we'), the person(s) spoken to (second person 'you'), or the person(s) or thing(s) spoken about (third person 'he, she, it, they').

	Singular			
	Nom.	*Acc.*	*Dat.*	*Gen.*
First person	**ich**	**mich**	**mir**	**meiner**
Second person	**du**	**dich**	**dir**	**deiner**
	Sie	**Sie**	**Ihnen**	**Ihrer**
Third person	**er**	**ihn**	**ihm**	**seiner**
	sie	**sie**	**ihr**	**ihrer**
	es	**es**	**ihm**	**seiner**
	Plural			
First person	**wir**	**uns**	**uns**	**unser**
Second person	**ihr**	**euch**	**euch**	**euer**
	Sie	**Sie**	**Ihnen**	**Ihrer**
Third person	**sie**	**sie**	**ihnen**	**ihrer**

Note   1) Apart from in the genitive, the third person pronouns have the standard case endings (usually without the **-e-**) [➤23c(i)]. Note the extended **-nen** of the dative plural and the shortened forms of the genitives **unser** and **euer**.

2) The genitives of personal pronouns are rare even in writing. They are avoided by rephrasing the sentence using, for example, verbs and prepositions (especially **von**) which do not take the genitive.

(ii)   *You, you and you: second person pronouns*

German second person pronouns are more complex than English.

(A) The 'familiar' singular **du/dich/dir** and plural **ihr/euch**, and their possessives **dein** and **euer**, are used when speaking to members of your family, to close friends and some fellow workers, to fellow pupils, students, sports club members etc., to anyone under about 16 – and to animals! Note that in letters, which is where they are most commonly written, they are also spelled with a small letter.

Lieber Max,	Dear Max,
wie geht's *dir*? **Hast** *du* **meinen**	How are *you*? Did *you* get my last
letzten Brief bekommen? Was	letter? What's *your* sister doing?
macht *deine* **Schwester? Zankt**	Do *you* still have such wonderful
ihr euch **immer noch so schön?**	quarrels? Give her my best wishes
Grüße sie bitte trotzdem von	all the same. See you soon!
mir. Bis bald! *Dein* **Tom**	*Yours*, Tom

(B) **Sie/Ihnen** and its possessive **Ihr** are used when speaking to all other adults (singular and plural). They are always spelled with a capital but are otherwise identical to the third person plural **sie/ihnen** 'they/them' and **ihr** 'their'. This is sometimes called the 'polite' second person, but it is simply the normal form of address to anyone not close to you. Foreigners do well to let native speakers make the first move in changing from **Sie** to **du**. (Note that **Liebe(r) Frau (Herr) ...**, followed by **Sie** etc., is perfectly acceptable if you know a person fairly well.)

Sehr geehrte Frau Dorsch,	Dear Mrs. Dorsch,
ich freue mich schon darauf, *Sie*	I am already looking forward to
kennen zu lernen und einige	meeting *you* and spending some
Zeit bei *Ihnen* **zu verbringen.**	time at *your* house/with *you*. I
Hoffentlich geht es *Ihrem* **Mann**	hope *your* husband is feeling
jetzt besser.	better now.

NOUNS AND NOUN PHRASES

(C) The plural **ihr** etc. is used to any group of people which includes someone you would say **du** to, for example, a close friend and her/his parents, or a group standing talking. It is also used with nationalities: **ihr Deutschen** 'you Germans'.

Ich höre von Max, dass *ihr* **alle ein paar Tage bei** *euren* **Freunden in den Bergen verbringen wollt. Das wird Ihrem Mann sicherlich gut tun. Mit freundlichen Grüßen**	Max tells me that *you* are all going to spend a few days with *your* friends in the mountains. I am sure that that will do your husband good.
Ihr Tom Hartley	Yours sincerely, Tom Hartley

(D) 'I say **du** to you' is **ich duze dich**, and 'I say **Sie** to you' is **ich sieze Sie**. Among native speakers **duzen** is normally associated with first names and **siezen** with **Herr/Frau** + surnames. But circumstances may alter this, especially with people from other countries where different rules apply.

(iii)   *Adjectives after personal pronouns*

As a rule, adjectives after personal pronouns have the standard case endings [➤24b(ii)B]. In the nominative plural, **-en** is more common than **-e**.

Sind *wir älteren* **Leute wirklich konservativer als** *ihr jungen*? **Oder umgekehrt?**	Are *we older* people really more conservative than *you young ones*? Or the other way round?

(iv)   *Prepositions and personal pronouns*

In general, German uses the same personal pronouns after prepositions as in any other position.

Tom ist eine Woche *bei uns* **geblieben. Er hat viel** *für mich* **getan. Unsere Kinder mochten ihn gern, und er hat oft** *mit ihnen* **gespielt.**	Tom stayed *with us* a week. He did a lot *for me*. Our children liked him, and he often played *with them*.

The main exceptions are:

(A) A preposition + 'it' or + 'them' referring to things contracts to one word, **da(r)** + preposition, as in the English 'therein, thereon' etc. The **-r-** is inserted when the preposition begins with a vowel.

Tom hatte ein schweizerisches Taschenmesssser. *Damit* **konnte man allerlei machen. Es hatte zahlreiche Klingen. Unsere Kinder wunderten sich immer** *darüber.*	Tom had a Swiss pocketknife. *With it* you could do all sorts of things. It had numerous blades. Our children always marvelled *at it/them.*

(B) **da(r)-** compounds cannot be formed with:

• the prepositions **außer, gegenüber, ohne, seit**. The normal phrases are:

außerdem	apart from that, besides
(ihm) gegenüber	opposite (it)
ohne (es)	without (it)
seitdem, seither	since (then), ever since

• prepositions taking the genitive. Some of these have equivalent adverbs or phrases; some others use **davon**.

an meiner/seiner/ ihrer Stelle (for **statt**)	instead of me/him/her/them etc.
trotzdem	in spite of that, all the same
währenddessen	during this, meanwhile
seinetwegen/ihretwegen/ unsertwegen	for his/her/their/our sake
deswegen	because of that
außerhalb/innerhalb davon	outside/inside it
oberhalb/unterhalb davon	above/below it

25c   *Reflexive pronouns*

Reflexive pronouns are simply personal pronouns which refer back to the subject of the sentence, as when you do something to yourself. In general, they are therefore treated just like any other personal pronoun. Their use with verbs is discussed in paragraph 8f.

Note   The examples below show how often German uses a reflexive where English does not.

(i)   *Use of reflexive pronouns*

• In the first person (**mich/mir, uns** 'myself, ourselves') and familiar second person (**dich/dir, euch** 'yourself, yourselves') German uses the normal personal pronouns as reflexives.

Setz *dich* **einen Augenblick, Tom, und schaue** *dir* **die Zeitung an. Ich werde** *mich* **schnell anziehen und** *mir* **einen Kaffee kochen. Wir müssen** *uns* **beeilen.**	Sit (*yourself*) down a moment, Tom, and have a look at the newspaper. I'll get dressed quickly and make *myself* a cup of coffee. We must hurry.

- In the third person there is only one reflexive pronoun: **sich** 'her/himself, themselves'. This is used in both singular and plural, accusative and dative, including after prepositions.

Hat dein Vater *sich* **jetzt von seiner Krankheit erholt? Hoffentlich haben deine Eltern** *sich* **in den Bergen gut ausgeruht. Sie sollten** *sich* **wirklich einen neuen Wagen kaufen. So ein alter bringt immer Probleme mit** *sich***.**	Has your father recovered from his illness now? I hope your parents had a good rest in the mountains. They really ought to buy *themselves* a new car. Such an old one always causes problems.

- If you use the ordinary third person pronouns **ihn/ihm, sie/ihr, sie/ihnen** 'him, her, them' then the action is being done to somebody else, not to the subject. (Compare the meanings of the next two examples.)

Kommt deine Schwester mit? Hat deine Mutter *sie* **an unseren Ausflug erinnert?**	Is your sister coming too? Has your mother reminded *her* about our outing?

- **sich** (still with small **s**) is also the reflexive pronoun for **Sie** 'you'.

Frau Dorsch, erinnern Sie *sich* **noch an den Tag, an dem Sie** *sich* **den Fuß verstaucht haben?**	Mrs. Dorsch, do you still remember the day when you sprained *your* ankle?

➤   I've cut *my* finger: possessives and reflexives ➤8e(iii).

(ii)   *Reflexive pronouns used reciprocally*

The plural reflexive pronouns **uns, euch** and **sich** can also be used 'reciprocally', that is, when people do something not to themselves but to each other.

einander, which never changes, can be used instead of the pronoun, especially to stress the meaning 'each other'. It must be used with this meaning after prepositions, when the two are written as one word. Otherwise, it is used more in writing than in speech.

Max und ich haben *uns* **auf einer internationalen Schule in Hannover kennen gelernt. Seitdem haben wir ziemlich viel** *miteinander* **zu tun gehabt.**	Max and I met *each other* at an international school in Hanover. Since then, we have had a great deal to do *with each other*.

 Do not confuse reflexives with the words we use to emphasize that it was the subject that did something, and not anyone else, as in **Sie hat es selber gemacht** 'She did it herself'.

25d The indefinite pronoun 'one'

(i) The *indefinite pronoun* **man** 'one' means 'people in general, you, they'. As such, it provides one alternative to the passive [➤15f(iii)].

Man **sagt, dass** *man* **auf solchen Schulen oft sehr interessante Freundschaften schließen kann.**	*People* say that *you* can often make very interesting friends at such schools.

(ii) **man** can only be used as the subject of the sentence. In the accusative **einen** is used, in the dative **einem**. The reflexive is **sich** and the possessive **sein**.

Wenn es *einem* **gelingt, sich mit Schülern aus anderen Ländern anzufreunden, kann** *man* **viel über die Sitten und Gebräuche ihrer Länder erfahren.**	If *one* succeeds in becoming friends with students from other countries, *one* can learn a lot about the customs and traditions of their countries.

 Do not confuse **man** with the quantity 'one' as in **einer aus der Gruppe** 'one of the group' [➤25h].

25e The impersonal pronoun 'it'

There are a number of constructions using the *impersonal* **es**. In some it has greater status in the sentence than in others.

(i)   **es** is used as an 'empty subject':

> • in **es gibt** + accusative 'there is/are ...'. Note that **es gibt** has no plural;
> • in constructions such as **es macht nichts** 'it doesn't matter', **wie geht es?** 'how are things?', **es gilt/geht um .../handelt sich um ...** 'it is a matter of';
> • when talking about the weather or time;
> • in constructions corresponding to English 'there is/was a ~(ing)'. Although empty of meaning, **es** is here the true subject and cannot be left out, even if some other word or phrase starts the sentence.

Es hat damals in Hannover viel geregnet. **Es** war auch kalt – einmal hat *es* sogar geschneit. *Es* gab aber viel zu tun, und abends *gab es* oft Partys. Eines Abends hat *es* an der Tür *geklopft/geläutet* – die Nachbarn meinten, *es* wäre Mitternacht, wir sollten bitte an sie denken! In solchen Fällen *gilt es,/geht es darum,/handelt es sich darum,* ihren Gesichtspunkt zu verstehen.	That time in Hanover *it* rained a lot. *It* was also cold – once *it* even snowed. But *there was* a lot to do, and in the evenings *there were* often parties. One evening *there was a knock/ring* at the door – the neighbors said *it* was midnight, could we please think of them! In such cases *it is a matter of* understanding/*you have to* understand their point of view.

(ii)   There are a number of idioms where **es** or **das** is the commonest subject but not the only possible one.

Hannover hat mir gut *gefallen*. **Es ist uns *gelungen*, die Stadt ein bisschen kennen zu lernen.** **Es *fehlte* uns leider die Zeit, um alles zu sehen.**	I *liked* Hanover. We *succeeded* in getting to know the city a little. Unfortunately we *lacked* the time to see everything.

(iii)   The 'caretaker' **es** can start a sentence, taking the place of the true subject, which then follows it. This may be done for emphasis or to place the main information later in the sentence [➤4e(ii)]. The verb agrees with the true subject (which may be plural), not with **es**. Because it is not the true subject, **es** can be left out if the sentence is re-arranged.

Es fanden manchmal/Manchmal fanden längere Ausflüge statt.	Sometimes longer excursions took place.

(iv) **es** can be used as the caretaker subject of a passive or reflexive verb to refer to an activity in general [➤15e]. Again, **es** is left out if it does not start the sentence.

Es wurde dann/Dann *wurde* viel gegessen und getrunken. *Es isst sich* in manchen deutschen Gaststätten sehr gut.	*There* was then a lot of eating and drinking. *You can eat* very well in many German inns.

(v) **es** or its emphatic alternative **das** is sometimes used as object or complement of the verb in cases where English would omit it or perhaps use 'so'. Note especially *ich* **bin's** 'it's *me*'. etc – in German the subject is always the person referred to, not **es**.

Das habe ich immer geglaubt, jetzt weiß ich *es* aber!	I have always thought *so*, but now I know!

(vi) **es ist/war** etc. + dative is used with idioms referring to feelings and sensations [➤8h].

25f   *Which one? Interrogative pronouns*

These are the question words listed in paragraphs 6d(i) to (iii).

(i)   *Wer?/Wen?/Wem? Was? Wessen ? 'Who(m)? What? Whose?'*

(A) As in English, **Wer/Wen/Wem?** can only refer to people. They have the full range of case usages, including after prepositions, but **Wessen ...?** is now usually replaced by some other construction, such as **Wem gehört ...?** 'Who does ... belong to?'.

Entschuldigen Sie, *wer* ist das da drüben? – *Wen* meinen Sie?	Excuse me, *who* is that over there? – *Who(m)* do you mean?
Wem gehört die Jacke mit dem Lederkragen?	To *whom* belongs the jacket with the leather collar?

(B) Was? has no other forms in current use [➤(D)below].

Das ist Magnus Krössis. *Was* wollen Sie von ihm?	That is Magnus Krössis. *What* do you want with him?

(C) The verb **sein** is plural after **Wer?** and **Was?** if they refer to more than one person or thing.

Und die Leute um ihn – *wer sind* die?	And the people around him – *who are* they?

(D) After most prepositions **Was?** becomes **wo(r)-** + preposition (compare **da(r)-**, ➤25b(iv)).

***Worüber* haben Sie mit Herrn Krössis gesprochen?**	*What* did you and Mr. Krössis talk *about*?

(ii)   Welcher? 'Which one?'

This has the same meaning and endings as its determiner [➤23c(i)].

Ich interessiere mich für einen seiner Leute. – Oh, für *welchen*? Und warum?	I am interested in one of his people. – Oh, *which one*? And why?

(iii)   Was für einer? Was für welche?   'What sort?'

einer is used in the singular, **welche** in the plural. Both have the same endings as **welcher** and the same meaning as the determiner **Was für ein ...?** [➤23c(ii)]. The case of **einer/welche** is decided by their function in the sentence, not by **für**.

Ich bin Berater. – *Was für einer*? – Ich berate Kunden. – Nein wirklich? *Was für welche*? – Reiche Kunden.	I am a consultant. – *What kind (of one)*? – I advise clients. – You don't say! *What sort*? – Rich ones.

25g   Pointing and showing: demonstrative pronouns

Demonstrative pronouns have the same meanings as the corresponding determiners [➤23f]. With the exception of **der** [➤(i) below] they have the same standard case endings [➤23c(i)].

(i) *der, die, das* 'this one', 'that one'

These are the most common demonstrative pronouns. They have the same forms as the definite article [➤23d(ii)].

	Masculine	*Feminine*	*Neuter*	*Plural*
Nominative	der	die	das	die
Accusative	den	die	das	die
Genitive	dessen	deren	dessen	deren
Dative	dem	der	dem	denen

(A) der, die, das is used alone as a more forceful alternative to **er/sie/es**. Its 'pointing' role is often reinforced with **hier** or **da**. The neuter **das** is the general purpose pointing word 'that'.

Und wer ist *die da*? – *Die*? *Das* ist Claudia. *Die* ist wirklich klasse.	And who is *that*? – *Her*?/*That one*? *That's* Claudia. *She's* really great.

(B) Followed by a genitive or **von** + dative noun phrase **der, die, das** translates English '~'s'. They can also be followed by other defining phrases.

Mein Wagen ist eine alte Kiste. Ich habe mir *den* meines Bruders/*den* von Max ausgeliehen.	My car is an old jalopy. I've borrowed my brother*'s*/Max*'s*.

(C) Followed by a relative clause it translates English 'the one(s) who/which ...'.

Claudia unterhält sich gern mit intelligenten Männern – besonders mit *denen*, die schnelle Sportwagen haben.	Claudia likes talking to intelligent men – especially to *those* who have fast sports cars.

(D) When referring to things, **der, die, das** can make **da(r)-** + preposition compounds, like personal pronouns [➤25b(iv)], but with the stress on the **da-**. It does not do this before defining phrases or clauses [➤(B) and (C) above].

Mein eigenes Auto nützt mir nichts – *da*mit komme ich nicht bei ihr an. Aber mit *dem* von Max – wer weiß!	My own car is no good to me – with *that* I'll never get anywhere with her. But with Max*'s* – who knows!

(E) dessen and **deren** can be used instead of the possessives **sein** and **ihr** [➤23h(iii)].

Meine Schwester hat sich gestern lange mit Claudia und *deren* Bruder unterhalten. Hoffentlich hat sie nur Gutes von mir gesagt.	Yesterday my sister talked for a long time with Claudia and *her* (Claudia's) brother. I hope she only spoke well of me.

(ii) The other demonstrative pronouns

These are:

• **dieser** 'this one', **jener, derjenige** 'that one', **derselbe** 'the same one' and **so einer, solche** 'one(s) like that'.
• With the following few exceptions they have the same endings and uses as the corresponding determiners [➤23f].

(A) The short form **dies** 'this' is used to point to things nearby, though **das (hier)** is often used instead.

Dies (Das) hier sind meine Traumwagen.	*These (This)* are my dream cars.

(B) so einer is used in the singular and **solche** in the plural, both with the standard case endings [➤23c(i)]. '... as such' is ...**als solcher**, agreeing with the noun referred to.

Ich bin ein paarmal *solche* Probe gefahren. *So einen* möchte ich haben. Das Auto *als solches* sagt mir wenig – nur seine Wirkung auf andere!	I have test-driven *ones like that* a couple of times. I should like to have *one like that*. The car *as such* means little to me – only its effect on others!

25h How much? How many? Indefinite quantities

Some *quantifiers* refer to the whole or none of something, others to some part or some members of it. All the determiners discussed in paragraph 23g can also be used as pronouns.

The following paragraphs deal with additional points relevant to these pronouns.

(i) *einer* 'one', *keiner* 'none'

These have the standard case endings [➤23c(i)]. **einer** has no plural.

	Masculine	*Feminine*	*Neuter*	*Plural*
Nominative	**einer**	**eine**	**ein(e)s**	**keine**
Accusative	**einen**	**eine**	**ein(e)s**	**keine**
Genitive	**eines**	**einer**	**eines**	**keiner**
Dative	**einem**	**einer**	**einem**	**keinen**

(A) einer usually means 'one of a number', when it is often followed by a genitive plural or a phrase with **von**. It can also mean 'someone' [➤**jemand**, (iii) below].

Einer meiner Söhne ist ein begeisterter Filmfan, aber Kinokarten sind teuer für *einen/ jemand*, der wenig Geld hat.	*One* of my sons is an enthusiastic movie fan, but movie house tickets are expensive for *someone* who doesn't have much money.

(B) keiner is used like **einer**, with the opposite meanings of 'none of ...' and 'no one' [➤**niemand**, (iii) below].

Keine der Lokalzeitungen enthält die Programme für die Großstadt. Keiner (Niemand) im Dorf wusste darüber Bescheid. Wir haben meine Eltern gefragt, aber keiner (der beiden) interessiert sich für Filme.	*None* of the local newspapers gives the program for the city. *No one* in the village knew anything about them. We asked my parents, but *neither* (of the two) is interested in movies.

(C) nicht einer means 'not one', usually implying **... sondern zwei** '... but two' etc. **kein Einziger** is 'not a single one'.

Übers Wochenende hat er *nicht einen*, sondern fünf Fernsehfilme gesehen! Dabei war *kein Einziger* sehenswert.	Over the weekend he watched *not one* but five TV movies! And *not one* was worth watching.

(D) The alternative form **der eine** has a plural **die einen** 'some'. The **ein-** has the **-e/-en** adjective endings [➤24b(ii)]. It usually refers to one of two people or things, or some of a group, often contrasted with **der andere, die anderen** 'the other(s)'.

Mein Sohn hat zweierlei Freunde: *die einen* **teilen seine Filmleidenschaft, die anderen nicht.**	My son has two kinds of friends: *some* share his passion for movies, (the) others do not.

(ii)   ***alles*** *'everything'*, ***alle*** *'everyone'*, ***beides*** *'both things'*, ***beide*** *'both people'*

These all have the standard case endings [➤23c(i)].

(A) The singular **alles** and **beides** generally refer to things and the plural **alle** and **beide** to people.

Alle **mögen aber** *alles*, **was mit Pop zu tun hat. Mein Sohn hat eben eine CD und eine Kassette gekauft.** *Beides* **spielt er unaufhörlich.**	But *they all* like *everything* which has to do with pop. My son has just bought a CD and a cassette. He plays *both* non-stop.

(B) The alternative forms **die beiden** and more emphatic **alle beide** are the usual translations for 'the two (of them)'.

Er hat einen Freund Antonio. *Die beiden/Alle beide* **sind Popfans.**	He has a friend Antonio. *Both/The two of them* are pop fans.

(C) **alles** may be combined with an adjective-noun taking the **-e/-en** endings, to mean 'everything ..., all the ... things'.

Alles Neue **fasziniert sie.**	*Everything new* fascinates them.

(D) The word **alle** is used colloquially to mean 'all gone'.

Sein Geld ist jetzt aber leider *alle*.	Unfortunately his money is now *all gone*.

(iii)   ***jeder*** *'each one, everyone'*

jeder has standard case endings, but no genitive. The more emphatic **ein jeder** 'just anyone, anyone at all' has all the sin-

PRONOUNS 25h

gular cases; the **jeder** (in **ein jeder**) has adjective endings [➤24b(ii)]. **jedermann** 'everyone' is now used only in formal writing and set phrases.

Jeder weiß, dass man so eine **Aufgabe nicht** *einem jeden* **geben kann. Das ist bestimmt nicht** *jedermanns* **Sache.**	*Everyone* knows that you cannot give a job like that to *just anyone*. It certainly isn't *everyone's* thing.

(iv) *jemand* '*someone*', *niemand* '*no one*', *etwas* '*something*', *nichts* '*nothing*'

These do not now usually have case endings, though they are possible with **jemand** and **niemand**. In colloquial speech **etwas** is frequently shortened to **was** and **nichts** pronounced **nix**. **wer** is sometimes used in place of **jemand**.

(A) Adjective-nouns after any of these words have standard neuter singular case endings, though accusative **-en** is also possible after **jemand** and **niemand**.

Niemand Vernünftiges hätte *so was Dummes* gemacht!	*No sensible person* would have done *something so stupid*!

(B) **irgendjemand/etwas** stresses '*just* anyone/anything'.

Hat *irgendjemand* denn *irgendetwas Sinnvolles* gemacht?	Has *anyone at all* done *anything sensible*?

(v) *einiges* '*some things*', *manches* '*quite a lot*', *vieles* '*a lot*', *weniges* '*not much*'

The neuter forms **einiges, manches, vieles** and **weniges** refer to things (to be) done. All but **einiges** are rather formal. The short forms **viel** and **wenig** are more usual.

Wir haben schon *viel(es)* getan – es bleibt aber noch *einiges* zu entscheiden. Mit *manchem* bin ich nicht einverstanden.	We have already done *a lot* – but there are still *some things* to be decided. There is *quite a lot* I don't agree with.

205

NOUNS AND NOUN PHRASES

25i *Belonging together: possessive pronouns*

Possessive pronouns are unique in that they represent two different nouns at once: the 'possessor' and the 'thing possessed'. Like possessive determiners [➤23h], they take their form from the possessor, and their gender and number from the thing possessed. Take care not to confuse the two: one person can own several things, and several people can be joint owners of one thing.

Natürlich sind ihre Hunde bessere Hauswächter als *seine.* **Sein Hundekorb ist bequemer als** *ihrer.*	Of course their dogs are better watchdogs than *his*. His dog basket is more comfortable than *theirs*.

(i) *Use*

The possessive pronouns are the same as the determiners except that they have the full standard endings [➤**einer**, 25h(i)]. In general, their use is similar to English, but note two common exceptions:

Gehört **dieser Hund** *Ihnen*? – **Ja, er** *gehört mir*. **Ein Freund von** *mir* **hat ihn mir gegeben.**	*Is* this dog *yours*? – Yes, it*'s* mine. A friend of *mine* gave it to me.

(ii) *Forms*

There are two alternative forms of possessive pronouns: endingless **mein** etc.; **der meine** etc. In the second, the possessive has the **-e/-en** adjective endings. These forms are used only in elevated style, and then often as nouns.

Ich habe *das Meine* **getan, tun Sie jetzt** *das Ihre*. **Sie verwechseln offenbar** *Mein* **und** *Dein*! **Herzliche Grüße an Sie und** *die Ihren*.	I've done *my bit*, now you do *your bit*. You obviously confuse '*mine*' and '*thine*' (take what is not yours)! Best wishes to you and *yours* (your family).

25j *Relative pronouns*

➤   *Whoever/Whatever it was, ...*: ➤5a(ii).

PRONOUNS **25j**

(i) *Use*

A *relative pronoun* 'relates' or links a noun to a 'relative clause', which always begins with a comma. They have exactly the same forms as the demonstrative pronouns **der, die, das** [➤-25g(i)].

• The clause closely follows the noun and defines it or comments on it [➤5b].

• Because it comes before the clause, the noun is known as the *antecedent*.

• Relative pronouns follow exactly the same rules as other pronouns [➤25a], that is, their gender and number are the same as for the antecedent, but their case depends on their use within the relative clause.

• The examples below show that German can never omit the relative pronoun or put prepositions at the end of the sentence as English often can. The order must always be:

... antecedent (...)**,** (preposition, if any) pronoun ...

Drüben steht *der Mann, der* **unseren Wagen stehlen wollte! – Ist das** *der Wagen, den* **Sie von mir gekauft haben? – Ja,** *der Wagen, mit dem* **wir in Urlaub gefahren sind.**	Over there is *the man who* tried to steal our car! – Is that *the car (which)* you bought from me? – Yes, *the car (which)* we went on vacation *in*.

(ii) *dessen or deren?*

The choice of **dessen** or **deren** for 'whose' depends on whether the antecedent is masculine/neuter (**dessen**) or feminine/plural (**deren**). The noun which follows has no effect on this at all. Any adjectives in the phrase have the standard case endings [➤24b(ii)B].

Gestern bin ich einem Bekannten begegnet, *dessen* **älteste Tochter Petra in meiner Klasse war. Wir waren in der Buchhandlung, mit** *deren* **neuem Besitzer ich befreundet bin.**	Yesterday I happened to meet a man I know *whose* eldest daughter Petra was in my class. We were in the bookstore, *whose* new owner I am friendly with.

207

(iii) A relative clause may be separated from its antecedent, especially by verbs at the end of the clause, but it should follow as soon as possible.

Die arme Petra ist von einem Lastwagen angefahren worden, der bei Rot durch die Ampel gefahren ist.	Poor Petra was hit by a *truck* *which* drove through a red light.

(iv) ***welcher*** *as a relative pronoun*

welcher, etc. sometimes replaces **der,** etc. in formal writing.

Fahrer, *welche* (die) sich so benehmen, sollten ihren Führerschein verlieren.	Drivers *who* behave like that should lose their driver's license.

(v) ***wer*** *'anyone who',* ***was*** *'what'*

wer and **was** can be used to mean 'anyone who' and 'what'. They normally begin the sentence. They may be picked up by **der** and **das** etc. in the main clause; this must be done if the **der/das** is in a different case from the **wer/was**. **was** may also have **das** as its antecedent.

***Wer* so handelt, mit *dem* will ich nichts zu tun haben/(*der*) ist zu allem fähig. (*Das,*) *Was* er getan hat, *dafür* muss er büßen/ist mir unbegreiflich.**	*Someone who* acts like that I won't have anything to do with/is capable of anything. *What* he did he will have to pay for/is incomprehensible to me.

(vi) ***was*** *as a relative pronoun*

was is used as a relative pronoun in several instances. Note the different English equivalents [➤also (v) above and (vii) below]:

(A) when it refers back to the whole idea expressed in the preceding sentence:

Manfred erscheint nie pünktlich zur Arbeit, *was* seinen Chef sehr böse macht.	Manfred never appears on time for work, *which* makes his boss very angry.

(B) when the antecedent is a neuter pronoun or neuter adjective-noun [➤24d(iii)]:

Er vergisst *alles, was* man ihm sagt.	He forgets *everything (which)* you tell him.
Er hat auch *etwas Seltsames* an sich, *was* uns alle misstrauisch stimmt. Er ist aber gutmütig – das ist *das Beste, was* man von ihm sagen kann.	He also has *something strange* about him *which* makes us all mistrustful. But he is good-natured – that's *the best (which)* you can say of him.

wer and **was** can never be used instead of **der** and **das** as normal relative pronouns. Their commonest use is to ask the questions **wer?** 'who?' and **was?** 'what?' [➤25f(i)].

(vii) Prepositions + relative pronouns referring to things may contract to one word: **wo(r)-** + preposition [➤25f(i)]. This is now little used even in formal writing. **wo(r)-** compounds are, however, normal when the pronoun is **was** [➤(vi) above].

Manfred scheint immer Geld zu haben, *worüber* ich mich sehr wundere.	Manfred always seems to have money, *about which* I am very surprised.

(viii) *Alternatives to relative clauses*

German relative clauses can be rather clumsy constructions. Perhaps for this reason, they are much less used in speech than they are in French or English, though they are common enough in writing. A favorite alternative is the identical demonstrative **der, die, das** with a main clause, though there are others.

Wir waren alle da außer Greta, *die* verreist war. or	We were all there except Greta, *who* had gone away. or
... außer Greta. *Die* war verreist.	... except Greta. *She* had gone away.
Es war schade um Greta, *deren* Sprachkenntnisse uns nützlich gewesen wären. or	It was a pity about Greta, *whose* knowledge of languages would have been useful to us. or

| ... um Greta. *Ihre* Sprachkenntnisse wären uns nützlich gewesen. | ...about Greta. *Her* knowledge of languages would have been useful to us. |

Note A relative clause cannot be replaced in this way if it defines the antecedent rather than just adding a comment.

| Greta ist die Frau, *die* letztes Jahr bei uns gewohnt hat. | Greta is the woman *who* stayed with us last year. |

25k   *Natural and grammatical gender: problems of agreement*

There are some nouns whose gender is different from the sex of the person they refer to. Most of these are neuter diminutives ending in **-chen** or **-lein**, but there are other examples [►20b(iv)]. If a pronoun referring to one of these nouns stands close to it, then the grammatical gender tends to be used; with relative pronouns this always happens. The further a pronoun is from its noun, the more the natural gender is likely to reassert itself.

| Plötzlich erblickte mich *das* Mädchen, *das* ich im Café gesehen hatte. *Es/Sie* kam zu mir herüber, und wir unterhielten uns eine Zeit lang. Dann fragte ich *sie*, wo *sie* wohne. | Suddenly the girl (*that*) I had seen in the café spotted me. *She* came over to me and we talked for a while. Then I asked *her* where *she* lived. |

26 Giving vent to your feelings: exclamations and interjections

26a   *Exclamations*

Exclamations express strongly felt wishes or emotions. Very often they are not complete sentences, though it is always obvious what the rest of the sentence might be. In writing they end with an exclamation point.

(i)   *Addition of modal particles for emphasis*

Said with force, almost any utterance can be an exclamation. One or more modal particles are often used to add emphasis, especially **aber, bloß, doch, erst, ja, nur** [➤29c(iii)].

Du bist mir *aber/vielleicht* einer!	You're a real/right one!
Das ist *doch/ja* die Höhe!	That really is the limit!

(ii)   *Expressing emotions*

welcher ...!, **was für (ein) ...!** 'what (a)' + noun phrase, and **wie ...!** 'how' + adjective or adverb express emotions such as delight, anger, surprise or fear. **was für** is more used colloquially than **welcher**. Unlike when the same words are used as questions [➤ch.6], if a verb is used, it is put at the end.

Was für/Welches Wetter! Wie heiß/kalt es ist!	*What* weather! How hot/cold it is!
Was für ein seltsamer Kerl! Was für wilde Augen er hat! Wie mager er doch/ja ist!	*What* a strange fellow! *What* wild eyes he has! *How* thin he is!

(iii)   *If only*

'If only!' wishes are often expressed by a free-standing conditional clause, either a **wenn** clause with the verb at the end or a clause starting with the conditional. [Simple conditional vs. **würde** + infinitive: ➤14d Note.]

| Wenn er *bloß/doch/nur/erst* anrufen würde! | *If only* he would call/ring up! |
| Hätte ich *nur* mehr Zeit! Wäre ich *bloß* nicht so beschäftigt! Könnte ich *erst* früher nach Hause! | *If only* I had more time! *If only* I were not so busy! *If* I could *only go* home earlier! |

(iv)   *Another way of expressing a wish*

Freestanding **zu** + infinitive clauses can also express wishes.

| Ach, immer hier *zu bleiben*! Nie wieder ins Büro gehen *zu müssen*! | Oh *to remain* here always! Never again *to have* to go to the office! |

26b   *Interjections*

Interjections range from words or short phrases, which are really cutdown exclamations through standard noises associated with various emotions, to whatever may be wrung from you in the heat of the moment. This is an area where non-native speakers need to be cautious – there is always the risk of making yourself ridiculous or causing offense.

Note   Interjections do not count in the word order of any following sentence.

(i)   *Addressing people*

Frau Biel, Sie haben den ersten Preis gewonnen!	Mrs. Biel, you have won first prize!
Martin, wir sind reich!	Martin, we're rich!
Sie da! Was machen Sie da?	You there! What are you up to?

(ii)   *Agreeing and disagreeing*

Ja! Nein!	Yes! No!
Doch!	Yes I have/do/am! (contradicting negatives)
Stimmt! Klar!	True! I agree!

(iii) *General emphasis*

Abgemacht!	Agreed/Done!
Aber, aber! Was ist hier los?	Now, now! What's going on here?
Leute, wir fahren in fünf	Hey folks, we're leaving in five
Minuten los!	minutes!
Mensch, was machst du nur?	Man, just what are you doing?
Mensch, (da) habe ich mich	Boy, was I wrong/angry!
aber getäuscht/geärgert!	

(iv) *Warning*

Aufpassen/Aufgepasst!	Look out! Careful!
Vorsicht!	

(v) *Startled surprise*

Du liebe Zeit!	Hell's bells!
Ach, du heiliger Bimbam!	Good heavens!
Auwei!	Oh dear!

(vi) *Swearwords*

Scheiße! is probably the most used, even by people who would avoid its English equivalent.

Scheiße! Verdammt/Verflucht	Shit! Damn(ation)!
(noch mal)!	
Verflixt! Diese	Blast! This damned/blasted
verdammte/verflixte Maschine!	machine!

E

LINKING AND MODIFYING MEANINGS: PREPOSITIONS AND ADVERBIAL EXPRESSIONS

27   Linking noun phrases into the sentence: prepositions

28   Types of adverbial expressions

29   What adverbial expressions do

27 Linking noun phrases into the sentence: prepositions

27a What does a preposition do?

A *preposition* is a connecting word. It links the noun phrase which follows it to various other parts of the sentence. This chapter deals mainly with the cases which follow German prepositions. The various links which prepositions can make are discussed in the following paragraphs:

➤ *With* a quick movement I put my hand in my pocket: adverbial phrases ➤28a.
I was relying *on* bluff: linking verbs to noun phrases ➤8g.
His reaction *to* my action was to draw a knife: linking two noun phrases ➤19h.
He tried to stab me *with* it: prepositions + pronouns referring to things (**da(r)**- compounds) ➤25b(iv).
He was pale *with* fury: linking adjectives to noun phrases ➤24g(ii).

27b Prepositions and the cases they take

German prepositions can be grouped by the case of the noun phrase which they govern. The following paragraphs list only the more commonly used prepositions. Note that a few sometimes follow the noun phrase.

(i) Prepositions followed by the accusative

Six common prepositions are always followed by the accusative:

• **bis** 'until, as far as, up to; by (a deadline)'. Always used with another preposition of motion except before place names, adverbs, and time phrases starting with a noun or a numeral (or equivalent).

Bis 1962 **wohnte ich in der DDR (Deutsche Demokratische Republik).** *Bis nächsten Freitag* **muss ich einen Artikel darüber fertig haben.**	*Until 1962* I lived in the GDR (German Democratic Republic). *By next Friday* I have to have an article on it finished.

• **durch** 'through'. Also 'across' (especially after **quer** 'crosswise') and 'throughout', often combined with **hindurch**.

| Damals lief die innerdeutsche Grenze mitten *durch unser Dorf.* | In those days the inner-German border ran *through* the middle of *our village.* |

durch 'by (means of)' shows how something happened [➤passive15c]. Hence **dadurch** 'thereby, by that means'.

| *Durch diese Grenze/Dadurch* wurde das Dorf entzweigerissen. | The village was torn apart *by this border/by it.* |

• **für** 'for'. With periods of time **für** means 'for ... in all' [➤(ii) below, **seit**]. Note **dafür** 'but (to make up for it)'.

| Das war *für uns alle* eine traurige Zeit. Nicht einmal *für einige Stunden* durften wir die Verwandten im Westen besuchen. | That was a sad time *for us all*. We couldn't visit our relatives in the west even *for a few hours.* |

• **gegen** 'against, towards; (at) about (numbers, time)'. With motion it tends to imply forceful contact.

| An einem Oktobertag *gegen Mittag* bin ich mit einem Traktor *gegen die Grenzsperre* gekracht und bin durchgekommen. | One October day *at about midday* I crashed a tractor *into the border barrier* and got through. |

gegen 'in exchange for; compared to'. Note **dagegen** 'but (on the other hand)'.

| Ich hatte mein ganzes Hab und Gut *gegen den Traktor* getauscht. | I had traded all my wordly goods *for the tractor.* |

• **ohne** 'without'. Often used without **ein** or a possessive where English would use one. **ohne** cannot form **da(r)**-compounds [➤25b(iv)], but it can be followed by a clause [➤27c].

PREPOSITIONS AND ADVERBIAL EXPRESSIONS

Ohne Traktor/Ohne ihn **hätte ich es nie geschafft.**	*Without a tractor/Without it* I would never have managed it.

• **um** 'round; at (clock time)'. With other time phrases it means 'around', often strengthened with following **herum**.

Schon *um Viertel nach zwölf* **war das ganze Dorf** *um mich* **versammelt.**	Already *at (a) quarter past twelve* the whole village was gathered *around me*.

um 'by, at (so much); concerning'. Note **darum** 'for that reason, that's why' and **um ... zu** + infinitive 'in order to ...' [➤27c].

Ich wollte *um jeden Preis* **bleiben. Es ging ja** *um meine Freiheit*.	I wanted to stay *at any cost*. After all, it was a matter *of my freedom*.

(ii) *Prepositions followed by the dative*

Nine common prepositions are always followed by the dative:

• **aus** 'out of (places and motives), made of (materials)'.

Als ich *aus dem Haus* **kam, sah ich einen großen Schlüssel** *aus Messing* **auf dem Bürgersteig.**	When I came *out of the house* I saw a large key *made of brass* on the sidewalk.

aus also describes causes and motives.

Aus Neugier **hob ich ihn auf.**	*Out of curiosity* I picked it up.

• **außer** 'except, apart from'.

Außer einem kleinen Kind **war niemand zu sehen.**	*Apart from a small child* there was nobody to be seen.

außer means 'out of, beyond' in certain expressions.

Der Geldautomat war *außer Betrieb*. **Ich war** *außer mir* **vor Wut.**	The cash machine/automatic teller was *out of order*. I was *beside myself* with rage.

- **bei** 'near to, at the house/shop of'.

Beim Apotheker wollte ich Aspirin kaufen. Da sah ich das Kind *bei* der Tür stehen.	I wanted to buy some aspirin *at the pharmacist's*. Then I saw the child standing *by* the door.

bei often indicates the background to something. **beim** + infinitive noun means 'while ~ing' [►10a(iii)]. Note **dabei**, with its many idiomatic usages.

Bei heißem Wetter bekomme ich oft Kopfschmerzen. *Bei dieser Gelegenheit* waren sie besonders stark. *Beim Zahlen* konnte ich die Münzen kaum sehen.	*In hot weather* I often get a headache. *On this occasion* it was particularly severe. *As I was paying* I could hardly see the coins.

- **gegenüber** 'opposite'. Always follows a pronoun. It can follow nouns, especially people, but more usually it precedes them.

Mir gegenüber stand eine ältere Frau, die *gegenüber der Apotheke* wohnte.	*Opposite me* stood an elderly woman, who lived *opposite the pharmacy*.

gegenüber '(in relation) to, in the face of'.

Meiner Familie gegenüber war sie immer sehr nett gewesen.	She had always been very nice *to my family*.

- **mit** 'with, at (the age of)'. [**damit** 'so that' ►5a(ii)].

Mit 40 Jahren hatte Sie ihren Mann verloren. Ich sprach einen Augenblick *mit ihr*.	She had lost her husband *at the age of 40*. I spoke *with/to her* for a moment.

mit 'by using ...' is more widely used than the English 'with', for example, for means of transport and parts of the body.

Ich wollte dann *mit dem Bus* nach Pasing fahren. Beim Einsteigen stieß ich *mit dem Kopf* gegen die Tür.	Then I wanted to go *by bus* to Pasing. As I was getting in I bumped *my head* against the door.

219

PREPOSITIONS AND ADVERBIAL EXPRESSIONS

- **nach** 'after (time)'. In the sense of 'following after' **nach** is used as a verbal particle [➤16e(ii)].

Nach einer Weile sah ich, dass Frau Gruber *mir nachgekommen* war.	*After a while* I saw that Mrs. Gruber had *followed me*.

nach 'to (a place)'. Used with towns and countries without articles [➤19e(i)], and adverbs. Note also **nach Hause** '(to) home' ['at home' ➤**zu** below].

Sie war ganz *nach hinten* gegangen. Ob sie auch *nach Pasing* (fahren) wollte?	She had gone all the way *to the back*. Did she also want to go *to Pasing*?

nach 'according to, judging by'. In certain phrases **nach** may follow the noun phrase.

Nach meiner Ansicht/Meinung benahm sie sich sehr seltsam.	*In my view/opinion* she was behaving very strangely.

- **seit** 'since, for (time)'. Refers to a period leading up to the time spoken of [➤12a(iv)]; compare **für** [➤(i) above].

Seit einiger Zeit folgte sie mir überall hin.	*For some time* she had been following me around everywhere.

- **von** 'from; of; by'. Often used to replace the genitive [➤22e], and with the passive [➤15c].

Dabei hatte ich aber nur Gutes *von ihr* gehört. Ich war *von der ganzen Sache* ziemlich verwirrt. Da sah ich *vom Busfenster aus*, dass wir in Pasing waren.	All the same, I had only heard good *of her*. I was pretty confused *by the whole affair*. Then I saw *from the bus window* that we were in Pasing.

- **zu** 'to (place, person)', but note **zu Hause** 'at home'.

Vom Bus ging ich direkt *zur Post*.	From the bus I went straight *to the post office*.

Da trat Frau Gruber ein und kam *zu mir* **herüber.**	Then Mrs. Gruber entered and came over *to me*.

zu 'for (purpose), to (effect), (made) into' and many other idiomatic usages.

Zu meinem Erstaunen **sagte sie** *zu mir*: „Polizei! Darf ich fragen, *wozu/zu welchem Zweck* **Sie den Schlüssel da gebrauchen wollen?"** – „*Zu keinem*!" **erwiderte ich. „Ich habe ihn gefunden. Das macht mich doch nicht** *zu einem Verbrecher*!"	*To my astonishment* she said *to me*: "Police! May I ask *what/what purpose* you are going to use that key *for*?" – "*(For) none*!" I replied. "I found it. That doesn't make me *(into) a thief*!"

(iii) *Prepositions followed by either the dative or the accusative*

Some prepositions are followed by the accusative to show movement into a position and by the dative to show the position itself. The dative is thus often the result of the accusative.

(A) The accusative is only used for movement to the position mentioned. The dative is used, for example, for walking along, behind, next to or between other people (often followed by **her**), running up and down between two objects, or flying around over a place.

(B) With a number of verbs, the accusative is used if the movement is emphasized, the dative if the position is uppermost in the speaker's mind. For example:

Accusative	
Maria hielt die Hand an *den* **Mund. Sie klopfte heftig an** *das* **Fenster.**	Maria held her hand to her mouth. She knocked hard on the window.
Dative	
Der Einbrecher hielt eine Taschenlampe in *der* **Hand. Da klopfte es an** *der* **Tür.**	The burglar was holding a flashlight in his hand. Then there was a knock at the door.

(C) In a few instances this leads to prepositions taking the accusative after the simple verb but the dative when the verb is linked to a verbal particle [➤16e(ii)]. For example:

PREPOSITIONS AND ADVERBIAL EXPRESSIONS

Beim Einkaufen *binde* **ich immer meinen Hund** *an eine* **Laterne.** /*... an einer* **Laterne** *an/fest.*	When I am shopping I always tie my dog (*on*)*to* a streetlamp.
Ich habe Ihre Zeichnung *an die* **Küchentür gehängt.**/*... an der* **Küchentür** *auf*gehängt.	I have hung your drawing (*up*) on the kitchen door.
Ich möchte mich lieber *auf das* **Sofa legen/setzen.**/*... auf dem* **Sofa** *hin*legen/*hin*setzen.	I should prefer to lie/sit down on the sofa.
Ich habe Ihre Namen *in mein* **Notizuch geschrieben.**/*... in meinem* **Buch** *auf*geschrieben.	I have written your names (*down*) in my notebook.

(D) If there is no reference to place, then **auf** and **über** are used with the accusative, the others normally with the dative.

(E) The accusative is normal with:

Ich baue/schließe an ... an.	I build/add onto ...
Ich beuge mich über ...	I bend over ...
Es grenzt an ...	It borders on ...
Es mündet in ...	It flows into ...
Ich schreibe es in ... (ein)	I write it in(to) ...
Ich sehe/blicke auf ...	I look/glance at ...
Ich stütze mich auf ...	I lean on ...
Ich verteile es an ...	I distribute it to ...
Ich bin in ... vertieft/verwickelt.	I am engrossed/involved in ...

(F) The dative is normal with all verbs of arriving and (dis)appearing, and with:

Ich befestige es an ...	I fasten it to ...
Ich bringe es an ... an .	I attach it to ...
Ich drucke es auf/in ...	I print it on/in ...
Ich notiere es in ...	I note it down in ...

(G) There are 10 common prepositions which may take either the accusative or the dative according to the rules described above. In the examples the accusative usages are in italics.

• **an** 'on (a vertical surface), by, at'.

Der Leiter des Jugendwettlaufs stand vorne am Tisch und heftete eine große Karte *an die Wand.*	The organizer of the youth competition stood at the table at the front and pinned a large map *to the wall.*

- **auf** 'on (a horizontal surface), at'. Note the use of **auf** + certain public places: **auf der Straße/dem Platz/dem Bahnhof** 'in the street/square/station'.

„So, Leute!", sagte er, „Wir fahren gleich *aufs Land*. Der Start ist auf dem Unterdorfer Kirchplatz.

"Right, folks!" he said, "We're driving *to the country shortly*. The start is in the Unterdorf church square.

- **entlang** 'along' + accusative describes movement alongside or down the middle of something. Here **entlang** follows the noun phrase.

Ihr lauft zunächst *den Waldrand entlang*.

First you run *along the edge of the woods*.

entlang 'along' + dative describes position alongside something. Here **entlang** precedes the noun phrase.

Vorsicht! Entlang dem Pfad ist ein Stacheldrahtzaun.

Watch out! Alongside the path there is a barbed wire fence.

an + dative + **entlang** is a common alternative for either motion or position alongside something.

Ihr lauft weiter am Zaun entlang auf eine kleine Hütte zu.

You go on running along beside the fence towards a small hut.

- **hinter** 'behind, beyond'. Note **hinter** + dative + **her** '(running/shouting) after ..., (walking) behind ...'.

Geht *hinter die Hütte*. Hinter der Hütte hängen nummerierte Zettel an einem Nagel.

Go *behind the hut*. Behind the hut there are numbered tickets hanging on a nail.

- **in** 'in'. With periods of time **in** + dative means 'after (so long from now)'. Note also **im Radio/Fernsehen** 'on radio/television', **im 4. Stock** 'on the 4th floor'.

Bald biegt der Pfad links *in den Wald* ein. Im Wald wird er sehr schmal.

Soon the path turns left *into the woods*. In the woods it gets very narrow.

- **neben** 'next to'. **neben** + dative can mean 'apart from' or 'compared to'.

Die nächsten Nummern findet ihr neben einer hohen Eiche. Ihr müsst euch dicht *neben die Eiche* stellen, um sie zu sehen.	You will find the next numbers next to a tall oak tree. You'll have to go and stand right *next to the oak* to see them.

- **über** 'across, over, above'.

Der Weg führt weiter *über eine schmale Holzbrücke*. Über der Brücke weht eine grünweiße Fahne.	The path leads on *across a narrow wooden bridge*. A green and white flag is flying over the bridge.

über + accusative can mean 'about (concerning)' or 'more than (a quantity)'.

***Über diese Fahne* haben wir schon gesprochen. Sie ist *über drei Meter* lang.**	We've already spoken *about this flag*. It is *over three meters* long.

- **unter** 'under, among, less than (a quantity)'.

Die Zettel liegen unter einem großen Stein verborgen. Ihr braucht nur die Hand *unter den Stein* zu stecken.	The tickets are lying hidden under a large stone. You only need to stick your hand *under the stone*.

- **vor** 'in front of'. Note **vor mich/sich hin** 'to myself/oneself'.

Links vor der Ziellinie sitzt die Schiedsrichterin. Ihr legt eure Zettel *vor die Richterin* auf den Tisch.	The umpire will be sitting in front of the finishing line on the left. You put your tickets on the table *in front of the umpire*.

vor + a dative time phrase means 'ago'.

Vor einem Jahr haben mehrere vergessen, das zu tun.	A year ago several people forgot to do that.

• **zwischen** 'between'.

Für das Schlussfoto sitzt ihr zwischen euren Eltern. Setzt euch also *zwischen eure Eltern.*"	For the final photo, you'll be sitting between your parents. So go and sit down *between your parents.*"

(iv)   *Prepositions followed by the genitive*

Many prepositions are followed by the genitive, but only a few are used outside formal, especially official, writing. The following are in common use, but even here some other phrasing is often preferred.

• **(an)statt** 'instead of'. The longer form is more formal.

Gestern haben Sie uns *statt der richtigen Stärke* 2,5-Millimeter-Blech geliefert.	Yesterday you delivered 2.5-millimeter sheet metal to us, *instead of the correct gauge.*

• **trotz** 'in spite of, despite'.

***Trotz unserer ausdrücklichen Anforderung* ist das jetzt zum dritten Mal geschehen.**	*In spite of our explicit request,* this is now the third time this has happened.

• **während** 'during'.

Der Fehler ist erst *während der Verarbeitung* entdeckt worden, als eine Maschine klemmte.	The error was only detected *during processing*, when a machine jammed.

• **wegen** 'because of'.

***Wegen dieses Fehlers* hat die Maschine einen schweren Schaden erlitten.**	*Because of this error,* the machine suffered severe damage.

• Eight prepositions of place also take the genitive. The four **-halb** prepositions are probably used more than the others.

außerhalb	outside	**diesseits/jenseits**	on this/that side of
beiderseits	on both sides of	**innerhalb**	inside

oberhalb	above	**unweit**	not far from
unterhalb	below		

27c Prepositions followed by clauses

The prepositions listed below can be followed by a **zu** + infinitive clause. If there is a change of subject, **außer**, **statt** and **ohne** can be followed by a **dass** clause. The equivalent for **um ... zu** is **damit** 'so that' [➤5a(ii)]; do not confuse this with **damit** 'with it' [➤25b(iv)].

• **außer** 'apart from'.

Außer jede Sendung extra *zu* messen, wissen wir nicht, was wir noch tun können. *Außer dass* die Reparatur teuer sein wird, verlieren wir auch Zeit.	*Apart from* measuring every delivery specially, we do not know what else we can do. *Apart from the fact that* the repair will be expensive, we are also losing time.

• **ohne** 'without'.

Ohne die Maschine auseinander *zu* nehmen, ...
Ohne dass diese Maschine in Betrieb ist, ...
    ... können wir nicht weiterproduzieren.
	Without taking apart the machine ...
	Without this machine being in operation ...
	    ... we cannot go on producing.

• **(an)statt** 'instead of'.

Statt einen neuen Lieferanten *zu* suchen, ...
Statt dass eine andere Firma uns versorgt, ...
    ... möchten wir lieber bei Ihnen bleiben.
	Instead of looking for a new supplier, ...
	Instead of another firm supplying us, ...
	    ... we would rather remain with you.

• **um** 'in order to'.

Um bei Ihnen **zu** bleiben, ...	*In order to* stay with you, ...
Damit unsere Produktion nicht leidet, ...	*So that* our production does not suffer, ...
... **brauchen wir Ihre Kooperation.**	... we need your cooperation.

28 Types of adverbial expression

➤ We *often* went *by bus to the seaside:* order of adverbials in the sentence ➤4c(ii).

28a What is an adverbial expression?

Adverbial expressions (often shortened to '*adverbials*') mainly answer the questions listed in paragraphs 6d(v) to (ix). We say that they 'modify' meanings, because they complete, alter or even contradict them. There are three types of adverbials: adverbs, adverbial phrases and adverbial clauses. They all play the same part in the sentence – you can often say the same thing using any one of them.

Vorher ...	*Beforehand ...*	(adverb)
Vor der Konferenz ...	*Before the meeting ...*	(phrase)
Bevor die Konferenz		
angefangen hatte, ...	*Before the meeting started ...*	(clause)
... hatte ich mit meiner Chefin gesprochen.	... I had spoken to my boss.	

28b Adverbs

These are single word expressions, of various types.

(i) Adverbs formed from adjectives [➤ch.24]

Most of these adverbs answer the question **Wie?** 'How?', though they can answer other questions. German has no special adverb suffix like the English '-ly', so these adverbs are the same as the adjective, without any ending. (Some English adverbs are also like this, for example 'fast' and 'late'.)

Ich hatte einen *dringend* gebrauchten Bericht *äußerst schnell* und nicht sehr *gut* verfasst.	I had written an *urgently* needed report *extremely fast* and not very well.

Adverbs can be formed from many adjectives by adding **-erweise**. These express the speaker's attitude to the event described [➤29b(iii)].

Glücklicherweise war die Chefin
an dem Tag abwesend, aber
dummerweise habe ich den
Bericht datiert.

Fortunately the boss was absent
on that day, but *foolishly* I dated
the report.

➤ We talk fast but he talks *faster/fastest* of all: comparatives and superlatives ➤24e.

(ii) Adverbs formed from nouns and verbs

The ending **-(s)weise** can be added to many noun and verb stems, mostly to express the sense of 'as a ~, in ~s, by ~'.

paarweise/gruppenweise/ massenweise	in pairs/groups/masses
ausnahmsweise/beispielsweise	as an exception/example
pfundweise/stückweise/ stundenweise	by the pound/ piece (piecemeal)/hour
teilweise/versuchsweise/ zeitweise	partly/experimentally/temporarily
beziehungsweise (often shortened *to* **bzw.**)	or, and ... respectively

Note These adverbs are increasingly used as adjectives, but only with nouns which describe a *process*, many of them formed from verbs.

eine teilweise Verbesserung	a partial improvement
schrittweise Fortschritte	gradual progress
massenweiser Protest	massive protest

(iii) Other adverbs

Many of the most common adverbs, especially those answering the questions **Wann?** 'When?' and **Wo?** 'Where?', are not formed from adjectives. These are dealt with in paragraph 29b(ii).

28c Adverbial phrases

Sometimes a noun phrase [➤19b] acts as an adverbial, as in **er redet *die ganze Zeit*** 'he talks *the whole time*', but most *adverbial phrases* begin with a preposition [➤ch.27 for full details].

PREPOSITIONS AND ADVERBIAL EXPRESSIONS

Auf den ersten Blick hat die Chefin gesehen, dass der Bericht *in aller Eile* verfasst und lange *nach dem Termin* eingeschickt worden war.	*At first glance* the boss saw that the report had been written *in great haste* and sent in well *after the deadline.*

28d   Adverbial clauses

Unlike the phrases, adverbial clauses contain a main verb and are introduced by a subordinating conjunction [➤5a(ii)].

Als sie nach mir geschickt hat, hatte ich ziemlich Angst, *weil sie Unpünktlichkeit hasst.*	*When she sent for me,* I was quite scared, *because she hates tardyness.*

29 What adverbial expressions do

29a The role of adverbs in German

German makes very extensive use of adverbs, often in expressions where English or French would normally use a verb. This is especially true of *nuance adverbs* like **ja, doch, wohl** [➤29c(iii)] and of adverbs which express a general attitude [➤29b(iii)].

Ich schwimme *gern*, aber ich spiele *lieber* Handball. *Allerdings* spiele ich nicht sehr gut. Ich bin *wohl* zu klein. Dafür kann ich *leider* wenig.	I *like* swimming but I *prefer* playing handball. *I must admit that* I don't play very well. *I suppose* I'm too small. *I'm afraid* there is not much I can do about that.

29b What do adverbials affect?

An adverbial expression may affect, or 'modify', the meaning of a verb, an adjective or the whole sentence.

(i) Adverbials modifying verbs

Adverbials modify verbs by supplying further information about the action or situation described, for example when, where, how or why it happened.

Ich will fit bleiben, *also* spiele ich *im Winter jeden Mittwoch im Freizeitzentrum* Handball.	I want to stay fit, *so in winter* I play handball *every Wednesday in the leisure center.*

(ii) Adverbs modifying adjectives and other adverbs

Adverbs which modify adjectives and other adverbs generally answer the question 'How?', though there are other types.

Ich spiele *höchst* energisch aber *nicht sehr* geschickt.	I play *extremely* energetically but *not very* skillfully.

PREPOSITIONS AND ADVERBIAL EXPRESSIONS

Meine *meist* älteren Mitspieler sind *gleich* ungeschickt. Nach *nur* wenigen Minuten sind einige *erstaunlich* müde.	My *mainly* older teammates are *equally* unskilled. After *only* a few minutes some are *astonishingly* tired.

(iii) Adverbs expressing an attitude

Some adverbs express an attitude to the whole statement [➤also 28b(i)]. For example:

allerdings/freilich/zwar	admittedly
angeblich	allegedly
bestimmt	certainly
gern/lieber	like/prefer [➤24e(i)]
hoffentlich	I/we hope that
leider	I'm afraid, unfortunately
möglicherweise	possibly
natürlich	of course, naturally
ruhig	by all means
vielleicht	perhaps
zufällig	by chance

29c What effect do adverbials have?

(i) Negative adverbs

nicht 'not' is by far the commonest negative. It is used very much as in English, but 'not a/not any' is normally **kein** [➤23g(ii)], and 'not anywhere, not ever' etc. is **nirgendwo, nie** 'nowhere, never' etc. [➤(ii) below]. Here are some common negative expressions:

(gar) nicht	not (at all)	**nicht mehr**	no longer
auch nicht	not ... either	**keineswegs**	not at all
nicht einmal	not even		

(ii) Adverbial expressions which answer questions

The question-words in paragraphs 6d(v) to (ix) are themselves adverbs. Each question-word has a corresponding group of adverbials.

Die Konferenz findet *morgen früh um halb neun* statt, *bevor wir nach Frankfurt fliegen.* (*Wann?*)	The meeting is *tomorrow morning at half past eight, before we leave for Frankfurt.* (*When?*)

Sie wurde *in aller Eile* arrangiert.	It was arranged *very hurriedly*.
Das Personal ist *telefonisch* informiert worden. (*Wie?*)	The staff has been notified *by phone*. (*How?*)
Sie wird *hier* stattfinden, *im Büro des Personalleiters*. (*Wo?*)	It will take place *here, in the personnel manager's office*. (*Where?*)
Unsere Vertreter kommen *aus ganz Europa*. (*Woher?*)	Our reps are coming *from all over Europe*. (*Where from?*)
Ich bedauere *sehr*, dass Sie nicht dabei sein werden. Es ist *äußerst* ärgerlich. (*Wie (sehr)?*)	I *very much* regret that you won't be there. It is *extremely* annoying. (*How (much)?*)
Frau Dr. Kraus kann nicht kommen, *weil sie krank ist*. Ich habe *also* ihren Stellvertreter eingeladen. (*Warum?*)	Dr. Kraus cannot come *because she is ill, so* I have invited her deputy. (*Why?*)

These are some of the commonly used adverbs which answer these same questions. Note how many are in fact compounds of other parts of speech, for example, **zuletzt, umsonst, überall, gleichfalls, beinahe**.

(A) Wann? 'When?': time. There are a large number of these.

erst mal/zuerst	first of all
dann	then (next)
zunächst	at first
zuletzt	in the end
damals	then (at that time)
jetzt	now
bald	soon
oft	often
manchmal	sometimes
selten	seldom
immer	always
nie(mals)	never
noch immer	still
noch nicht	not yet
schon	already
erst	not until, only
heute	today
heute früh/Abend	this morning/evening
(vor)gestern	(the day before) yesterday

(über)morgen	(the day after) tomorrow
heutzutage	nowadays
sofort/(so)gleich	at once, immediately
neulich/vor kurzem	recently

(B) Wie? 'How?': manner, methods, means. This is a very broad group, which includes most adverbs made from adjectives [➤28b(i)] and phrases answering questions like **Mit wem?** 'With whom?' and **Womit?** 'With what?'. See also the adverbs which express an attitude to the whole statement [➤29b(iii)]. Other adverbs include:

ebenfalls/gleichfalls	likewise
rundheraus	bluntly
sonst	otherwise
unversehens	by mistake
umsonst/vergebens	in vain

(C) Wo? 'Where?': place. Adverbs of place are often used with prepositions like **auf** or **in** where English would have 'at the top of ...' etc.

hier	here
dort	there
da	there, here
oben/unten	at the top/bottom, upstairs/downstairs
vorne/ hinten	at the front/back
außen/innen	on the outside/inside
draußen/drinnen	outside/inside
mitten	in the middle
überall	everywhere
irgendwo	anywhere
nirgendwo/nirgends	nowhere
anderswo/woanders	somewhere else
oben auf dem Haufen	at the top of the pile
draußen vor der Tür	outside the door
mitten im Wald	in the middle of the woods

(D) Wohin? Woher? 'Where to? Where from?': direction. **hin/her** combine with adverbs of place [➤(C) above] to make adverbs of movement away from/towards the speaker. They are also used by themselves after prepositional phrases to emphasize the direction. Note the use of **von/nach oben** etc. to indicate motion from or towards a position.

| hierher | (to) here |
| dahin | (to) there, away |

dorther	from there
dorthin	(to) there
irgendwoher	from anywhere
anderswohin	(to) somewhere else
von unten her	from below
nach vorne hin	up to the front
zum See hin	to the lake
von der Gaststätte her	from the inn

(E) **Wie ... ?** 'How ... ?': degree. Adverbs of degree usually modify adjectives or other adverbs. Many of those made from adjectives are colloquial and are used mainly by certain groups or ages, for example, **unheimlich** 'incredibly (eerily!)', **echt** 'really (genuinely)'. More humdrum adverbs include:

äußerst/höchst	extremely
beinahe/fast	almost/ nearly
besonders	especially
bloß	merely
durchaus/überaus	totally/thoroughly
ganz	entirely, quite
genau	exactly
größtenteils	for the most part
kaum	hardly
nur	only (not of time)
recht	really
schlechthin	absolutely
sehr	very (much)
so	so (to such an extent)
ungefähr/etwa	approximately/ about
verhältnismäßig	relatively
ziemlich	fairly, quite
zu	too

(F) **Warum?** 'Why?': reason, cause. Reasons are usually given in phrases or clauses. The few adverbs of reason all have the general sense of 'therefore'. In approximate order of frequency they are: **also, darum, daher, deshalb.**

(iii)   *Nuances of meaning: modal particles*

Like many other Germanic languages, German has a range of very useful short adverbs which express the speaker's attitude to what s/he is saying. Adverbs listed in paragraphs above are not repeated in the selection below, though many of them are used in this way. English often has no real equivalents, so the translations given are only approximate.

Wo bleibt *denn* der Manfred? Er sollte von Bonn herüberfahren. Hat er *denn* keinen Führerschein?	Where has Manfred got to *then*? He was going to drive over from Bonn. Hasn't he got a driver's license *then*?
– *Doch*! Er ist *doch* Rennfahrer! Das wissen Sie *doch*.	– *Yes of course*! He is a racing driver *after all*. You *know* that.
– Er ist *eben* vergesslich. Wir müssen *eben* Geduld haben.	– He is *just* forgetful. We will *just* have to be patient.
– Das ist *ja* die Höhe! Er hat *ja* versprochen, pünktlich zu sein.	– That *really* is the limit! *You know* he promised to be punctual.
– Hören Sie *mal*, Sie könnten ihn *mal* anrufen.	– Listen, you could *just* give him a call.
– Das *schon*, aber *schon* der Gedanke daran macht mich wütend.	– *True enough*, but *just* the thought of it makes me furious.
– Wo kann er *wohl* sein? Er hat sich *wohl* verfahren.	– *I wonder* where he can be? He has *probably* lost his way.
– Er ist *zwar* intelligent, aber er ist nicht sehr pünktlich.	– He *may* be intelligent, but he is not very punctual.

F
USING NUMBERS

30   *Numerals*

31   *Times and dates*

Numerals

30a Counting: cardinal numbers

(i) The forms of the cardinal numbers

These are the German numbers which you should know. All the others follow the same patterns. Note especially the irregularities in the numbers shown in italics.

0 null	21 einundzwanzig
1 eins	22 zweiundzwanzig
2 zwei	23 dreiundzwanzig
3 drei	24 vierundzwanzig
4 vier	25 fünfundzwanzig
5 fünf	26 sechsundzwanzig
6 sechs	27 siebenundzwanzig
7 sieben	28 achtundzwanzig
8 acht	29 neunundzwanzig
9 neun	30 *dreißig*
10 zehn	40 vierzig
11 elf	50 fünfzig
12 zwölf	60 *sechzig*
13 dreizehn	70 *siebzig*
14 vierzehn	80 achtzig
15 fünfzehn	90 neunzig
16 *sechzehn*	100 hundert
17 *siebzehn*	101 hundert(und)eins
18 achtzehn	102 hundertzwei
19 neunzehn	200 zweihundert
20 *zwanzig*	

1000 tausend	1 000 000 eine Million
1001 tausend(und)eins	1 000 001 eine Million eins
1002 tausend(und)zwei	2 000 000 zwei Millionen
2000 zweitausend	1 000 000 000 eine Milliarde

777 777 **siebenhundertsiebenundsiebzigtausendsiebenhundert- siebenundsiebzig**

Note 1) As the last example shows, numbers under a million are written as one word, but in practice, numbers above 19 with more than one part, like **vierunddreißig** or **hundertzehn**, are always written as figures.

2) Figures over 1000 are written with spaces or periods every three digits, not commas [➤30c(iii)].

3) When taking down tens and units, it is quicker to write the unit down as you hear it, then insert the ten before it. Especially on the telephone, **zwo** is often used for **zwei**, to avoid confusion with **drei**.

(ii) *Numbers as nouns*

(A) eine Million and **eine Milliarde** are always treated as feminine nouns. Other numbers are also feminine nouns when they refer to the number itself and to things like buses and trams [➤20b(ii)]. They all add **-(e)n** for the plural.

In Erdkunde kriege ich normalerweise *eine Drei*.	In geography I usually get *a three*.
Dreimal hat er *zwei Sechsen* **geworfen**.	Three times he threw *two sixes*.
Das hat € 2 500 000 (zwei Millionen fünfhunderttausend Euro) gekostet?!	That cost 2,500,000 euros?!

(B) ein Dutzend is a neuter noun of quantity [➤3d]. The plurals **Dutzende, Hunderte, Tausende, Millionen** and **Milliarden** describe approximate numbers of people and things. The first three add **-n** in the dative and, if used without a determiner, **-er** in the genitive.

In dem Winter sind *Hunderte* **von Menschen erfroren**.	In that winter *hundreds* of people froze to death.
Die Neugierigen sind in *Tausenden* **gekommen**.	The curious came in *thousands*.
Das schlechte Essen hat den Urlaub *Dutzender* **von Familien verdorben**.	The bad food spoiled the vacations *of dozens* of families.

(iii) *Numbers and case endings*

(A) eins, which does not change, is used for counting and as a feminine noun [➤(ii)above].

• The pronoun **einer,** etc., refers to one of a group [➤25h(i)]. It has the standard case endings.
• The form **ein** is used before a noun, with the same endings as the indefinite article [➤23e(ii)], but always fully pronounced.

USING NUMBERS

der eine ~ etc. also makes it clear that 'one ~' is meant, not 'a ~'.
• 'Only one' is **ein einziger ...** or **nur ein ...**

Erich kann schon von *eins* **bis hundert zählen. Er ist** *eines* **der begabtesten Kinder seiner Spielgruppe.** *Nur ein* **anderes Kind ist mit ihm zu vergleichen.**	Erich can already count from *one* to a hundred. He is *one* of the most gifted children in his playgroup. *Only one* other child can compare with him.

(B) Other numbers do not normally have case endings except that:

• in writing, **zwei** and **drei** quite often have genitives **zweier** and **dreier**;
• in certain set phrases the numbers 2 to 12 have a dative in **-en**.

Die Liebe *zweier* **junger Menschen – wie schön! Während die Erwachsenen** *zu zweien und dreien* **herumstanden, kroch Erich** *auf allen vieren* **zwischen ihren Beinen.**	The love *of two* young people – how lovely! While the adults stood around *in twos and threes*, Erich crawled *on all fours* between their legs.

(iv) *Numbers as measurements*

Adjectives are made from cardinal numbers by adding **-er**. They refer mainly to money and to years, though sometimes also to other measurements. They can also be used as nouns, if it is clear what they refer to. The adjectives do not take case endings, but the nouns have the usual noun endings [➤22b].

Leute, die in den *Achtzigern* **sind, erinnern sich noch an die** *zwanziger* **Jahre. Die normalen** *Zehner* **und** *Hunderter* **waren wertlos.**	People in their *eighties* still remember the *twenties*. The normal *tens* and *hundreds* (*ten and one hundred mark notes*) were worthless.
Leider habe ich nur einen *Fünfziger*.	I'm afraid I've only got a *fifty* (euro note).

30b *Arranging in order: ordinal numbers*

(i) *Formation of ordinal numbers*

Ordinal numbers are formed simply by adding **-te** to cardinal numbers from 2 to 19, and **-ste** to all other numbers. First, third, seventh and eighth are irregular. Ordinals are always used after a determiner and have the normal adjective endings [➤24b(ii)].

1. der *erste*	11. **der elfte**
2. **der zweite**	12. **der zwölfte**
3. **der** *dritte*	13. **der dreizehnte**
4. **der vierte**	20. **der zwanzigste**
5. **der fünfte**	21. **der einundzwanzigste**
6. **der sechste**	30. **der dreißigste**
7. **der** *siebte*	40. **der vierzigste**
8. **der** *achte*	70. **der siebzigste**
9. **der neunte**	80. **der achtzigste**
10. **der zehnte**	90. **der neunzigste**

100. **der hundertste**	200. **der zweihundertste**
101. **der hundert(und)erste**	1000. **der tausendste**
103. **der hundertdritte**	1 000 000. **der millionste**

2345. **der zweitausenddreihundertfünfundvierzigste**

Note   As shown in the list above, in German ordinal numbers are written with a period after them [➤also 31b(iv)].

(ii) *Firstly, secondly*

For 'firstly, secondly' etc. **-ens** is added to the stem of the ordinal numbers.

Ich komme nicht, *erstens* **weil**	I am not coming, *firstly* because I
ich keine Zeit habe, *zweitens*	have no time, *secondly* because I
weil ich nicht will.	don't want to.

(iii) *Second/third best*

For 'second/third best' etc., superlative adjectives are added to the stem of the ordinal numbers.

Käthe ist die *zweitbeste* Läuferin ihrer Klasse, aber im Schwimmen ist sie immer die *Drittletzte*.	Käthe is the *second best* runner in her class, but in swimming she is always *third from last*.

30c *Dividing into parts: fractions and decimals*

(i) With the exception of 'half' [➤(ii) below], fractions are neuter nouns made by adding **-el** to the stem of the ordinal numbers.

• Before a noun any determiner takes its gender from the noun, not the fraction.

• There is no **und** between a full number and a following fraction.

Drei Viertel des Essens und *neun Zehntel* des Weins waren weg. Wir teilten den Rest auf. Jeder bekam ein *Drittel* Brot und eine *zehntel* Flasche Wein. Ein *Zehntelliter* ist nicht viel! Vom Obst blieben nur noch *zwei ein Viertel Melonen*.	*Three-quarters* of the food and *nine-tenths* of the wine were gone. We divided up the rest. Each of us got a *third* of a loaf and a *tenth* of a bottle of wine. A *tenth of a liter* is not much! Of the fruit only *two and a quarter* melons were left.

(ii) 'Half' may be a noun, adjective or adverb:

(A) The noun is **die Hälfte**. 'Half the/this/that/my ...' etc. is usually **die Hälfte** followed by a genitive or **von** + dative.

Karl hat mir *die Hälfte* seines Brots/von seinem Brot gegeben.	Karl gave me *half* (of) his bread.

(B) The adjective is **halb**. 'Half a ...' is normally **ein halber** ... etc., taking the normal adjective endings. **das Halb** refers to the number itself.

Ich hatte noch *einen halben* Apfel übrig.	I had *half an* apple left over.

(C) The adverb is **halb**.

Das hatte ich *halb* vergessen.	I had *half* forgotten that.

> **(D)** 'One and a half' is **eineinhalb** or **anderthalb**, followed by **zweieinhalb, dreieinhalb** etc.

Nach *viereinhalb* Tagen sind wir zu einem Dorf gekommen. Wir waren *eineinhalb* Monate unterwegs gewesen.	After *four and a half* days we came to a village. We had been traveling for *one and a half* months.

(iii)   As in most languages other than English, German decimals are written with a comma, not a point/period.

Ich hatte *10,5* Kilo verloren.	I had lost *10.5* kilos.

Times and dates

31a   Clock times

(i)   Hours and minutes

The following list shows the everyday way of telling the time. Note especially:

• **(die) Uhr** means 'clock, watch' ('hour' is **die Stunde**).
• Half-hours are always reckoned as 'half way to the next hour', so **halb eins** is 'half past twelve', not 'half past one'. In South Germany quarters are often reckoned in the same way, but this is not general throughout the country.
• '25 past/to' is often reckoned as '5 to/past' the half hour.

1.00	**ein Uhr/eins**
1.05	**fünf (Minuten) nach eins/ein Uhr fünf**
1.10	**zehn (Minuten) nach eins/ein Uhr zehn**
1.15	**Viertel nach eins/viertel zwei**
1.20	**zwanzig (Minuten) nach eins/ein Uhr zwanzig/** **zehn vor halb zwei**
1.25	**fünfundzwanzig (Minuten) nach eins/ein Uhr fünfundzwanzig/** **fünf vor halb zwei**
1.30	**halb zwei**
1.35	**fünf nach halb zwei/fünfundzwanzig vor zwei**
1.40	**zwanzig vor zwei**
1.45	**Viertel vor zwei/drei Viertel zwei**
1.50	**zehn (Minuten) vor zwei**
1.55	**fünf (Minuten) vor zwei**
2.00	**zwei Uhr**

(ii)   The 24-hour clock

The 24-hour clock is normal in official and business contexts such as railroad timetables and announcements, times of meetings, opening and closing times. It is always spoken as 'hours . minutes (if any)'.

00.15	**null Uhr fünfzehn**
07.30	**sieben Uhr dreißig**
10.45	**zehn Uhr fünfundvierzig**
12.00	**zwölf Uhr**
13.12	**dreizehn Uhr zwölf**

17.26	**siebzehn Uhr sechsundzwanzig**
21.57	**einundzwanzig Uhr siebenundfünfzig**
24.00	**vierundzwanzig Uhr**

(iii) Clock time phrases

Note how ways of saying 'a.m./p.m.' vary according to how early or late it is.

Wie viel Uhr ist es?/Wie spät ist es?	What time is it?
Wie viel Uhr haben Sie?	What time do you have?
Es ist (Punkt/genau) halb elf.	It is (exactly) half past ten.
Wann/Um wie viel Uhr fährt der Zug ab?	When/At what time does the train leave?
um zwölf Uhr (mittags)/um Mittag	at twelve o'clock (twelve noon)/ at noon
um vierundzwanzig Uhr/ um Mitternacht	at 24.00 hours/at (twelve) midnight
um zwei Uhr nachts/nachmittags	at two a.m./p.m.
um acht Uhr vormittags/abends	at eight a.m./p.m.
gegen acht Uhr morgens	at about eight a.m. or not quite eight a.m.
vorm./nachm.	a.m./p.m.

31b Days, months and years

All names of days, months and seasons are masculine.

(i) Days of the week

Sonntag	Sunday
Montag	Monday
Dienstag	Tuesday
Mittwoch	Wednesday
Donnerstag	Thursday
Freitag	Friday
Samstag	Saturday (used everywhere)
Sonnabend	Saturday (only in the North)
am Montag	on Monday, etc.
montags	on Mondays, etc.

(ii) Months and seasons

Januar	January

Februar	February
März	March
April	April
Mai	May
Juni	June
Juli	July
August	August
September	September
Oktober	October
November	November
Dezember	December
der Frühling	spring
der Sommer	summer
der Herbst	fall/autumn
der Winter	winter

Es ist/wird bald Winter.	It is/will soon be winter.
Der Juli/Der Sommer war wirklich heiß.	July/The summer was really hot.
Im November/Im Herbst regnete es jeden Tag.	In November/the fall it rained every day.
bis Anfang/Mitte/Ende Mai	up to/by the beginning/middle/ end of May
Wir fahren nächsten Juni in Urlaub.	We are going on vacation next June.
letzten/vorigen/ vergangenen Januar	last January

(iii) Major festivals in Germany

das (der)Neujahr(stag)	New Year's (Day)
der Fasching	(pre-Lent) Carnival
der Aschermittwoch	Ash Wednesday
der Karfreitag	Good Friday
(zu) Ostern	(at) Easter
Ostermontag	Easter Monday
Pfingsten	Pentecost/Whitsun
(Christi) Himmelfahrt	Ascension Day
Mariä Himmelfahrt	Assumption of the Virgin Mary (15th August)
Allerheiligen	All Saint's
der Heilige Abend	Christmas Eve
(zu) Weihnachten	(at) Christmas Day

Frohe Weihnachten!	Merry Christmas!
Zweiter Weihnachtstag	Day after Christmas Day
Silvester(abend)	New Year's Eve

(iv) Dates

Days of the month are ordinal numbers, as in English
[►30b(i)]. They are always written as figures, with a full stop/
period, never as words. Note that (for example) 'in 1993' is
either just **1993** or **im Jahre 1993**. [Spoken versions are given
in square brackets below to show the endings.]

Den Wievielten haben wir heute?	What's the date today?
Heute ist der 16. [sechzehnte] August.	
Wir haben heute den 16. [sechzehnten] August.	Today is the 16th of August.
Sie ist am 20. [zwanzigsten] April geboren.	She was born on the 20th of April.
Sie hat am 20. April Geburtstag.	Her birthday is on the 20th of April.
Er ist 1833/im Jahre 1833 gestorben.	He died in 1833.
Sie fangen (am) Montag, den 6. September an.	You/They start on Monday, September 6th.
Hamburg, (den) 28.3.98/(den) 28. März 1998	Hamburg, 28 March 1998 (at head of letter)

G
INDEX

INDEX

Note **(1)** The symbol ⟦D⟧ indicates that this term is defined in the paragraph shown.

(2) The sign ➤ refers you to another part of the index.

A **aber** 5a(i)
Accusative ➤ *Cases*
 object 8d(i)
Active verbs ⟦D⟧11c
Adjective-nouns ⟦D⟧24d
 with small letters 24d(iii)Note
Adjectives ⟦D⟧24a
 + **dass** clauses 24g(ii)B
 + prepositions + noun phrases 24g(ii)
 + **zu** + infinitive 24g(ii)B
 after pronouns 25b(iii)
 comparative ➤ *Comparatives*
 compound 3b(ii)
 endings 24b
 formed from other parts of speech 24f
 governing noun phrases 24g(i)
 not in the noun phrase (predicative) 24c
 rule for endings 24b(i)
 superlative ➤ *Superlatives*
 unchanging (invariable) 24f, 24b(iii)C, 30a(iv)
 used as nouns 24d
 with **-e/-en** (weak) endings 24b(ii)A
 with noun understood (omitted) 24b(iii)B
 with only comparative and superlative forms 24e(i)F
 with spelling changes 24b(iv)
 with standard (strong) endings 24b(ii)B
 within the noun phrase (attributive) 24b
Adverbial expressions (adverbials) ⟦D⟧28a
 answering questions (time, place, etc.) 29c(ii)
 clauses 28d
 negatives 29c(i)
 order in sentence 4c(ii)D
 phrases 28c
Adverbs 28b
 comparative ➤ *Comparatives*
 expressing the speaker's attitude 29b(iii), 28b(i)

formed from nouns and verbs (~**(s)weise**) 28b(ii)
formed from adjectives 28b(i)
modifying verbs ⒟29b(i)
modifying adjectives/other adverbs ⒟29b(ii)
role in German 29a
superlative ➤*Superlatives*
Agreement, verb with subject ⒟ 4c
all- (quantifier) 23g(iii); 25h(ii)
allein (conjunction) 5a(i)
allerlei, etc. (demonstratives) 23f(vi)
Alphabet 2b
als (conjunction) 5a(ii); (after comparatives) 24e(ii)B
als ob 5a(ii)
an (preposition) 27b(iii)
anstatt (preposition) 27b(iv)
Antecedent ⒟5b, 25j(i)
Apposition ⒟3c
Article, definite ⒟23d
    indefinite ⒟23e
    used instead of possessive 23h(iii)
Attributive adjectives ⒟24b
außer (preposition) 27b(ii), 27c
außerhalb (preposition) 27b(iv)
auf (preposition) 27b(iii)
aus (preposition) 27b(ii)

B   Bare infinitive ⒟8h(i)
bei (preposition) 27b(ii)
beide(s) (quantifier) 23g(v); 25h(ii)
beiderseits (preposition) 27b(iv)
bevor 5a(ii)
bis (conjunction) 5a(ii); (preposition) 27b(i)
by, with passive 15c

C   Cardinal numbers (1,2,3 ...) ➤ *Numerals*
Caretaker subject (**es**) 25e(iii), 10a(iv)Note
    with passive 15d, 15e
Cases ⒟22a
    accusative, uses of 22d
    dative, uses of 22f
    -e/-en (weak) adjective endings 24b(ii)A
    endings on nouns 22b
    genitive, uses of 22e
    nominative, uses of 22c

standard (strong) endings 23b, 23c(i)
Clauses, main D4d(i)
    participle clauses 10b(v)
    relative 5b
    subordinate D4d(ii)
    zu + infinitive 10a(iv)
Clock time 31a
Clothing 8e(iii)
Colon 2d(iii)
Commands ➤*Imperative*
Commas, use of 2d(ii)
    with **zu** + infinitive 8h(ii)
Comparatives, formation 24e(i)
    ~er than 24e(ii)B
    as ~ as 24e(ii)C
    more and more ~ 24e(ii)D
    the more ~, the more ~ 24e(ii)E
    irregular 24e(i)C/D
    meaning *fairly ~* 24e(ii)A
    with Umlaut 24e(i)B
Complement D8c
Compound words 3b
Compound tenses 17c
Conditional D tense usage 14d
    compound 17c(iii)
    past (perfect) 17c(iii)
    simple or compound? 14c(iii)B, 14d(iv)Note
    tenses (simple, compound, past) 14b
    wenn clauses 14d
Conjugation of verbs D16a
Conjunctions D5a
    coordinating 5a(i)
    subordinating 5a(ii)
Consonants, double 2c(iii)
Content words D1b
could (have) 9c(ii)

D   **da** 5a(ii)
    da(r)- compounds 8gNote, 25b(iv)
        + **dass** clauses 8i, 24g(ii)B
        + **zu** + infinitive 8h(ii)D, 24g(ii)B
    dass 5a(ii)
    dadurch dass 5a(ii)
    damit (conjunction) 5a(ii)
    Dates 31b(iv)

Dative ➤*Cases*
   object 8d(ii)
Days of the week 31b(i)
Decimals ➤ *Numerals*
Definite article **der** [D]23d
Demonstratives ➤*Determiners, Pronouns*
denn (conjunction) 5a(i)
der (article) 23d; (demonstrative) 23f(i); 25g(i); (relative) 25j
derjenige (demonstrative) 23f(iii); 25g(ii)
derselbe (demonstrative) 23f(iv); 25g(ii)
Descriptive passive [D]15g
dessen/deren (relative) 25j(ii); (as possessives) 23h(iii)
Determiners [D]23a
   definite article **der** 23d; after prepositions 23d(iv)
   demonstratives [D]23f
   indefinite article **ein** 23e
   interrogatives 23c
   possessives [D]23h
   quantifiers [D]23g
dieser (demonstrative) 23f(ii); 25g(ii)
diesseits (preposition) 27b(iv)
Direct speech [D]5c(i)
   questions [D]6a
Direct object 8d(i)
durch (preposition) 27b(i)
dürfen 9c(i)

E   *each other* 25c(ii)
ein (article) 23e
ein bisschen, ein paar (quantifiers) 23g(ix)
einer (pronoun) 25h(i)
einig- (quantifier) 23g(vi); 25h(v)
Empty subject (**es**) 25e(i)
entlang (preposition) 27b(iii)
entweder ... oder 5a(i)
es sei denn 5a(ii)
etlicher (quantifier) 23g(viii)
etwas (quantifier) 23g(i); 25h(iv)
Exclamation mark/point, use of 2d(iii)
Exclamations 26a

F   **falls** 5a(ii)
Fractions ➤ *Numerals*
Full stop/period, use of 2d(i)

für (preposition) 27b(i)
Future tenses 12c

G **gegen** (preposition) 27b(i)
gegenüber (preposition) 27b(ii)
Gender ⒟20a
    by meaning 20b
    different from sex 20b(iv)
    nouns with double gender 20c
Genitive ➤*Cases*
    object 8d(iii)
gern 9c(iii)
Governed, by a verb ⒟8a
    by adjectives 24g

H **haben**, full conjugation 18a
    + noun idioms 8k
    as auxiliary 17c(i)B
hinter (preposition) 27b(iii)
Hyphen, use of 3b(iii)

I *If only ...* 13d(ii), 26a(iii)
Imperative ch.13
    alternatives to 13b
    first person 13d(i)
    formation 17d
    infinitive used as 13c(i)
    past participle used as 13c(ii)
    reported requests and commands 5e
    second person 13b
    third person 13d(iii)
Impersonal pronoun **es** ➤ *Pronouns*
Impersonal verbs 8d(ii), ⒟8j
in (preposition) 27b(iii)
Indefinite article **ein** ⒟23e
indem 5a(ii)
Indicative ⒟ch.12
Indirect object ⒟8e
Indirect speech ⒟5c(ii)
    commands 5e
    questions ⒟5d
    tense usage 14c
    word order 14c(ii)

Infinitive ⒟, formation 10a(i)
    after verbs 8h
    as imperative 13c(i)
    bare ⒟ 8h(i)
    clauses 10a(iv)
    in opening block 4e(1), 8h(i)Note
    infinitive-nouns 10a(iii)
    with particles 10a(i)
    with **zu** 8h(ii)
-ing form, equivalents in German 10b(ii)
innerhalb (preposition) 27b(iv)
Inseparable prefixes ➤*Prefixes, on verbs*
Interjections 26b
Intransitive ➤ *Verbs*
Inverted commas/quotation marks, use of 2d(iii)
irgend- 23g(x); 25h(iv)B

J   **jeder** (quantifier) 23g(iv); 25h(iii)
    jemand 25h(iv)
    jener (demonstrative) 23f(iii); 25g(ii)
    jenseits (preposition) 27b(iv)

K   **kein** (determiner) 23g(ii)
    keiner (pronoun) 25h(i)
    Konjunktiv ⒟ 14c
        I/II in reported speech 14c(i)
        tenses 14b
    können 9c(ii)

L   Languages 19f
    lassen 9c(vii)
        sich lassen instead of passive 15f(v)
    Let's ... 13d(i)
    Letters needing care 2c(i)
    lieber 9c(iii)

M   Main clause ⒟ 4d(i)
    Main verb ⒟ 9c(vi)
    manch- (quantifier) 23g(vii); 25h(v)
    man ➤ *Pronouns, indefinite*
    Measurements 3d
    mehrere (quantifier) 23g(viii)

mit (preposition) 27b(ii)
Modal verbs ch.9 (*see also individual verbs*)
    in conditional 9b(ii)
    infinitive-past participle 9b(i)
    perfect in subordinate clauses 9b(iii)
    tenses 9b(i), 16c(ii)B
    with understood infinitive 9b(iv)
mögen 9c(iii)
Months 31b(ii)
müssen 9c(iv)

N   **nach** (preposition) 27b(ii)
nachdem 5a(ii)
Names of people 19d
    of places 19e
Nationalities 19f
neben (preposition) 27b(iii)
Negatives 29c(i)
nichts 25h(iv)
niemand 25h(iv)
Nominative ➤ *Cases*
Non-finite verb forms ⒟ch.10
Noun phrases ⒟19b
    with noun understood 24b(iii)B
Nouns ⒟19a
    cases ➤ *Cases*
    compound 3b(i)
    formed from other parts of speech 19g
    governing phrases and clauses 19h
    masculines adding **-n(s)** 22g(ii)
    names of places 19e
    names of people 19d
    nationalities and languages 19f
    plurals ➤ *Plural*
    proper or common? 19c
    singular or plural? 21e
    weak masculines 22g(i)
Numerals ch.30
    cardinal 30a
    case endings 30a(iii)
    decimals 30c(iii)
    firstly etc. 30b(ii)
    fractions 30c(i); *half* 30c(ii)
    ordinal 30b
    referring to money, years, etc. 30a(iv)

second best etc. 30b(iii)
    used as nouns 30a(ii)
nun da 5a(ii)

O   **ob** 5d
    oberhalb (preposition) 27b(iv)
    Objects ⒟8d
        dative 8d(ii)
        direct (accusative) 8d(i), 8e
        genitive 8d(iii)
        indirect (dative) ⒟8e
        prepositional ⒟8g
        reflexive 8f
        two accusatives 8e(iii)Note
        word order 4e
    obwohl 5a(ii)
    oder 5a(i)
    of, with place names 3c
    ohne (preposition) 27b(i), 27c
    Ordinal numbers (1st, 2nd, 3rd ...) ➤ *Numerals*

P   Participles 10b
        as adjectives 10b(iv)
        in opening block 4e(1)
        participle clauses 10b(v)
        past 10b(iii); used as imperative 13c(ii)
        present 10b(i)
        sein + past participle (descriptive passive) 15g
        with particles 10b(i)B, 10b(iii)D
    Particles, verbal (separable prefixes) !D 16e(ii), 16e(iii)
        with infinitives 10a(i)
        with participles 10b(i)B, 10b(iii)D
    Parts of speech ⒟1a
    Parts of the body 8e(iii)
    Passive verbs ch.15, ⒟11c, 15a
        alternatives 15f
        by (agent, instrument or means?) 15c
        descriptive passive (**sein** + past participle) 15g
        full conjugation 18d
        tenses 15b
        with no subject 15e
        with verbs + dative 15d(i)
        with verbs + prepositions 15d(ii)
    Past participle, formation and use 10b(iii)

INDEX

Perfect tense 12b
Period, use of 2d(i)
Personal pronouns ➤ *Pronouns, personal*
Pluperfect tense 12b(ix)
Plural, groupings 21b
    nouns with double plurals 21c
    predicting 21a
    with no singular 21d
Possessives ➤*Determiners; Pronouns*
Predicate ⒟4c
Prefixes, on nouns 19g(iv)
    on verbs (inseparable) ⒟16e(i), 16e(iii)
    on adjectives 24f(ii)
Prepositional objects ⒟8g
Prepositions ⒟27a
    + accusative 27b(i)
    + accusative/dative 27b(iii)
    + dative 27b(ii)
    + genitive 27b(iv)
    + infinitive-nouns 10a(iii)Note
    + **zu** + infinitive/**dass** clauses 27c
Present tense 12a
Present participle, formation and use 10b(i)
Prices 3d
Pronouns ⒟25a
    agreement 25a
    demonstratives 25g
    impersonal (**es**) 25e; as empty subject ⒟25e(i);
      as caretaker subject ⒟25e(iii);
      as object/complement 25e(v)
    indefinite (**man**) 25d; instead of passive 15f(iii)
    interrogatives 25f
    personal: forms 25b;
      2nd person **du/ihr/Sie** 25b(ii);
      +adjectives 25b(iii); after prepositions 25b(iv)
    possessives ⒟25i;
    alternative constructions 25i(ii)
    problems of agreement 25k
    quantifiers ⒟25h
    reflexive ⒟25c;
    used reciprocally (*each other*) 25c(ii)
    relative ⒟25j(i);
      alternative constructions 25j(viii)
Punctuation 2d

Q Quantifiers ➤ *Determiners; Pronouns*
Quantities 3d
Question mark 2d(iii)
Questions, direct ⒟6a
    indirect ⒟5d
    with question-words ⒟6d
    with tags ⒟6c
    Yes/No ⒟6b
Quotation marks 2d(iii)

R Reflexive pronouns ➤ *Pronouns, reflexive*
Reflexive verbs ⒟8f
    instead of passive 15f(iv)
Relative clauses ⒟5b
Relative pronouns ➤*Pronouns, relative*
Reported speech ➤*Indirect speech*

S Second person pronouns **du/ihr/Sie** 25b(ii)
sein, full conjugation 18b
    + dative idioms 8k
    + past participle (descriptive passive) 15g
    as auxiliary 17c(i)A
seit (preposition) 27b(ii)
seit(dem) 5a(ii)
Semi-colons 2d(iii)
Sentences ⒟4a
    types of 4d
Separable prefixes ➤*Particles, verbal*
sich (reflexive pronoun) 25c(i)
Simple past tense 12b
sodass 5a(ii)
sobald 5a(ii)
sofern 5a(ii)
solange 5a(ii)
solch- (demonstrative) 23f(v); 25g(ii)
sollen 9c(v)
sondern 5a(i)
soweit 5a(ii)
sowie 5a(i)
sowohl ... als/wie 5a(iii)
Spelling 2a-c
ss or **ß**? 2c(iv)
Standard (strong) case endings ⒟23b, 23c(i)
statt (preposition) 27b(iv), 27c

Strong verbs ⏛16d
　　full conjugation 18b/c
　　list of principal parts 18e
Structure words ⏛1b
Subject ⏛4b
　　caretaker **es** 10a(iv)
　　change of 8i
Subjunctive ➤*Konjunktiv*
Subordinate clauses ⏛4d(ii)
Suffixes, on nouns 19g(iii)
　　on adjectives 24f(i)
Superlatives, formation 24e(i)
　　am ~**sten** 24e(iii)B
　　der ~**ste** 24e(iii)A
　　irregular 24e(i)C/D
　　meaning *extremely* ~ 24e(iii)C
　　of adverbs 24e(iii)B/D
　　with Umlaut 24e(i)B
Syntax 4a, 4e

T　　Tenses ⏛11a
　　active 11d
　　basic form (base) of simple tenses 17a
　　compound conditional 14c(iii)B,
　　　14d(iv)Note; (formation) 17c(iii)
　　compound future 12c; (formation) 17c(ii)
　　endings 17b
　　formation ch.17
　　future perfect 12c(iii); (formation) 17c(ii)
　　haben or **sein** in perfect? 17c(i)
　　past (perfect) conditional (formation)17c(iii)
　　past (simple, perfect, pluperfect) 12b
　　present 12a
　　simple and compound ⏛11b
Times and dates ch. 31
Transitive ➤*Verbs*
trotz (preposition) 27b(iv)
trotzdem (conjunction) 5a(ii)

U　　**über** (preposition) 27b(iii)
　　um (preposition) 27b(i), 27c
　　und 5a(i)
　　unter (preposition) 27b(iii)
　　unterhalb (preposition) 27b(iv)

unweit (preposition) 27b(iv)

V   Verb tables ch.18
       Verbs (full) D7a
           + bare infinitive 8h(i)
           + prepositions 8g
           + subordinate clauses 8i
           + **zu** + infinitive 8h(ii)
           auxiliary D7b
           basic form (base) of simple tenses 17a
           compound (prefix or particle?) 16e;
           conjugation 16a
           haben in perfect 17c(i)B
           impersonal 8j, 8d(ii)
           infinitive D, formation 10a(i)
           intransitive D 8b
           irregular strong 16d(iii)
           irregular weak 16c(ii)
           linking D8c
           main D4c
           modals D9a
           non-finite forms Dch.10
           reflexive D8f
           regular or irregular? D16a(i)
           sein in perfect 17c(i)A
           strong D, formation 16d(i); classes 16d(v)
           tense endings 17b
           tenses D11a
           transitive D8d(i)
           weak D, formation 16c(i)
           with particles 16e(ii), 16e(iii)
           with fixed prefixes 16e(i), 16e(iii)
       viel (quantifier) 23g(ix); 25h(v)
       von (preposition) 27b(ii)
       vor (preposition) 27b(iii)
       Vowels, long 2c(i)

W   **während** (conjunction) 5a(ii); (preposition) 27b(iv)
       wann? 6d(v), 29c(ii)A
       warum? 6d(ix), 29c(ii)F
       was für (ein)? 6d(iv), 23c(ii), 25f(iii)
           exclamation 26a(ii)
       was? 6d(ii); (as relative pronoun) 25j(v/vi)
       Weak masculine nouns 22g(i)

INDEX

Weak verbs 16c
    full conjugation 18a
weder ... noch 5a(i)
wegen (preposition) 27b(iv)
weil 5a(ii)
welcher? 6d(iii), 23c(i), 25f(ii)
    as relative pronoun 25j(iv)
    exclamation 26a(ii)
wenig (quantifier) 23g(ix); 25h(v)
wenn 5a(ii); ➤ *If only*
wer? 6d(i), 25f(i); (*anyone who*) 25j(v)
werden, full conjugation 18c
    as auxiliary 17c(ii)/(iii)
whoever, wherever etc 5a(ii)
wie (conjunction) 5a(ii)
wie? 6d(vii), 29c(ii)B/E; (exclamation) 26a(ii)
wie viel? 6d(viii), 23c(iii)
wo? wohin? woher? 6d(vi), 29c(ii)C/D
wo(r)- compounds 25j(vii)
wollen 9c(vi)
Word order 4e
    central block 4e(ii)
    final block 4e(iii)
    opening block 4e(i)
    outside the blocks 4e(v)
    questions and commands 4e Note
    subordinate clauses 4e(iv)

Z   **zu** + infinitive: after verbs 8h(ii)
    after prepositions 27c
    expressing wishes 26a(iv)
zu (preposition) 27b(ii)
zumal 5a(ii)
zwischen (preposition) 27b(iii)